D0860286

The Evolution of *Allure*

The MIT Press

Cambridge, Massachusetts

London, England

The Evolution of Allure

Sexual Selection from the Medici Venus to the Incredible Hulk

George L. Hersey

This book was set in Meta by The MIT Press.

Printed and bound in the United States of America.

Library of Congress Cataloging-in-Publication Data

Hersey, George L.

The evolution of allure : sexual selection from the Medici Venus to the Incredible Hulk / George L. Hersey.

p. cm.

Includes bibliographical references and index.

ISBN 0-262-08244-6 (hc : alk. paper)

1. Sex role in art. 2. Art and society. I. Title.

N8241.S.H47 1996

700—dc20

95-38927

CIP

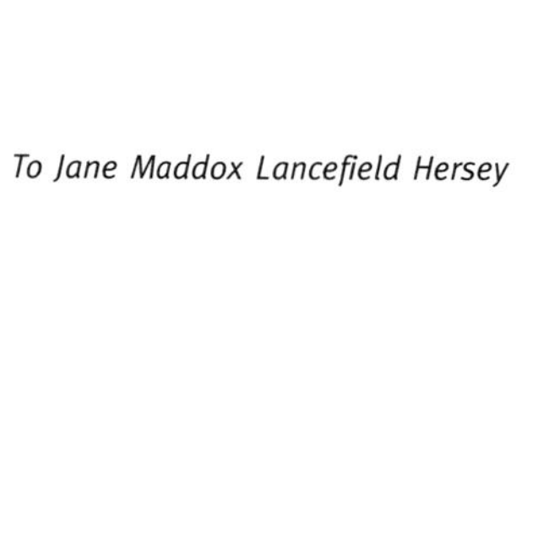

To Jane Maddox Lancefield Hersey

Contents

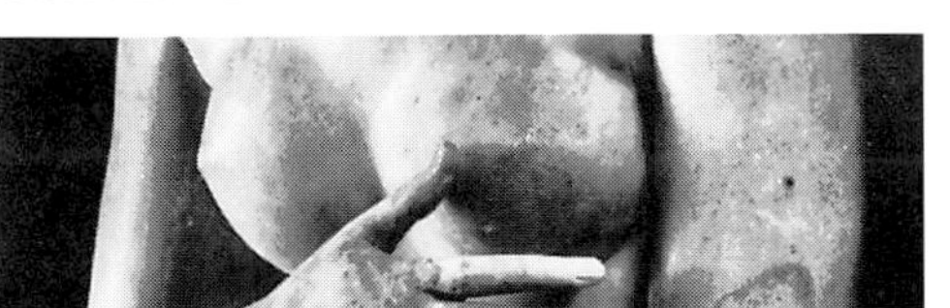

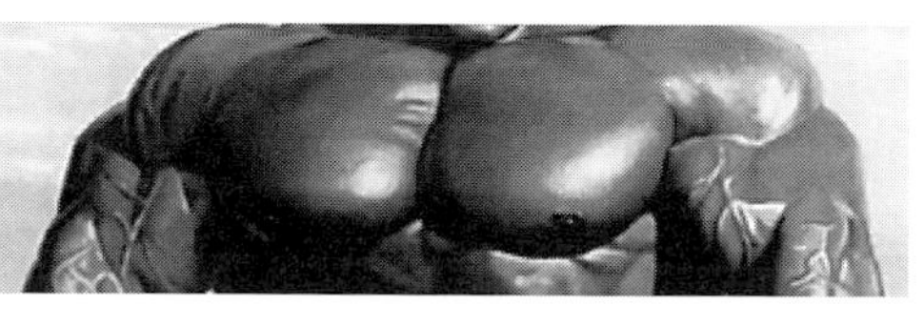

Acknowledgments

I would like to give special thanks to Jon Marks, Jules Prown, and Robert Jan van Pelt, each of whom has read the manuscript and provided many a necessary correction from the respective viewpoints of biology, physical anthropology, and art history. I also thank the readers for the MIT Press: Barbara Maria Stafford, Randy Thornhill, Anne Hollander, and a fourth reader who remains anonymous. Their often face-saving suggestions have served me well. I have also discussed my ideas with many others who have read sections of the book, offered useful advice and corrections, or have at least listened patiently: Martin Berger, Victor Bers, Eve Blau, Arnaldo Bruschi, Caroline Bruzelius, Giorgio Ciucci, Joseph Connors, Elisabeth Cropper, Angela Dalle Vacche, Debórah Dwork, Melissa Errico, Donald Fiske, Gabriele Guercio, Donald Hersey, James Hersey, John Hollander, Marta Huszar, Ellery Lanier, Esther da Costa Meyer, Geoffrey Miller, Talbot Page, Théo Page, Justine Richardson, Judith Rodin, Ron Rosenbaum, Vasily Rudich, Susan Ryan, Gustina Scaglia, Vincent Scully, Jane Sharp, Francesca Stanfill, Mark Zucker, and successive generations of Yale graduate and undergraduate students. Many people at the MIT Press have been helpful, and more than that, especially Roger Conover, with whom I have fruitfully discussed the manuscript over many months, Daniele Levine, Terry Lamoureux, Jeannet Leendertse, and my superb editor, Alice Falk.

Introduction: Aphrodite's Daughters

Perhaps the most celebrated bodily stance for female self-presentation in Western art is that of the so-called Venus Pudica. The goddess stands erect, face turned slightly away, with one hand over her breasts and the other shielding her groin. The Medici Venus is probably that pose's best-known embodiment (0.1). The implication is that the goddess, bathing, has noticed that someone—the viewer, the artist—has caught sight of her (cf. *Greek Anthology* 16.159ff.) and she is doing her best to cover herself. But she is hardly panicked. As generations of observers have always noted, the result is paradoxically both chaste and inviting.[1]

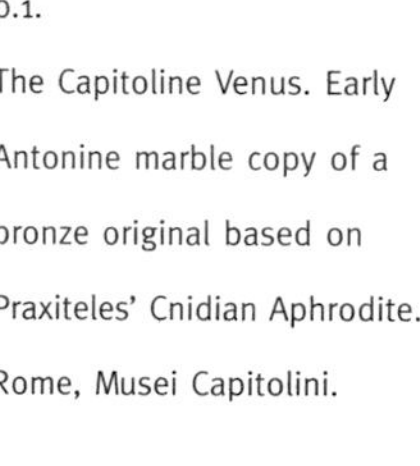

0.1.

The Capitoline Venus. Early Antonine marble copy of a bronze original based on Praxiteles' Cnidian Aphrodite. Rome, Musei Capitolini.

And, too, the image, as a type, represents something quite new in Greek sculpture: it is so female. It is so different from earlier Greek images of women—for example, the korai, who are bony and boyish. In this new vision we see a wide, upright elliptical body mass at the center; short, soft arms and legs; and none of the korai's musculature. The Medici Venus's legs are delicately placed, the right slightly bent, the main weight on the left. The refined small determined face turns its profile, with its full, almost grieving lips and marked triangular brows, firmly to her left. Her hair is elaborately prepared—wreathed and crisscrossed by a sea of knots and curls. As a mammalogist might say, this goddess is "presenting."

Later portraits depict women similarly, either directly as the Medici Venus or in some recognizable variant of that image's pose. Even when fully clad, a baroque lady, for example, will flutter one hand somewhere near her breasts

0.2.

Thomas Gainsborough. *The Honourable Mrs. Graham,* 1775. Edinburgh, National Gallery of Scotland. The image has been flipped horizontally in order to establish its likeness to the Medici Venus.

0.3

Bronze Age Paphiote goddess. Copenhagen, Nationalmuseet (inv. 3719).

0.4.

An advertisement from *D-Cup Superstars*, February 1992.

and dangle the other near her pelvis. The viewer is supposed to recognize that she is attractive yet modest—or "modest." The Honourable Mrs. Graham, in Gainsborough's portrait (0.2), indolently but recognizably stands exactly so. And she has further equipped herself with what in this book will be called attractors: the hand near her groin holds a plume that matches the other plumes in her hat. The hand near her breast has relaxed to fondle a part of her pannier that has turned into a flyaway piece of drapery. Other sexual proclamations take the form of pink knotted ribbons, oval gatherings of overskirt, and a deep-cut curved neckline fenced all around, as especially desirable territory, by zigzagging battlements of lace.

Mrs. Graham is unquestionably ladylike. Nonetheless it has been suggested that her much-repeated "borrowed attitude," like the attitude of the Medici Venus herself, originated in certain Cypriote images (0.3). C. S. Blinkenberg was the scholar who first seems to have thought of this source for the type.[2] The Paphiote image is a typical Bronze Age Cypriote temple hetaira. She wears her woven *thomingos* or prostitutes' crown and boasts the huge earrings and necklaces with which she and her sisters so often ornament themselves. More important, like these other statuettes she not only points to, but massages, her organs.

Yet, as Blinkenberg asks, is not the Medici Venus's switch from messaging to shielding simply a subtler way of continuing to focus on her reproductive system? In that paradox of modest immodesty lies the whole later meaning of the pose.

Indeed, I can provide the Medici Venus, Mrs. Graham, and the hetaira with an even earthier subtext. That the goddess's gestures, all along, have really been acts of sexual self-presentation is even more forcefully implied when we compare the pose with the ads in today's skin mags: in this case a certain Mistress Tanya (0.4), who offers phone sex while blatantly—and, I am sure, unconsciously—miming all three previous ladies.

But there is a big difference among these four images. Tanya's pose, and those of Venus and Mrs. Graham, may be in the same mode as the Paphiote hetaira's, yet the latter's bodily proportions differ markedly from those of the other three women.[3] That is, measuring in heads (as artists traditionally do, as I will do throughout this book, and as physical anthropologists never seem to do), the hetaira's nipples, navel, and groin come at the points marked respectively by distances of 1 3/4, 2 1/2, and 3 heads. For the period in Western art that ran from c450 BCE to c1900 CE, these proportions are far too short; and note that the image's arms are shorter still—only 2 heads. Blinkenberg's hetaira exhibits readiness, she presents; but she does not, like her three sisters, have what I will call selectable proportions. Venus, Mrs. Graham, and Tanya, on the other hand, all have nipples, navel, and groin respectively at 2, 3, and 4 heads, and they all have arms-and-hands equal to 3 heads' length. These are the normative male and female proportions for canonical body design in Western art in the period specified. They are also the normal proportions for Western men and women during that period.

It is the thesis of this book that Western art has reinforced a general preference for these proportions. There is, of course, no truly scientific way of proving this. Or at least I can think of no practical experiments that would do so (but see chapter 2). In Karl Popper's sense my thesis is unfalsifiable, and therefore probably "unscientific." But that does not mean that it cannot be put forward, discussed, and elaborated—or, for that matter, that it isn't true.

And thus by corollary does one confront a possibility that I will propose, but not be able to do justice to in this book: that in the Bronze Age human bodies, or at least those bodies that were being portrayed as sexually desirable, may have had greater proportional diversity than do such bodies nowadays. Mistress Tanya, in other words, would not have been chosen to pose for the photo in *D-Cup Superstars* if her body had been designed like the hetaira's. But just as clearly the hetaira embodied the cult of Aphrodite, goddess of love and beauty, and was made and used as an image of female desirability.

And, to push the point further still, perhaps our race has quietly been bred, over the last twenty centuries, *toward* the body design we see in Venus Pudica/Mrs. Graham/Tanya and *away* from that of the hetaira. This point is discussed again, and further illustrated, in chapter 1 and at the beginning and end of chapter 3. If my gently offered hypothesis is correct, in other words, our part of the human race would have lowered the statistical frequency of Paphiote-type bodies, in art and possibly also in life. And they would have produced, biologically and artistically, more bodies of the pudica design. (I should add that the proportional numbers described in the following pages apply equally to males and females.)

The present book, then, can only crouch in Lilliputian awe before its Brobdingnagian subject. There is a great deal more to be said about art and sexual selection, about art and body measurement, about racism and art, about biocultural decadence and reproductive goals, and all the other matters listed in the table of contents. There is much more to be said, on both sides, about whether or not culture determines, or helps determine, biological adaptations in general, and about whether canonical physiques of the Medici type are in fact such adaptations. I am starting these hares but will probably not be around when they reach the finish line—if they ever do. Furthermore, at heart the book is involved almost entirely with classical, Renaissance, and baroque cultures. But here I do not apologize for the limitation. These were the three periods, in the West, when the canonical body as a reproductive goal was of supreme concern.

As to other cultures that have been body conscious in various ways—for example, those of Japan, Hindu India, or of the Western Middle Ages—much valuable and relevant research that I will have to ignore is being done. The work of Caroline Walker Bynum is just one example.[4] Western medieval concepts of the body are a fascinating, indeed eloquent contrast to those I address. She writes, "there is something profoundly alien to modern sensibilities about [the body's] role in medieval piety. . . . Medieval images of the body have less to do with sexuality than with fertility and decay. Control, discipline, even torture of the flesh is, in medieval devotion, not so much the rejection of physicality as the elevation of it—a horrible yet delicious elevation—into a means of access to the divine."[5]

But though the thinkers and artists I deal with equally divinize the body, this happens, for them, not through its subjection, torture, or decay but so as to celebrate its allure and to analyze the attributes of that allure.

1 Sexual Selection

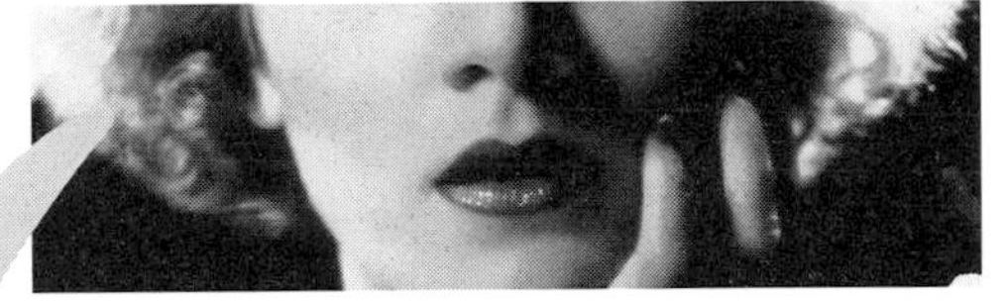

BEAUTIFUL STATUES FASHIONED AFTER BEAUTIFUL MEN REACTED UPON THEIR CREATORS, AND THE STATE WAS INDEBTED FOR ITS BEAUTIFUL MEN TO BEAUTIFUL STATUES.

Gotthold Ephraim Lessing, *Laocoön* (1766)

Humans, like many other animals, have always made sexual choices. In this sense all the phrase "sexual selection" means is that two potential partners consider each other more desirable, or at least less impossible, than other potential mates, and act accordingly. To at least some extent, and often to a large extent, their choices are made on the basis of each other's personal style and appearance—face, body, hair, clothes. To put it in the language of this book, the choice is made on the basis of the other person's body design and the quality of his or her attractors.

At the simplest level this is merely a matter of mate choice. But in evolution, sexual selection is the sort of mate choice that helps bring on permanent change.[1] In this sense one could (rather inelegantly) rephrase Lessing in the epigraph above and say: "Beautiful statues reacted upon their creators, and beautiful women and men selected each other when they looked like those statues. Because of this, beautiful children were born." Or as Darwin writes in *The Descent of Man* (1871): "Mr. Winwood Reade informs us that the Jollofs, a tribe of negroes on the west coast of Africa, 'are remarkable for their uniformly fine appearance.' A friend of his asked one of these men, 'How is it that every one whom I meet is so fine-looking, not only your men, but your women?' The Jollof answered, 'It is very easily explained: it has always been our custom to pick out our worse-looking slaves and sell them.'"[2]

Darwin does not explain how slave status among the Jollofs related to breeding status: Were beautiful slaves promoted to citizenship and ugly citizens sold as slaves? Or were only slaves ever ugly? Nonetheless the population seems consciously to have bred itself for beauty. Presumably, if they kept it up for several centuries, ugly Jollofs would be born with ever-greater infrequency. That would be sexual selection for beauty.

But what does sexual selection have to do with art? The answer lies, once again, in Lessing's statement quoted above. Figure art has urged us to breed, like the Jollofs, for beauty. It has presented and endorsed ideal human physical types. These have constituted the visual images of our gods, saints, and heroes. In our churches, museums, monuments, and homes, hundreds of generations of worshipers have stared at and meditated on these painted, carved, modeled, and molded bodies and faces. The human types that were portrayed during this long reign of the physically ideal (a reign now virtually ended in high art but not in low) still proliferate in our media. We do not, like the Jollofs, get rid of those among us who fail to meet the standards. But we have kept repeating and reaffirming the standards themselves.

And these ideal types have played their cultural role both for good and evil. On the innocent side there are beauty queens, Mr. Universes, and the like. On the evil side are writers like the early nineteenth-century French essayist Arthur de Gobineau, who frequently cites the beauty of classical statues as proofs of the superiority of the European over other races.[3] Almost a hundred years later Hitler's racial guru, Alfred Rosenberg, was saying much the same (see chapter 8). Even today, plenty of people believe it.

As I have implied in the introduction, I will also show that from the Greek fifth century BCE and on to the twentieth-century nudes of Rodin or Maillol, these ideal physiques have been extraordinarily similar. The real, easily verified extremes of human biovariation (see figs. 3.16, 3.17) have been ignored. The ideal physiques have been the body types that viewers secretly or publicly wished to find in their spouses—and themselves. They are types that form a vigorous contrast in specific proportions, muscularity, and fat content, as well as in their uniformity, to the bodies in the art that preceded what the canonical period offered (e.g., figs. 3.1, 3.3).

For most of history, furthermore, at least in the West, the outward aspect of these bodies and faces has also entailed certain conclusions about the minds and souls inside them. Since our saints, angels, gods, and heroes inhabit these physiques, the physiques have been equated with superior mental and spiritual qualities. I am well aware that this notion, beauty = excellence, has often been denied. But, psychologists have shown, this is an equation more honored in the breach than in the observance.[4] In any case, this book is not concerned with the truth of such claims; rather, it deals with them as historical phenomena, as beliefs that were acted on, as affirmations that were repeated over and over again for centuries.

But clearly not all admiration of another person's face and body, and not all mate choice, involve reproduction. Many people are willing to have sex with partners they would never dream of producing children with; and, of course, with same-sex couples reproduction is impossible. I grant these points. But I will also assume that, with ourselves as with all other animals and many plants, the core message of the attractors has involved reproductive prediction: What kind of offspring would result from this union? Nonreproductive attraction, indeed, is not a refutation of the attractors' original purpose but simply an elaboration of it. Darwin cites the case of the peacock that, lacking females to impress, displayed his myriad attractors to poultry and even some pigs.[5]

Nonreproductive sexuality nonetheless complicates the question; what complicates it even more is that throughout most of nature there is no indication that the selectors and selectees really knew that sex made babies. At whatever level of consciousness females and males may examine, admire, or reject each other, the underlying drive to select mates has been mainly instinctive. So, for many species, though obviously not our own, conscious sexual selection is independent of the reproductive success that ensues from good choices. And therefore when two humans choose each other with no thought of children, they are simply reverting to well-established prehuman behavior. My expression "reproductive goal," then, has to be taken as meaning a goal that can be partly or fully unconscious.

Another caveat can be discussed here. It is sometimes objected that sociobiologists, and perhaps others, make cross references and analogies between species that are not warranted due to the evolutionary space between the two taxa—for instance, ants and humans. Perhaps this can be the case. But when *I* make that sort of connection it will at least have the following justification: in wearing attractors, the men and women in question themselves borrow from distant species. They wear peacock feathers and sealskin or muskrat coats. They appropriate skins, fur, feathers, shells, flowers and leaves (real and artificial), leopards' spots, and alligators' hides. They shape their ornaments to resemble insects or their nests (e.g., beehive hairdos), and almost any other plant or animal you can think of. So in this case it is the subjects of inquiry themselves, and not the investigators, who are making trans-species analogies. Here, in other words, that analogy is not the wrong way to study the subject—it *is* the subject. We will see in chapters 6, 7, and 8, in fact, that at one time humans who wore nonhuman attractors were accused of devolving biologically back to animal or even plant status.

Sexual selection is actually a subset of two processes: the natural selection that Darwin defined and the artificial selection used for centuries by breeders. Above all sexual selection tends to emphasize, perfect, and exaggerate certain qualities. Pronounced attractors signify greater fitness to survive. If the chosen individual is more rather than less symmetrical, stronger rather than weaker, and so on, he or she will be better at overcoming disease, predators, and the like, and hence will be more likely to produce fitter offspring. And if that same individual is more rather than less beautiful, those offspring will in turn have a better chance of being so, too, and thus of being attractive to the fittest available mates.

These principles, often in subtle and prolonged forms, apply to a vast range of species running from flowers and tiny insects to humans. Sexual selection is often concerned, therefore, with adornment, courtship, and self-presentation. It cajoles, persuades, or seduces the reproductive act with the beauty of a richer plumage, a sweeter song, a more bewitching dance, or a more irresistible perfume. In analyzing sexual selection in the following pages I will posit the following four types of attractor manipulation: augmentation, borrowing, translation, and exchange.

Augmentation

William G. Eberhard, an entomologist and authority on sexual selection, explains the evolution of the more hyperbolic sort of attractors by invoking a principle of augmentation.[6] The attractor, whatever it may be, simply evolves so as to get larger and large. Thus in a classic 1982 article Malte Andersson showed that the extremely long tail of the male African widowbird had evolved through the active choice, by females, of males who boast particularly large and splendid tails.[7] Even more appropriately for the present study, Wolfgang Wickler has proved that among primates, female sexual selection is often based on the comparative size, color, and beauty of the males' genitals.[8] Larger testes, in particular, seem to be interpreted as containing more sperm and hence as better bets for reproductive success.[9] Sperm competition, indeed, is currently the subject of intense research. More generally, many experimenters are finding that when they artificially augment an attractor—say the length of a tail feather—far beyond what nature achieves, the females will usually go for it despite its unprecedented size.

Eberhard particularly stresses the importance for females of large, flashy male organs.[10] Some species, for example the scorpion fly, put enormous energy into the production of these appendages. Eberhard's thesis is that female body design has selected for elaborated male genitals because females have desired increasing amounts of vaginal stimulation through ever larger areas of physical contact. While for insects and the like this has been a tactile rather than a visual matter, it is difficult to ignore the visual aspect of Eberhard's illustrations. These penises (1.1, 1.2), though greatly enlarged in the drawings, nonetheless suggest visual stimuli—the massing of contrasting textures, the filamented tissue, glossy hair, and fine skin set against pitted, feathered, rutted, and dotted areas, here like shells, there like leafy branches. We see these things as extravagant biofantasies that nature has been led to provide. On reading Eberhard's text we soon see that his phrase "genitalic extravagance" (and note the author's very name!) is more than appropriate for a wide range of creatures. Throughout nature, though not universally among all species, he concludes, male genitalia, in perhaps the wildest range of forms that nature has ever produced, are as much the objects of female taste and judgment as are the tail feathers of birds, the antlers of elk, the fierce spurs of fighting cocks—and, for that matter, the money of a millionaire, the brains of an intellectual, or the muscles of a bodybuilder. If some of these structures are duplicated, enlarged, and transposed to other parts of the body, if some are shaped into weapons, helmets, or ornaments, and even if the members of one sex borrow the other sex's most potent attractors—these things all constitute visual foretastes of tactile stimulation.[11]

Others besides Eberhard have published on these themes.[12] R. V. Short has printed diagrams mapping the relative body size of male and female primates, including humans, along with the geometrically proportioned sizes of their respective sex organs when erected (1.3; tables 1.1, 1.2).[13] Note that the gorillas and orangutans have considerable sexual dimorphism with respect to total

1.1.
Hemipenes (i.e., one of a pair) from eight species of the snake genus *Rhadinaea*, inflated as when inside the female. From Eberhard, *Sexual Selection*.

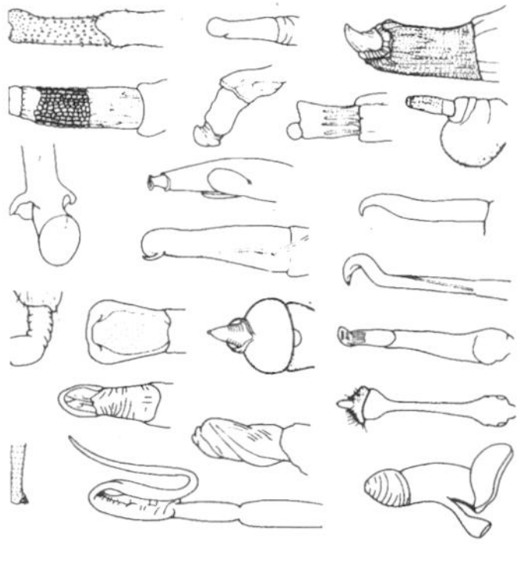

1.2.
Mammalian penes in the flaccid state, drawn to different scales. The top two rows are all from primates. From Eberhard, *Sexual Selection*.

Table 1.1

Primate Testes Size Variation

	Ratio between Testes and Body Weight	Factor of + or – Difference
Gorilla	0.017	4x+
Orangutan	0.048	2x+
Chimpanzee	0.269	3x–
Human	0.079	0

Table 1.2

Size Variation of Primate Ovaries

	Ratio between Ovaries and Body Weight	Factor of + or – Difference
Gorilla	0.012	0
Orangutan	0.006	0
Chimpanzee	0.010	0
Human	0.014	0

body size, while male and female humans and chimpanzees, respectively, are roughly the same.

As I measure them from Short's diagram, for orangutans and chimps penis volume increases about 250% and that of the testes about 500%. Human testes, meanwhile, remain roughly gorilla- or orangutan-size in proportion, but our penises are fully 400% larger than those of gorillas or orangutan, and considerably bigger, too, than those of most chimps except bonobos. This is evidence,

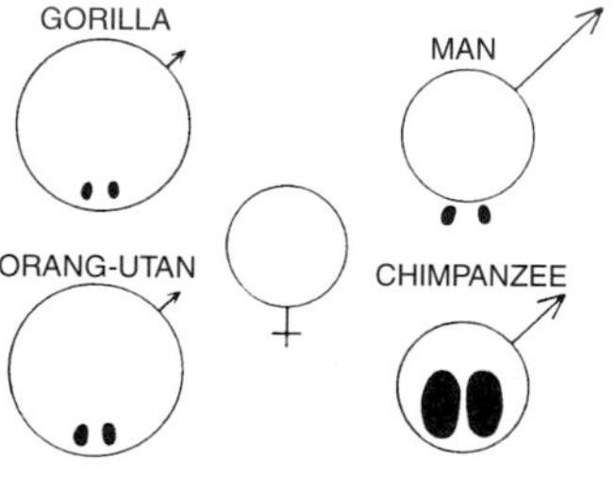

1.3.
Female primates' views of their males. The paired black blobs map the size and position of the testes (in humans they hang below the groin; in other primates they are on it). From R. V. Short, "Sexual Selection."

Table 1.3

Variation in Penis Length in Works of Art

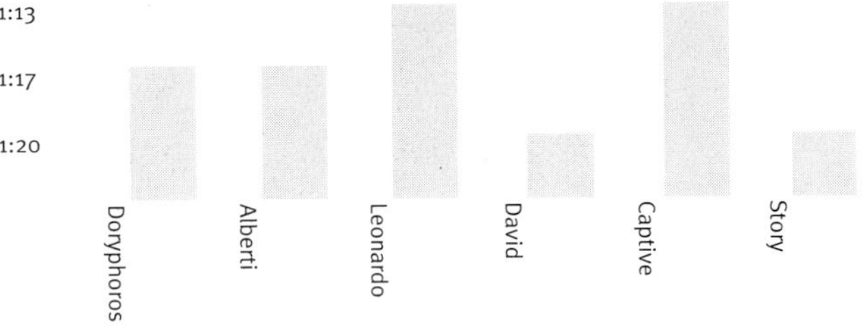

it would seem, that female chimps have selected for large penises *and* testes, while female humans have concentrated their selective force on penis size alone. (Probably vagina length has evolved so as to match these size-enhanced possibilities for stimulation.)

Among human males, furthermore, as measured in art, there is considerable variation in penis size (table 1.3). The table shows the gonad measurements (including testes and pubic hair) for some of the canonical bodies discussed in the following pages.

Borrowing, Translation, and Exchange

Augmentation, both in size and number, is thus a main mode of sexual advertisement. But there are three others, which I call borrowing, translation, and exchange. Plants, which have inspired so much of the ornament that we humans often borrow for sexually selective ends, are themselves sexually selected. Their striking blossoms, often together with perfumes, have evolved out of reproductive competition. And that competition has been a race to seduce insects and birds, which do not even belong to the same kingdom; so here, once again, sexual selection borrows attractors from alien species.

Flowers are in fact little more than bisexual attractors (1.4); their sole purpose is reproduction. Among humans, they are particularly associated with females.

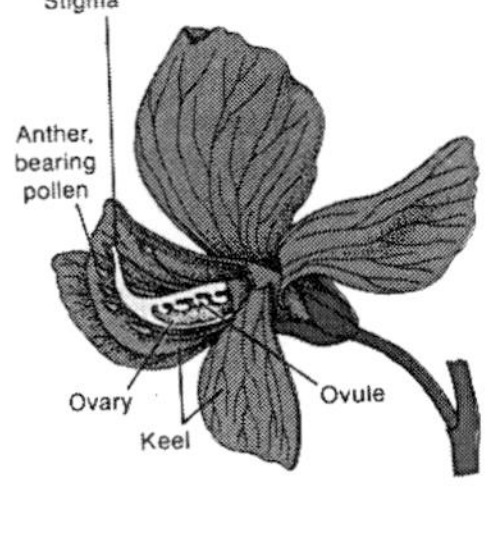

1.4.
Peaflower with one of two keels enclosing the sex organs cut open. The ovary is also shown in section. After J. B. Hill, H. W. Popp, and A. R. Grove, Jr., *Botany,* 4th ed. (New York, 1967).

1.5.
Cecil Beaton. Portrait of Marlene Dietrich with orchid, 1932. From the exhibition "Flora Photographica," Malibu, J. Paul Getty Museum.

Many women, for example, are named for flowers, which is not true of men. And no wonder Cecil Beaton photographed that archtemptress Marlene Dietrich as an adjunct to an orchid (1.5). Perhaps this is also the place to mention that orchids take their name from the Greek 'όρχις, a word that means *human* testicles or ovaries. The implications of Dietrich's face and head, with its halo of fine-spun golden hair, are developed by the petals, pistils, stigmata, and other come-ons that her orchid flaunts. The flower transforms her eyes, nose, and mouth, her lengthy lashes and pensively arrayed fingers, into analogues of its own beauty traps.

We will meet up with other examples of attractor borrowing. As to the exchange and translation of attractors between the sexes of the same species, or between different parts of the body, this can happen when, in an act of symbolic solidarity, males display symbols of sexual readiness that mimic those of females. Wickler illustrates this in baboons (1.6). The primary display is a brightly distinguished pattern around the female's clitoris. Not only does the male gelada exchange his unornamented chest for one that is ornamented like a female's, but the female meanwhile also translates her clitoris decoration to her chest. In their purely decorative form the ornament's framing elements become more geometrical—two pink triangles set vertically, point-to-point.[14]

1.6.
Attractor borrowing: female and male gelada. Sexual skin of a female gelada (left), female gelada from front (center), and male gelada (right). From Wickler, "Socio-Sexual Signals."

There are plenty of other examples. Among red and olive colobus monkeys, says J. H. Crook, both males and females erupt with "remarkable ischial [hip] swellings." These are almost identical—one being functional for reproductive purposes and the other, the male's, an ornamental dummy (1.7).[15] It is my view that in their symmetry, bright colors, frames, and contrasts of texture and composition, these primate ornaments reflect genetic drives similar to those that have produced sexually selective human clothing.

Sperm Competition

Thus do augmentation, borrowing, translation, and exchange constitute modes of attractor manipulation. We will meet with many other examples of all four. But sex and its attractors are often linked with violence as well as with seduction. In a large number of species, for example, males compete with each other for females and the latter choose the winners. As we have already seen, sometimes a very few males, or only one, will get all or most of the mating opportunities. In other cases there will be more democratic assortings but with competition and choice still present. Darwin calls this "the law of battle."[16] And there is plenty of battling to be seen. Sperm competition proper takes place when, after a female has received one partner's ejaculate, another partner tries to replace that sperm with his own. The process seems to endow spermatozoa, almost as if they were conscious individuals, with a fierce desire to beat out rivals, to stymie them, to crowd them out of the vagina and prevent them from fertilizing the egg. For some experts Richard Dawkins's famous selfish gene has an equivalent in the selfish spermatozoon. Throughout nature, sperm competition has led to all sorts of developments in the evolution of mating systems, the size and appearance of reproductive organs, copulation behavior, modes of establishing paternity, and territoriality and parenting instincts. Even the lovely dawn chorus of birds, it has been claimed, occurs partly because unmated males want partners, partly because some mated males are warning rivals from

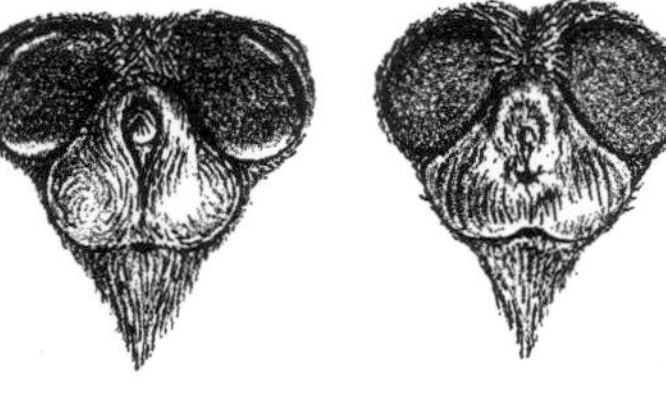

1.7.
Attractor borrowing: female and male red colobus monkeys. The buttocks of a female red colobus with genital swelling (left) and the imitation of these in a young male's groin (right). Drawing by Hermann Kacher. From W. Wickler, *The Sexual Code,* translated by Francisca Garvie, translation copyright © 1972 by Doubleday, a division of Bantam Doubleday Dell Publishing Group, Inc. Used by permission of Doubleday, a division of Bantam Doubleday Dell Publishing Group, Inc.

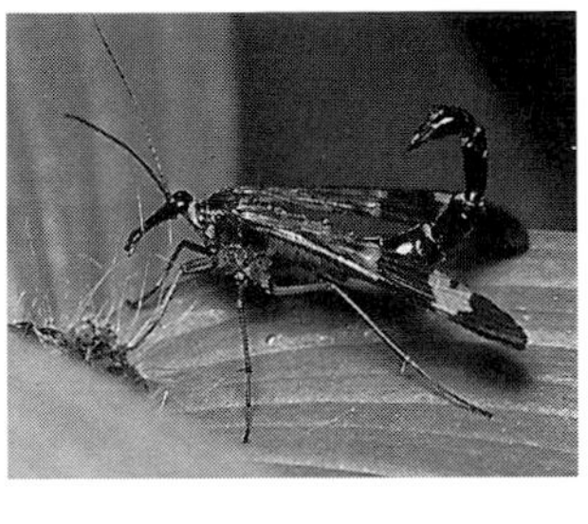

1.8.
The common Japanese scorpion fly with genitalia deployed. From Thornhill, "The Allure of Symmetry." Hiroshi Ogawa, Nature Productions.

1.9.
German jousting armor, c1500. New York, Metropolitan Museum of Art.

their territory, and partly because other mated males are adulterously trying to attract attached females. In addition, the dawn chorus gains its particular intensity because females are then most fertile; hence both the warnings and the invitations are particularly powerful.[17] It is a bit like one of those Rossini or Donizetti ensembles in which the singers all express their inmost thoughts, utterly contradicting each other, and yet with a superbly harmonious result.

These notions of competition put male attractors in a new light—they not only fascinate females but are often simultaneously the means by which males eliminate rivals. Even penises, quintessential inseminating devices though they are, can serve also as weapons. No wonder that horns, swords, spears, and suchlike are so often the penis's surrogates. Usually these phallic displays are secondary sexual growths or, in the case of humans, artifacts. In the rest of nature, however, some organisms do fight off sexual rivals directly with their erect penises. The scorpion fly, for example (1.8), transforms his rear-mounted penis into a battering ram, a black shiny segmented hook curving upward between his wings. This occupies approximately half his total body length. The fly duels with another male by poking and hitting at his enemy's weapon. Note that the weapon (coincidentally?) mimics the shape of the fly's head but is larger and more deadly looking.[18] Thus even at the level of the order Mecoptera there is visual attractor translation from groin to head.[19] The sixteenth-century German jousting armor in figure 1.9 is an example of the same translation among humans. The knight who wears it jousts for a female's favor in a courtly love tournament. Note that to complete his intimidating display, he has borrowed, from another mammal, the sinuously inflected horns used in that animal's own erotic duels. The horns take the form of a lyre; so in its human setting the associations of music's sweetness combine with those of death-to-rivals—which is exactly the double meaning of many male attractors.

Mammals are much more apt to go in for serious battling over these questions than are other taxa.[20] Human males' most obvious attractors, their relatively large muscles, may exist more for this reason than as instruments of work. Darwin himself makes the claim.[21] Men, he says, developed muscles because women consistently fancied these organs. And, I will add, they probably did so because such muscles promised that their owner could outstrip rivals as well as eliminate predators. One might observe that in many human societies today, traditional or not, the well-muscled, taller, heavier males do less heavy lifting than do the females.[22] In these cases the men's muscles are all the more the fruit of sexual selection, armament as a come-on, just as the muscles of a contemporary bodybuilder function as attractors, that is, as the artifacts of sperm competition (see chapter 9).

Clothes as Genital Maps

Recently, sexual selection experimenters have been providing artificial attractors to birds and other animals, or, conversely, removing the animals' own natural attractors so as to test changing responses in the opposite sex. Nancy Burley, who works with zebra finches, put red or green bands on the males' legs. Red bands on males attracted females and green repulsed them. Males, meanwhile, preferred black or pink bands on females and disliked light blue ones.[23] Anders Møller did something similar with swallows: those whose tails he lengthened with extra feathers found mates sooner, produced more offspring, and had more extracurricular affairs than did birds with normal tails.[24] And Jakob Höglund and his team enhanced the white tail feathers of male great snipes with white-out, which allowed them to lure more females into copulations than did birds without this brighter coloration.[25]

By providing extra feathers, paint, and leg bands to these animals, the experimenters have in effect been dressing them in clothes and adorning them with makeup. Though their articles do not mention it, the scientists are moving toward the point I want to make throughout the rest of this chapter: not only are human clothing and adornment often sexually selective, but they make use of our four manipulative modes—augmentation, translation, borrowing, and exchange—to intensify their effects.

When we dress in such clothes—and these of course are not the only kind of clothes that exist—our bodies become large-scale mappings of our reproductive

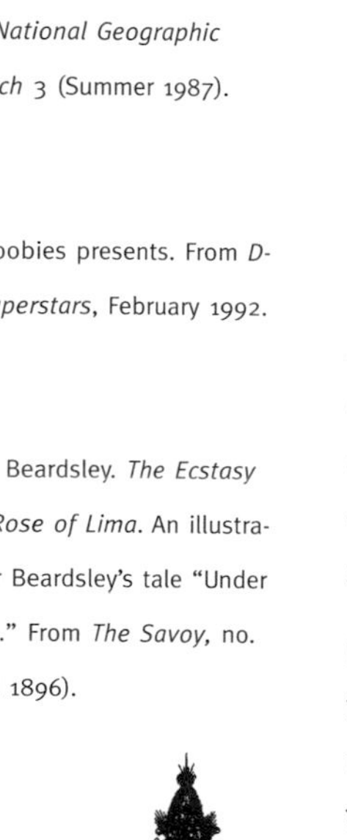

1.10.

Bonobo *(Pan paniscus)* chimpanzee. From Frans B. M. de Waal, *National Geographic Research* 3 (Summer 1987).

1.11.

Suzi Boobies presents. From *D-Cup Superstars*, February 1992.

1.12.

Aubrey Beardsley. *The Ecstasy of St. Rose of Lima.* An illustration for Beardsley's tale "Under the Hill." From *The Savoy*, no. 2 (April 1896).

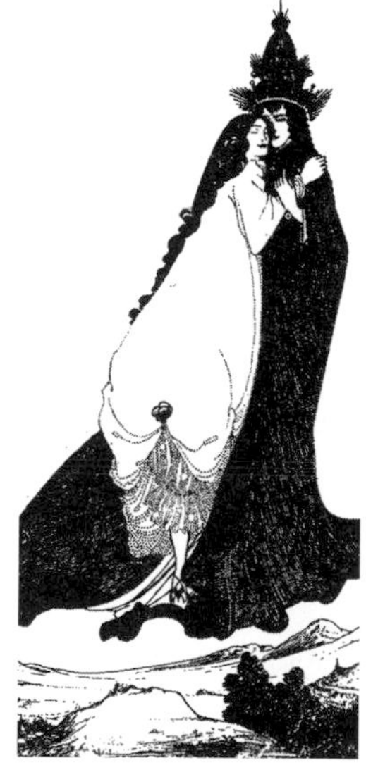

systems. The mappings may reproduce or symbolize our genital arrangements in situ, or they may transpose genital images to the head, face, or other parts of the body. We just saw the same thing, produced by nature rather than by clothing, in gelada baboons (1.6). Human clothing of this type also makes use of what I call "vectors"—ornamental indicators that point to or enframe the primary or secondary sex organs. We might note, too, that when we borrow ornaments from other species we mostly borrow their attractors. And we use these borrowed attractors to reportray our own or other organisms' primary and secondary reproductive apparatus, dramatizing select areas of bare skin by enframing it with hair or other accessories, and even modeling the process of dishabille. One could easily write a book—and it would be necessarily incomplete—focusing on headgear for both sexes seen as transposed, hyperbolized reproductive organs.

Female sexual display has also been commonplace, as we saw in the introduction. The Romans had a custom known as *ostentatio genitalium* in which both men and women indulged (e.g., Diodorus Siculus 1.85.3). In doing so they imitated other primates: the female bonobo chimpanzee's clitoris and its surrounding tissue blossom, when she is estrous, into a large pink swag (1.10). Strikingly similar presentations can reappear among humans with no conscious attempt at either the imitation of chimpanzees or the revival of ancient human practices (1.11). One is tempted to start thinking of G-strings as instinctive efforts to repair the evolutionary damage done when human females developed the interior clitoris. Less blatant versions are bustles, bows, and other things tied above or on the buttocks; the bottoms of two-piece swimsuits, especially bikinis, and especially when ornamented; and fanny packs. Beardsley's drawing of St. Rose of Lima embracing Christ the King (1.12) places the saint's namesake symbol exactly over the place where a chimpanzee's exterior clitoris would be, a fact emphasized and enlarged by the vector-festoons of the saint's panniers.

In antiquity, military clothing was constructed almost entirely so as to augment attractors, with seduction and threat, as usual among males, intermixed. The Greek military helmet, originally based on a simple leather cap, developed into a huge display modeled on horns, antlers, and bird crests. A great plume, usually of horsehair, sprang from a socket on the helmet's crown. This socket, appropriately, was called the *phalos* (but note: with one *l*).

Menelaus, raising high his silver-studded sword,
Struck forth at the phalos *on Paris's helmet. (Iliad 3.361–362)*

Otherwise classical armor was a sort of hollow inhabited statue that flatteringly resculptured the wearer's body: mainly, it exaggerated his muscles. In Homer the terms for body armor are almost always framed by adjectives of beauty; and the ancient Greek words for the body parts themselves are often the same, or almost the same, as those for the armor that covers those parts. A warrior doesn't put on greaves, breastplate, and baldric but dons his "beautiful calves," his "shining chest," and his "glorious shoulders." Note how Hypnos's head (1.13) becomes huge in its helmet and crest, so that it is a human equivalent to the kind of attractor-crest we see throughout nature. Note also that the painter has rendered the folds of the god's tunic, projecting along his upper arms and legs, as a fringe of dangling multiple phalloi. Thus the image exemplifies two kinds of augmentation—of size and of number—as well as translation.

1.13.
Euphronios Painter. Krater, c515 BCE. Detail. The god Sleep helps lift the body of Sarpedon to take it to the underworld. New York, Metropolitan Museum of Art.

Roman breastplates (1.14) were even more anatomical than Greek ones. Augustus's muscular abdomen, however, is overlaid with tiny political and mythological scenes that caress his pectorals and abdominals. These exemplify another type of auqmentation: increasing the apparent size of Augustus's

1.14.
Augustus from Primaporta, c20 BCE. Rome, Vatican Museums.

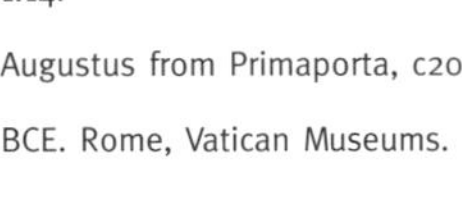

1.15.
Pheidias. Three goddesses from the Parthenon, Athens, c435 BCE. London, British Museum. Copyright British Museum.

1.16.
Nike fastening her sandal. From the parapet of the temple of Athena Nike, Acropolis, Athens, c410 BCE. Athens, Acropolis Museum.

muscles via a contrast of scale. Note too the complex genital enlargement as the cloak sweeps powerfully past the groin to fall over the left arm in a flood of corrugated folds. Within that complex a second host of pendants dangles around the emperor's upper legs. Here is an excellent specimen of attractors combining territoriality (the imperium) with reproductive fascination.

Greek nonmilitary dress, in art, could be equally bold. But we are so used to it that the messages have weakened. Let us look at the three goddesses, usually called Leto, Artemis, and Aphrodite, from the east pediment of the Parthenon (1.15). Their ocean of drapery creates an obbligato to the bodies beneath, framing and re-presenting knees, thighs, breasts, and bellies in an enfolding froth. Aphrodite's shoulder and breasts (she is on the right) free themselves from the fabric as from a shower of falling water. Just below them the folds begin a further animated descent, gaining in fullness and multiplicity as they emphasize the narrowness of her waist by burgeoning away from it. Whirlpools churn over all three laps. Notice the huge V-shape these folds make as they encase Aphrodite's haunches, while, in contrast, thin vertical ripples feed into the V across her lower stomach. Below, the turmoil thins out as the fabric tightens over her lower legs. The result is the visual enlargement or augmentation of the open ovals of the goddess's genitalia by the repetitions, framings, and outlinings of folds of material.

Nearby, just west of the Parthenon and slightly earlier in date, is a temple to Athena Nike. Here there was a frieze in which the goddess adjusted her sandal (1.16). Athena's breasts and abdomen are fully shown, though a few rivulets of fabric course over them. Then, around the pelvic area, deep concentric ovals, most complex and numerous at the groin, fan out and diminish as they

1.17.
Francesco Solimena. *The Risen Christ Appearing to the Virgin,* c1710. Detail. The Cleveland Museum of Art, Mr. and Mrs. William H. Marlatt Fund, 71.63. Copyright © 1995 The Cleveland Museum of Art.

descend to the floor. No garment could create more clearly an enlarged mapping of the reproductive complex onto the rest of the body. And this is achieved, once again, by concentrically repeating the ovals at larger and larger scale—by augmentation, in other words, both of size and number.

Ever since, draperies in works of art have continued to shimmer with these fantastic but fascinating and informative undulations.[26] In baroque art, for example, we see garments that would fall to the ground were not something mysterious—a breeze or other exhalation?—filling the fabric and wrapping it strategically around the figure (1.17). Francesco Solimena's Christ reveals his body to his mother to affirm the incarnation and to establish his role as king of heaven and his mother's as queen. Note the large fabric vector directly in front of his groin. It is in fact the central form in a floating bannerlike cloth—stiff, complicated, strong-shadowed, triangular, and not really a garment—that curls and clambers around his body and peeks out under his right armpit. We shall see that the doctrine of the incarnation amply justifies this fleshly exercise on Solimena's part.

Less often, but quite memorably, the public display of large, apparently erect male members, often in a context of luxury gear, has been used to enhance selectability. Among humans the most famous such garment is the codpiece: a permanent erection made out of stuffed cloth worn between the cleavage of breeches or trunk hose.[27] (Suits of armor frequently included metal codpieces, often of fanciful sculptured shape, which are now normally displayed separately from the armor itself.) In Bronzino's portrait Lodovico Capponi (1.18) wears

1.18.

Agnolo Bronzino. *Portrait of Lodovico Capponi,* 1555–1559. New York, Frick Collection.

1.19.

Robert Mapplethorpe. *Man in Polyester Suit*, 1980. Copyright © 1980 The Estate of Robert Mapplethorpe.

one that is covered with goffered white satin.[28] And note that the rest of his clothing showcases the codpiece. Vertical seams in the black doublet plunge directly to the groin, which is emphasized by brilliant puffed white breeches. Even the silver-white sleeves, padded and quilted to suggest immense muscles within, and socketed into the contrasting receptacles of the black epaulettes, are phallic and unconsciously create forms similar to the penises in figures 1.1 and 1.2. (A codpiece would probably have been a must for a male Capponi, since the name tropes "capon.")

Such Renaissance codpiece portraits also form the perhaps unconscious subtext to Robert Mapplethorpe's photograph *Man in Polyester Suit* (1.19). Even the gesture of the left hand framing the penis, and the brilliant white accent of the shirttail against the black semi-erection (the same colors as in the Bronzino, but reversed), echo the Frick painting; so does the shock value of formal dress and blatant sexual boast and the back-and-forth reflectings in the two portraits between fingers and penises. More intricately, the *frisson* in this comparison is a set of oppositions—black versus white, real penis versus false, and Capponi's sumptuous silks versus the photograph's suiting—stiff, slippery, plastic, yet sedately formal.

The codpiece is essentially a groin-guard. It protects or hides, while at the same time proclaiming, the penis. Groin-guards and the like are apt to be translated to other parts of the body. When the codpiece migrates it becomes a horn, a hat, or even an ornamental breast covering worn by women. The Greek *mitra* began life in Homeric times as a studded groin-guard, and its subsequent career is a good example of this genital out-migration, as we learn from the *Thesaurus Linguae Graecae* (s.v.). But it remained a device for sexual display; indeed Herodotus (1.131) says the Persian name for Aphrodite *is* Mitra, which is an appropriate (but perhaps etymologically distinct) name, certainly, for the penis's protectress, who is also mistress of the gods Phallos and Priapus and was herself formed out of Uranus's giant penis. And in Christian times the mitra turned into the bishop's mitre.[29]

We leap forward to the Victorian age. Perhaps the greatest reproductive improvement provided by clothes as opposed to fur or natural feathers is that clothes allow the wearer more control of the messages sent by his or her attractors. Francis Galton, the Victorian biostatistician, writes:

If a pea-hen should take it into her head that bars would be prettier than eyes in the tail of her spouse [the peacock], she could not possibly get what she wanted. It would require hundreds of generations in which the pea-hens generally concurred in the same view before sexual selection could effect the desired alteration. The feminine delight in indulging her caprice in matters of ornament is a luxury denied to the females of the brute world, and the law that rules changes of taste, if studied at all, can only be ascertained by observing the alternations of fashion in civilised communities.[30]

Galton's words are worth dwelling on. The phrase about female caprice in matters of ornament sounds, at first, like a reference to women's desire to adorn *themselves*. But he cannot and does not mean this. His women are indulging their ornamental caprices *by judging the appearance of men*. For men, Galton says, unlike peacocks, can be made to wear whatever clothes and ornaments they or their womenfolk think increases the men's erotic magnetism. Galton lived in a period—as Darwin shows when he condemns the European practice of selecting males for brains, strength, and so on, and females for beauty[31]—in which clothes made just this point. Men's dress emphasized their heads and hands,[32] women's their reproductive systems (though of course head and hands are important in lovemaking). But the men's real attraction was their ability to support their wives and children. It is in this sense that heads and hands are primary attractors. Thus do we find in the typical Victorian cravat-and-collar ensemble, its long, stiff thick necktie-penis hanging beneath a pair of collar-tes-

1.20.

Charles Dana Gibson. From *Sketches and Cartoons* (New York, 1898).

ticles, a translated and augmented reproductive system that makes an analogy between the head, with its brain, and the gonads. The effect is often further augmented by a beard or moustache and other artificial hair-skin-and-mouth patternings that can mimic the pattern and structure of the pubic area. Perhaps this pairing goes back to the age-old belief that sperm resides in the head.

And here (1.20) is Victorian reproductive dress in action. The two men wear evening dress, which increases the size and scale of the jacket opening and allows the tie-and-collar complex to turn snowy white against the suit's dramatic blackness. This powers up the genital-vector V formed by the jacket and vest. The young lady, meanwhile, borrows her attractor complex from the bisexual yet feminine world of flowers. The cone of her straight, solid skirt forms a plinth for her breasts, which emerge like a gadrooned vase from her narrow belted waist. As for primary genital expression, she carries a loose, ribboned bouquet of roses just in front of her groin. The roses = organs motif is continued in the embroidery around her bosom and the puffed sleeves, which thus suggest more roses and also additional breasts, especially via art—that is, the heavy loose parallel lines with which the artist has indicated both. The woman's father has just been asked if he is exhibiting at the horse show this year, and he replies, "Yes, I am sending my daughter." Arriving at a mating ground where the females display for a jury of males, she will find, one hopes, a partner worthy of the hypercharged reproductive success her outfit prophesies.[33]

Sexual selection, as originally defined by Darwin and then as reexplored in recent science, plays a huge role in nature. It has helped determine, in us and in most other animals, the appearance, cultural achievements, and differences between females and males. Or as Darwin puts it:

He who admits the principle of Sexual Selection will be led to the remarkable conclusion that the nervous system [Darwin's euphemism for the sex drive] not only regulates most of the existing functions of the body, but has indirectly influenced the progressive development of various bodily structures and of certain mental qualities. Courage, pugnacity, perseverance, strength and size of body, weapons of all kinds, musical organs, both vocal and instrumental, bright colours and ornamental appendages, have all been indirectly gained by the one sex or the other, through the exertion of choice, the influence of love and jealousy, and the appreciation of the beautiful in sound, colour or form.[34]

The clothes we have been looking at exemplify Darwin's words. They project sexual readiness and reproductive desirability in Darwin's sense of an evolved "indirect gain." Such gear may be contrasted with nonsexual clothes, whose message is often precisely that of unavailability, nonreproduction. But the message about selectability is most clearly understood only when there is contrasting dress with the opposite meaning. Thus the celibate priest, rejecting the sexual diagramming of the man of the world, will wear a Roman collar—that is, he eloquently omits the genital vector and phallic cravat, and, for similar reasons, might prefer a skullcap to a topper. Similarly, women in Iran must not only shroud their bodies, they must omit all the reproductive metaphors in which Western dress delights. Sexual unavailability is proclaimed not only by hiding the reproductive organs themselves but by ignoring the places to which those organs are metaphorically transposed and, even more, by banning the transposed and augmented forms those organs then take: the tailoring and fitting, the tubular sleeves and legs, the spiraling centrifugal hairdos, hats, and all strong demarcations between the upper and lower body. In contrast sexually selective clothing, as in Bronzino's portrait of Lodovico Capponi, a family portrait that would hang in the salon of the family palazzo, enshrines most of the meanings of a displaying primate; moreover, it declares to posterity the eminent selectability of the Capponi line.

2 Incarnate Christs and Selectable Saints

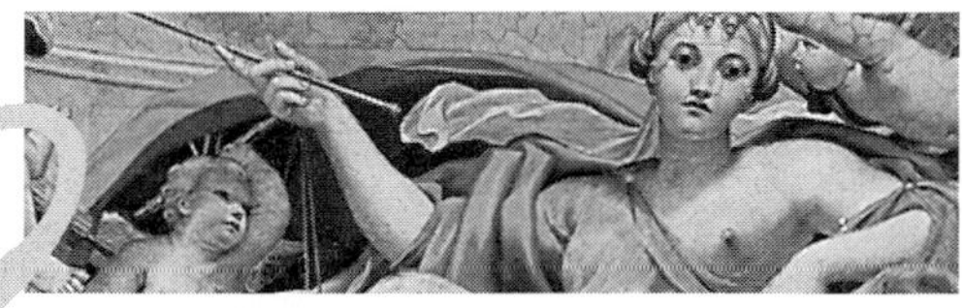

In the West, Christianity and Christian art have exercised enormous influence on sexual selection. One reason is that Roman Catholicism, in embracing the arts, was embracing media that had long been committed to depicting selectable people. Christianity only brought new energy to the process, beginning with the New Testament itself: Saints Peter and Paul recommended that Timothy constitute himself a living model for his flock (1 Tim. 4.12) and said that the elders of every congregation should do the same (1 Pet. 5.3).

The Incarnation

Of course this advice was meant spiritually. But physical and spiritual modeling were strongly interconnected, in part because of the Christian doctrine of the incarnation. This holds that God made himself into a being, Jesus Christ, who was fully divine but also fully human, who would take upon himself the full burdens of human life, and indeed through this incarnation—literally, his being made flesh—would act as the universal agent of salvation.

This taking-on-of-flesh by God has another aspect that reflects on ideas about the human body—that the worshiper who receives Communion during Mass eats Christ's flesh and drinks his blood, thus taking Christ's fleshly body into his or her own. This means that in a sense the body of the worshiper becomes at least partly Christ's.

That Christ is God-made-flesh has other, generally unspoken, corollaries. At a certain level Christian saints and heroes have exercised on those who worshipped them a selective force more like that of Aphrodite and Apollo—through their physical attractiveness, their power not only to fascinate but to ravish. And the relationships that resulted were often less chaste than appeared. They could even be incestuous. The Virgin Mary (like Ishtar, Ashtaroth, and most of the other Near Eastern goddesses she partly descends from) was both Christ's mother and his spouse. Nor was she his only real or dream partner. Mary Magdalen was famously termed Christ's lover, and her beauty and grande tenue were spiritually seen.[1] Another of Christ's lovers was his mystical fiancée, Catherine of Alexandria. There is even a tinge of homoeroticism in such figures as St. John the Evangelist, the beloved disciple, and in that wounded Eros, St. Sebastian.

Even though most saints were unmarried and the ideal of chastity has frequently pervaded the ranks of Christian heroes, their involvement with fleshliness and hence with sexual selection is not really diminished. Chastity may be the proper road for saints, monastics, priests, and some others; yet it is they, these chaste priests, who as confessors, pastors, authors, and preachers supervise the marriage choices of their flocks. They may not sexually select for themselves but, like stockbreeders, or like village elders in prescriptive marriage systems, they do so for others.

Christ's fleshliness in art is often celebrated in the form of a divinely beautiful male body. Moreover, as Leo Steinberg has shown, Christ in his humanity was not only subject to human passions and desires but even to human sexual feelings.[2] Like the Virgin, he was, in the language of the papal bull on the immaculate conception, *Ineffabilis Deus*, "preserved from sin but not concupiscence."[3] Some of the images that Steinberg publishes show Christ with an erection. At first this may seem shocking; but what is the virtue in renouncing a temptation that is not felt? Indeed theologians in the past have made a good deal of this point. As Johann Landsberger put it in his *Pharetra divini amoris,* first published in 1532: temptation "augments the merit of the reward, because the person who is tempted, and by resisting overcomes the temptation, is more praiseworthy than he who has not been tempted."[4]

In fact, any sort of obvious male sexual temptation is one of those things that the visual arts, unlike verbal expression, cannot gloss over or omit—though presumably the formula "concupiscence but not sin" still holds. Baldung Grien even portrayed the infant Christ (2.1) with the Virgin exhibiting his naked body while St. Anne, in an act that today would rank as child abuse, fondles his penis with

2.1.

Hans Baldung Grien. *Holy Family*, 1511. From Steinberg, *Sexuality of Christ.*

2.2.
Maerten van Heemskerck. *Ecce Homo,* c1525–1530. From Steinberg, *Sexuality of Christ,* fig. 95. Used with permission.

2.3.
Priapus anointing his penis. Bronze statuette, first century CE. Naples, Museo Nazionale (RP 7332).

two fingers. The three elders present, Mary, Anne, and (behind the wall) Joseph, calmly study what is clearly intended as a profitable subject for pious meditation.

Christ's erections can occur even after the crucifixion, which suggests not only life and its seed transcending the grave, immortality, and the joys of heaven, but also the eternity of Christ's incarnate nature. As Steinberg has shown, Heemskerck's Man of Sorrows (2.2), for instance, displays a Christ who shows forth his physical wounds to humankind and with his erection proves himself to be, as St. Paul says, "one who has been tempted as we are in every respect, yet without sinning" (Heb. 4.15).[5] Heemskerck's priapic Christ would of course also be the selectable Savior, Christ the cynosure, displaying the ultimate mark of procreative power.

In utilizing the formula of the draped erection, Heemskerck is indebted, of course, to the contemporary fad for codpieces; but he also draws on a pagan tradition, as shown in the statuette of Priapus reproduced here (2.3). The god's tunic falls in elegant wavelets down the back of his legs as, in a contrary gesture, an enormous crescent-shaped phallus thrusts upward to receive drops of consecrating oil. Like Christ, Priapus was a religious symbol of renewed life, resurrection, and joy.[6] Priapus, indeed, is much the same as an incarnation of the divine, a god whose name is troped with ποιέω, "create." In several texts Priapus is the creator-god whose seed created us all.[7]

We have noted that, in males especially, muscles are attractors, and we see this in much Renaissance and baroque art. If we look at the figure of Christ in Rogier's famous Escorial *Deposition* (2.4), painted seventy years or so before

2.4.

Rogier van der Weyden. The Escorial *Deposition,* c1435. Detail. Madrid, Prado.

2.5.

Peter Paul Rubens. *The Elevation of the Cross,* 1610. Detail. Antwerp Cathedral.

muscular saints began to appear with any frequency, we see a much older tradition that portrays an ectomorphic Christ with skeletal minimalism: all emphasis is on rib cage and bones, the muscles thin, strung out, and anonymous. But the Rubens Christ (2.5) exploits a new drama of hypermusculature. Note the huge deltoids, abdominals, and thigh and calf muscles. They are all prominent, if relaxed, and sag dramatically as the body is raised on the cross. Their very relaxation, into interweaving crescents and islanded mounds that twist and run beneath the skin, portrays surrender and renounced power as no bony quattrocento body would have done.

Painters like Rubens seem to have conceived of human muscles as elements in a discourse that could persuade and convert—muscles as the pictorial equivalent of epideictic oratory, leading viewers to empathize with a pain whose imagined impact was heightened by the detail and truth of the anatomies through which that pain flowed. There were additional reasons, in the age of the baroque, for depicting saints and divine figures as muscular beauties. For believers, in this age, the good people of the Bible and of Christian tradition all still existed, in heaven, as they had been seen and known on earth, but now in a state of grace. In other words, through Christ's sacrifice they had achieved, or reachieved, the primal innocence and nudity of Eden. And, as St. Roberto Bellarmino put it, in heaven the greatest joy of the senses will be the sight of beautiful human forms. There, even narcissism is utterly innocent. When the saved soul gains the kingdoms of the blessed "it will rejoice first in the splendor and pulchritude of its own body," and later in the sight of the bodies of the martyrs. Their very wounds, says Bellarmino, will become as jewels. And the supreme joy of the newly arrived soul will be the beauty of the body of Christ, unclothed on the cross.[8] Would that Blake could have been Bellarmino's illustrator.

Thus does Christ acquire male sexual beauty. But he does not lose his older role as a living model for human behavior. A distinguished modern writer on monasticism remarks that the purpose of that institution is to reshape each adherent into a living "icon or image of God's beauty."[9] Aside from Christ himself, the greatest of models, whose face more than any other reflects his features, is the Virgin Mary.[10] Indeed Mary's cult is seen by modern theologians as above all one of imitation, based less on her authority than on what they call her fascination. The living image of the Madonna, it is claimed, is stored in each Christian's soul as a visual incarnation. And the successful believer will, little by little, see his or her own body and face transformed into hers.[11] As noted, disclaimers were made to the effect that all of this was meant spiritually, not physically. But in the visual arts there is, unavoidably, considerable overlap between the two.

This same tradition of *imitatio* relates to epideictic preaching, which typically laces its sermons with adjurations: "Look on the face of this saint! Look at the sorrow of that lovely countenance! Look at the wounds, the emaciation, of that body! Is she (or he) not worthy of admiration and emulation? Can we not make ourselves more like this wonderful person in action and aspect?" The preacher may even be pointing or referring to a specific picture or statue. And if we go look closely at that image we will in most cases find that it is in fact a being whose fundamental beauty, despite the ravages of torture, suffering, and even age—perhaps because of them—has not dimmed.[12]

The Immaculate Conception

Aside from the doctrines of the incarnation and the real presence of Christ's body and blood in the edibles and drinkables of Communion, the Catholic doctrine of the immaculate conception is the most tremendous outlet for these feelings, once aroused. The doctrine, which has long been a matter of contention and is often misunderstood,[13] has considerable importance in this book because it deals with reproductive biology and a host of allied concepts in ways not found in paganism.[14] In normal usage the words refer not to Christ's having been immaculately conceived—most Christian denominations, Catholic or not, have no disagreement about that issue—but to the immaculate conception of his mother Mary in the womb of her mother, Anne. This latter belief is more or less limited to Roman Catholics.

An immaculate (literally, unstained) conception preserves the mother's virginity. The egg is fertilized without normal sexual intercourse, which in biological terms means either without sperm (asexual reproduction) or, as with flowers, through self-fertilization in which the mother supplies both the sperm and the egg. Another method, particularly relevant given the actual circumstances both of this immaculate conception and Christ's own, entails the transferral of sperm to the mother's womb by spermatophores, as bees transfer pollen from the anthers of one flower to the ovules of another. Mary's impregnation with God's sperm, variously ascribed to agencies such as the angel and the dove, shows how this botanical analogy could apply. In just such a mood one of the earliest theorists of the immaculate conception, the twelfth-century theologian Eadmer, proposed that Mary appeared from Anne's womb not in the unpleasant conditions of normal birth but as a chestnut appears from its spiny shell—sweet-smelling, unblemished, and hence "immaculate."[15]

In any event, ordinary conception via ordinary sexual intercourse was sinful, partly because it was linked to lust but also, and more important, because it created a fetus who had not been baptized and thereby freed from original sin, the sin of Adam, which infects all unbaptized persons. Baptism relieves a child of this weight; until it occurs, the mother has carried about, as a part of her body and for many months, a being infected with original sin. Even today, after giving birth, mothers in some faiths must be ritually cleansed ("churched").[16]

Yet, paradoxically, the Virgin, however pure she may have been as a result of her immaculate conception, was often seen as the successor to the maculate and impure Aphrodite. The idea was that sacred love followed after and triumphed over profane love, but without entirely losing the latter's trappings. Since Mary's immaculate conception meant that she had been preserved from original sin but not "from concupiscence,"[17] she is, like Christ, to be seen as subject to normal human drives and, perhaps, even as someone who can excite these drives in others. This is more true in art, once again, than in the world of written texts. When, as is common, Mary plays Venus less erotically, say as a fully clothed Venus Pudica, she gives the pose a new meaning: rather than hiding her nakedness or reproaching the viewer as a voyeur, she proclaims with this modest gesture that her loins and breasts are unstained by any unregenerate body in her womb. Or else: it is through *these* loins, *these* breasts, that the Christ Child, embodiment of all purity, immaculately conceived by an immaculately conceived mother, comes into the world. And still, such an image of the Virgin remains sexually selective. For in that world, Christ will serve as a reproductive goal so that humankind will breed itself into a fitter state and eventually gain the kingdom of Heaven.

But the most tremendous part of this tremendous doctrine is this: Mary was chosen for the high honor of immaculate conception long before her own birth, before St. Anne, before even Eve, before the creation of the world. The Virgin of the immaculate conception, in fact, is the oldest thought in the mind of God.[18] The Immacolata, described as all beautiful and all pure, is therefore nothing less than the conception of everything—of the heavens through which she descends and of the earth on which she lands. And it is at this point that we must think again of Aphrodite and her own epic descent from heaven, similarly bringing a religion of beauty and love and having the same purpose: namely, to foster, through upgraded sexual selection, what is godlike in human nature (Hesiod, *Theogony* 176ff.; Empedocles frags. 6, 7).

Art has had its own way of dealing with all these intricate crosscurrents.[19] Most frequently the immaculate conception is shown in a way that emphasizes the precedence of the action as God's earliest thought about creation. The Virgin stands alone, a young woman (and hence not only already conceived but grown up). She is descending to earth from heaven. A crown of twelve stars circles her head. Her foot is set on a crescent moon, and sometimes also on a serpent. She may extend her arms, fold her hands in an attitude of prayer, or put her hands over her heart. She is praying for the whole cycle of creation, fall, and salvation that will unwind from this descent. Her eyes look down at the round earth far below. Often, too, she is attended by angels. Sometimes she is surrounded by the instruments of Christ's Passion, showing that this Passion, with its death on the cross and ascent into heaven, was prophesied from the very first. Inscriptions from the Bible are frequently involved—for example, from the Song of Songs, *Tota pulchra es, amica mea, et macula non est in te:* "You are all beautiful, my friend, and there is no stain upon you." To these symbols were sometimes added the closed garden, the fountain, the well of living waters, the cedar, the olive, the lily, the rose; also the unstained mirror, the tower of David, the City of God, and the Gate of Heaven: all symbols applied to the Immacolata but drawn from the Song. Passages from the Apocalypse (Rev. 12) provide other artifacts—a pearl necklace, stars, the sun, the silver crescent moon, and the star of the sea that Mary and Venus share.[20]

There are strange conjunctions of imagery in these borrowings. The passage in the Apocalypse describes a *mulier amicta sole*, a woman clothed in the sun, who treads on a crescent moon and has twelve stars as a crown. She brings forth her child by herself, screaming and suffering, as she descends through the skies (Rev. 12.1–3). Meanwhile the lovers in the Song of Songs see each other directly, almost purely, as sexual objects. Like the Virgin Mary, they have not been kept from concupiscence—far from it. "Let her kiss me with the kisses of her mouth, for her breasts are better than wine" (1.1), sings the man. She in turn praises him, whose beauty, combined with hers, will make their marriage bed blossom. "Rise and come, my friend, my beauty," they say to each other. She asks him to remove her clothes and wash her feet. And, she adds later, "my spouse put his hand upon my hole, and my belly trembled at his touch."[21]

Like the Blessed Virgin herself, the woman in the Song is a projector of fascination, "beautiful and black like a cedar tabernacle." Her eyes are like doves. Her breasts are like two fawns, or else like twin goats feeding on lilies. The husband likens her beauties, natural and acquired, to weapons—her neck is like a fortified tower hung with shields, and her hair and eyes are fearsome weapons that besiege his heart. I would suggest that these animal and other figures represent the woman's pendants, rings, necklaces, and bracelets; they might also (or alternatively) represent fabrics embellished with such things. The Immacolata, then, succeeds the spouse in the Song of Songs just as she succeeds Aphrodite, complete with lilies, roses, clouds, stars, moon, and so on, but without the *sponsus*. He, instead, is the absent presence, God, in whose thought this startling apparition precedes all other happenings.

Authors who have confronted the paradoxes of the Virgin's different simultaneous roles in these scenes tend to grant, even celebrate and extend, her links with earlier goddesses; and the "evolutionary" gloss that was put on them was not denied but emphasized. The Victorian iconographic writer Anna Jameson, in a Darwinian mood, proposes (though without definitely approving) that the Virgin is the fitter final version of a series of flawed predecessors: "As, in the oldest Hebrew rites and Pagan superstitions," she writes, "men traced the Old Testament, and even the demigods of heathendom became accepted types of the Person of Christ—so the Eve of the Mosaic history, the Astarte of the

Assyrians . . . Ashtaroth . . . the Isis nursing Horus of the Egyptians, the Demeter and the Aphrodite of the Greeks, the Scythian Freya, have been considered by some writers as types of a divine maternity, foreshadowing the Virgin-Mother of Christ."[22]

Jameson does not say so, but one has to note that these goddesses, with their full measure of sensuousness, ruthlessness, and infidelity, not to mention murderousness, make odd forerunners for the mild and supremely chaste Virgin. But perhaps their wickedness only strengthens and exalts the contrast with the moral regeneration that comes with the mother of Christ. By the same logic Mary's child is the antitype of such types or foreshadowings as Eve's children, Cain and Abel; as Semiramis (daughter of Astarte); and as Anchises and Eros (Aphrodite's sons). Mrs. Jameson even claims, quoting Dante, that, thus seen, the Virgin ennobles all earlier and future women, thereby ennobling earlier and future men (a more difficult task, one gathers).[23] Thus is the "growth" from, say, Isis to the Virgin an evolutionary map.

In Guido Reni's Immacolata (2.6), the Virgin's oval form floats majestically, her hands delicately joined in prayer just in front of her breasts, her eyes cast luminously upward for a last look at heaven as she descends, her body wrapped in a thickly flowing gown. This massive mantle constructs, within the outer oval of the figure's silhouette, an inner opening enframing Mary's breasts and abdomen, while at the same time it establishes a powerful vectored V of highlighted fabric over her groin. Beneath this point the Virgin's gown turns into a flurry of verticals from which her feet just emerge. While she primly lacks the wind-tossed hair of an Aphrodite, say Botticelli's (2.7), the ends of the veil wound through her hair flower out into hairlike tendrils. Forming another, concentric outer oval

2.6.
Guido Reni. *The Immaculate Conception*, 1627. New York, Metropolitan Museum of Art.

2.7.
Sandro Botticelli. *The Birth of Venus*, 1482–1486. Detail. Florence, Uffizi.

to frame all this is a cloudbank of infant angels or erotes. Thus this picture, like almost all Immacolatas, constructs her quintessential shape of egg and womb. Below, two symmetrical winged adorers float beside the Madonna, arms crossed on their bosoms in attitudes of prayerful awe. The Virgin meanwhile stands on a crescent moon, a horned symbol of fatherhood, which is borne upward to her by three winged Eros-heads or thrones, suggesting that we are looking at the actual impact between God's seed and the Virgin's egg.

If we continue to compare Guido's Immacolata with the Botticelli, we immediately see how, and why, Guido's Virgin is revising her pagan predecessor's physical attitude. One may even say that the Medici Venus has shifted her hands from breast and groin so as to pray, turning the goddess's gesture of sexual self-revelation (this womb, these breasts) into one of supplication. Or: Guido has shown Botticelli's Venus clothed in the mantle that, in Botticelli's picture, is being offered to the goddess on the right; the surrounding pagan beings, that is, Flora and certain winds, become Guido's angels, as the shell turns into the crescent moon. And Venus's eyes, cast down upon the earth and sea that will be her home, now, as the Virgin's eyes, turn upward to God whence she has come. Art emphasizes the fleshly or incarnational aspects of the texts used to support the doctrine of the immaculate conception. It thus goes directly against the long-standing purely verbal tradition that has sought to explain away all erotic aspects of these visions—for example, the claim that when the lover of the Song talks of resting between the breasts of his lady he is really saying that the breasts are the Old and New Testament, or that his long night of pleasure is the long night one consecrates to the study of scripture.[24]

There is a further biological way in which we can study the Madonna. Recent sexual selection theory has proposed that animals at quite a few different evolutionary levels select mates on the basis of their bodily symmetry. Researchers are also examining "fluctuating asymmetry," which refers to mismatchings, in an individual, of normally symmetrical features such as wings, fins, hands, feet, eyes, or ears. It appears that women whose sexual partners have nearly equal measurements in these respects, irrespective of the partners' general sexiness or handsomeness, tend to have more orgasms than when they copulate with partners whose hands, ears, and so on suffer from fluctuating asymmetry.[25] Symmetry, of course, has long been equated with or linked to beauty and attractiveness, though these latter, at least for many evolutionists, are only a subset of fitness.

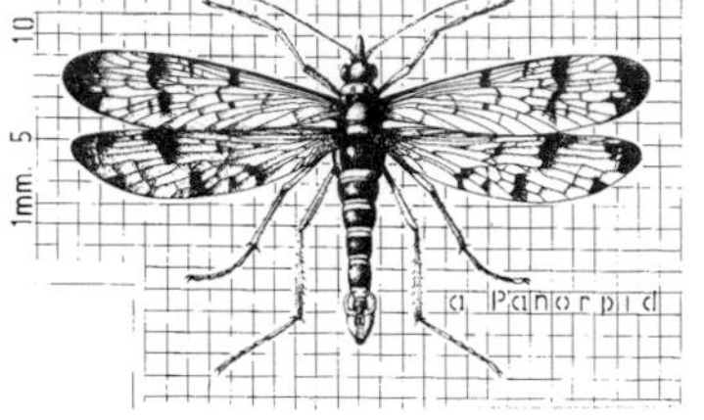

2.8.
Male panorpid (scorpion fly). From *Insects of the World.*

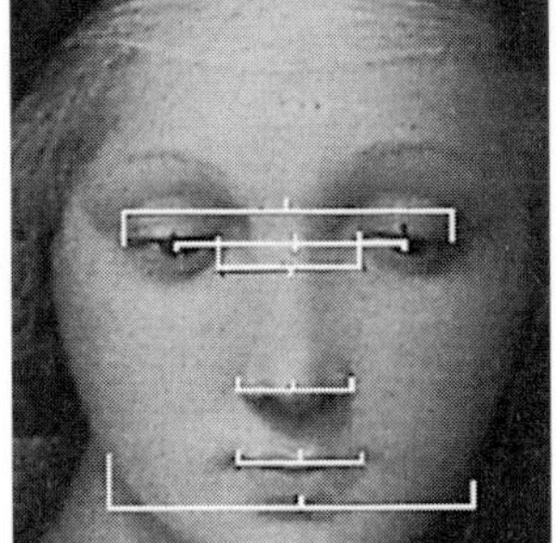
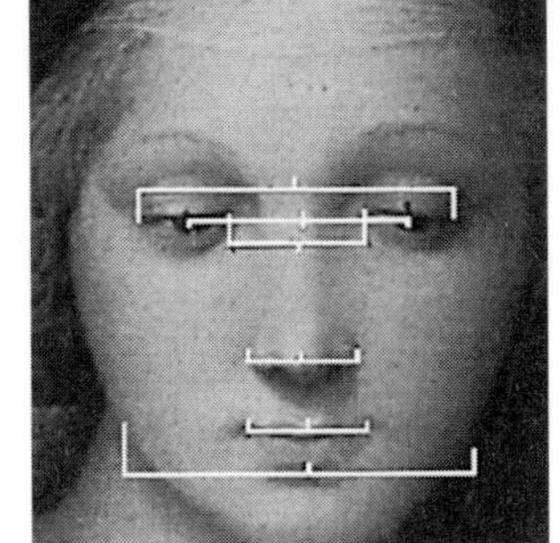

2.9.
Raphael. *Madonna del Granduca,* c1504. Florence, Pitti Gallery. Madonna's face with horizontal symmetries mapped according to the Thornhill system. The vertical axis has been straightened.

Scorpion flies (2.8), for instance, have proven more adept at food gathering the more symmetrical they are.[26] As to fitness, it is certainly true that many motor activities involving grasping, chewing, or moving are probably easier and more effective when the appendages that do these things are well matched.

Let's see how the Madonna's symmetry, she being the most perfect of all women, plays into this. Few human faces are perfectly symmetrical. Even the greatest master of the perfect face, Raphael (2.9), gives the Madonna a slightly asymmetrical countenance, as measured by the system developed by Randy Thornhill and others. In addition, we instantly perceive that the system does not map such keys to symmetry/asymmetry as the curves of the cheek, chin, and forehead. Note that in the Raphael, while the jaw, mouth, nose, and eyes are symmetrically centered, the outer curves of the head, left and right, are all different. There is also the slightly different horizontal angle of the Madonna's left eye. Thus, she suffers from a very slight case of fluctuating asymmetry. However, more generally her face has the proper markers for high estrogen endowment—a generous mouth and a delicate jaw.[27]

Magdalen and Teresa

Many female saints are highly selectable and, like Raphael's Virgin, exhibit unusual endowments of estrogen. The most prominent of these is probably Mary Magdalen, who has acted as a useful bridge between paganism's salient sexuality and the chaster but still erotic ideals of the Christian life. By her heyday, when a sexualized piety was more firmly reestablished in baroque Italy, Spain, and France, Magdalen had a special and overwhelming appeal. Unlike many saints she was all too human: after all, as a prostitute she had been tempted and fallen not once but thousands of times, and yet she rose to final, famous sanctity. In art she is often portrayed as still being highly sexed despite having renounced her old life. As with similar portrayals of Christ, this showed that her renunciation really meant something. Yet the Magdalen never really renounces the old lifestyle and its artifacts. Thus she is the patron of perfume, cosmetics, jewelry, fashion. And of hairdressers. (Thus an unnamed French preacher quoted by Mrs. Jameson, who proposes Magdalen as a model for all women, first of all defends her makeup and finery by claiming that in ancient Israel the art of pleasing men ranked as highly as any other.)[28]

Similarly, in his 1671 *Oeuvres poétiques,* P. Le Moyne published a sonnet on a Guido Reni *Converted Magdalen* that partly goes as follows:

Her luxury, converted, becomes religious, the spirit of her perfumes is that of devotion like her own, her rubies are ardent with her new fire, and her pearls become the tears in her eyes. Beautiful eyes, sacred channels of a precious flood, innocent corrupters of your amorous judge! You will never be without your flames and darts. But at least for a moment stay your charms. The earth still smokes with the fire of your glances, and already you sear the heavens with your tears.[29]

This might be described as a hymn to sacralized attractors; thus does Magdalen vie with Aphrodite as a magnet before whom humans and the very heavens are powerless, as is Christ, her "amorous judge."

The Magdalen of legend was developed out of three biblical Marys: first, Mary of Magdala, and second, Mary of Bethany, the sister of Martha and Lazarus. The third Mary (identified in scripture only as a *peccatrix)* appears at the feast of Simon the Pharisee (Luke 7.37). A fourth source figure, less certain, is the Mary who participates in the events of the Passion along with the Virgin. The "Magdalen" of Simon's feast brings a jar of ointment and, carried away by Christ's words, weeping and repentant, in devotion anoints his feet and dries them with her hair. Christ knows she is a sinner; but, he says, much is forgiven her for she loved much. The Magdalen who exists in later lore as the repentant prostitute was often offered as proof, to those who believed too rigidly in predestination, that true contrition can, through the soul's free will, achieve salvation and indeed the greatest sanctity. Magdalen's role in art is that of a beautiful, regretful, and submissive-seeming follower. Yet she has a volcanic potential. Her scarlet times are over, perhaps, but, in art at least, she frequently seems not to have cast aside her passionate nature.

Mary Magdalen is the object of a considerable postscriptural legend. After the resurrection she traveled to southern France, where she established herself in a cave near Marseilles called the Sainte-Baume (holy balm, a reference to her ointments).[30] There she pondered her guilt and sought, through visions of Christ's crown of thorns and of the spikes that had nailed him to the cross, to obtain further forgiveness. Sometimes she even saw a vision of the crucified savior.

Most often, however, she appears in art as an object for meditation. And these Penitent Magdalens normally deploy the full armament of arousal. Often, for example, the saint is shown before her conversion, among her jewels and ointments. Modern writers have ridiculed these images as absurd attempts to package porn as uplift. Without completely denying this, one should add that what is also revealed, in this very derision, is the critics' own confusion about the role of sexuality in Renaissance and baroque religious art. Most of us, conditioned by Judaeo-Protestant-Tridentine puritanism, make absolute antitheses of sexuality and religion. Yet the Magdalen's fleshly qualities, Christ's erection, and the Immacolata's eroticism and that of many other saints all explore the many dimensions of the incarnation, which, of course, must involve the whole of the human condition, all human drives, and the entire human body.

2.10.

Titian. *The Penitent Magdalen,* c1565. Florence, Pitti Gallery.

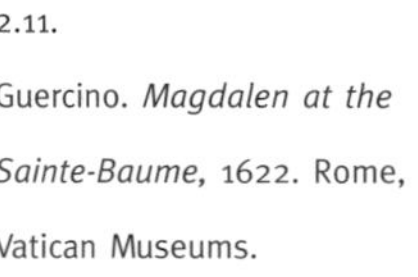

2.11.

Guercino. *Magdalen at the Sainte-Baume,* 1622. Rome, Vatican Museums.

Thus Titian's *Penitent Magdalen* (2.10) shows the saint at prayer in her French cave. But still, and though she is now outdoors, she is ensconced in her attitude as a demimondaine at her toilette. In dishabille, and with lacy white and gaily striped shawls revealing her upper body, the skull and book she contemplates are joined by her makeup jar. And we realize, looking at this picture, that the ointment with which she anointed Christ's feet was part of her prostitute's arsenal of attractors—as, for that matter, was the hair with which she dried

those feet. (Christ, indeed, singles out this ointment, along with Magdalen's kisses, as marks of her contrition and conversion; Luke 7.45ff.) Earthly love has turned to heavenly, yes, but retains some of the latter's artifacts and yearnings. And though she fasts rigorously, the Magdalen unlike other hermit saints almost always appears healthy and vibrant, as here. This, we are told, is because her frequent abductions, by angels, to heaven and its joys fulfill all her needs, bodily as well as spiritual.[31]

As Titian shows her, too, the Magdalen adopts the pose of the Medici Venus, except that the hand that, in the classic version, hides her breasts has here moved to her heart, thus proposing that she is now penetrated with the love of Christ and that his love has replaced the physical love invoked by Aphrodite's gesture. The expression on the Magdalen's full, solemn, weeping face is one of hope after forgiveness. Her golden hair curls and runs around her head and neck, tumbling past her breasts, as if charged with sanctifying grace.

The Magdalen's angelic abductors often appear in art. In Guercino's picture (2.11) the saint, her lower body masked in deeply invaginated folds, reveals her upper body. She kneels at a stone altar, hands clasped, face averted, eyes oval and large, hair flowing over her shoulders and breasts. The young angel in the center points to two more angels in a cloudy sky tinged with red. The angels are not only her heavenly hosts—literally—but symbols of evolution, earthly into heavenly love.[32] The participants all contemplate the nails and crown of thorns that had "adorned" Christ on the cross. One angel actually offers a nail to Magdalen: the way to heaven through Christ's Passion. Yet the whole setup remains that of a woman at her dressing table.

Magdalen, then, like so many other saints, draws on various pagan prototypes. The second most famous selectable female saint, after the Magdalen, is probably Bernini's St. Teresa (2.12). And for good reason. Looking at it brings to mind one of Correggio's best-known erotic pictures, his *Venus, Cupid, and a Satyr* in the Louvre (2.13). Having fallen asleep, the goddess and her son are unaware that a satyr has lifted their coverlet and stares down in tender fascination. The satyr's interest is understandable; after all, he is looking at the incarnation of physical love. In just the same way Teresa's angel, in Bernini's celebrated composition, remarks on a comparable epiphany. Such scenes once again merge the Christian notion of heavenly and earthly love, the spirit-flesh of incarnation, with holy *ravissement*.

2.12.
Gianlorenzo Bernini. *The Ecstasy of St. Teresa*, 1646. Rome, Santa Maria della Vittoria.

2.13.
Engraving by F. Basan of Correggio's *Venus, Cupid, and a Satyr*, 1520s. Detail. Paris, Louvre.

The arrow that penetrates Teresa's heart in Bernini's sculpture is the arrow of Christ's love, propelled by an angel of transcendent beauty who smiles tenderly on the saint as she writhes and stiffens in passion. Note, by the way, the contrasts in the draperies, and the partial dishabille of the angel. A dark flame of shadow licks his loins as he kneels on Teresa's cloudy bed. And note too that he gently begins to lift, with his left hand, the huge drapery encasing her. Thus, we must surmise, will he bare her bosom for the arrow's plunge. What he will then see is possibly not too different from the sleeping Venus Correggio painted. But Teresa's costume, contrasting with the angel's, makes no comment on her sexual centers. It is anatomically mute, a lavalike burial of the weakening body. Yet the global agitation of the mantle does express the idea of a whole body within, suffused and penetrated, veins and muscles engorged with holy fire. Nor is this eroticism Bernini's gratuitous creation. Rather, it comes out of the tradition we have been referring to and, even more than that, is taken from the saint's own writings. As William James has said, "her idea of religion seems to have been that of an endless amatory flirtation—if one may say so without irreverence—between the devotee and the deity."[33]

In the Renaissance, as in so many other periods, artists used themselves and their relatives as models in depicting these Christian cynosures. This only strengthened and humanized the bond between the divine reproductive goal and the art's viewers. For these reasons among others, Christianity could conceivably offer a way of proving, or at least buttressing, my claim that art has helped shape Western society's reproductive goals. One can imagine a small medieval village with a stable population and, let us say, an altarpiece or two in which a certain distinctive type of face and physique dominates. More specif-

2.14.
The Master of the Flémalle (Robert Campin?). *Nativity with Two Wise Women*. Detail of Virgin. Musée de Dijon.

2.15.
Same artist. Merode altarpiece, c1425–1428. Detail from its Annunciation panel. New York, Metropolitan Museum, The Cloisters.

ically, let us propose a village in the Hainault province of Belgium with an altarpiece by Robert Campin (probably the artist also known as the Master of Flémalle). Before the full advent of mass media imagery in the sixteenth century, such images would have been nearly unique within their village contexts. The villagers themselves would have known few other pictorial representations of the human figure, if any. Furthermore, generations of worshipers would have been adjured to behave and believe like the saints and angels depicted in that altarpiece. It would be unsurprising if they attempted to look like those holy persons and selected mates who did the same.

There would have been generations, even centuries, of selective pressure toward the painted figures' dark-lidded orbical eyes, their long noses and rosy bee-stung lips, their elevated foreheads and softly pointed chins, their high, trim waists, narrow chests, and elegant arms and thighs (2.14, 2.15). As a result of this art-fostered sexual selection, the village would in fact have bred toward the painted phenotype. Would not this be mainly how the Christian could store the living image of the Madonna in the soul and see the body and face transformed into hers?

Of course one must also account for feedback, and allow that the painters of the altarpieces had employed local models who already possessed these privileged faces and bodies. The genes for the desired phenotypes would probably have had to be in the population already. But this really only means reciprocal selecting: by being turned into saintly role models, by being portrayed and then worshipped, the real people who were models for the saints would simply have been consecrated as living reproductive goals. They would have been selected, as particularly holy, on the basis of their faces and figures.

In other words, there is probably a certain amount of feedback or two-way influence between the saint in art, the real-life model for that saint, and the worshiper who is supposed to model herself or himself on the saint. Saints in pictures and statues frequently represent not only themselves but other, more immediate personages. For example, in the Borgia Apartments in the Vatican (Pinturicchio and assistants, 1492–1495) we see, in an overdoor, a fresco of Giulia Farnese, Alexander VI's mistress, portrayed as the Virgin Annunciate, with Alexander himself kneeling nearby adoring in full pontificals—a sort of second Gabriel.[34] As is the case here, artists often endowed these holy images of real relatives or lovers with considerable sexual attraction. In the fifteenth century, Savonarola thundered against Florentine pictures in which the Madonna appeared as a luscious blonde wearing gold and jewels, her head immodestly unveiled and her features those of some famous or infamous local lady. The friar even struck a selective, or rather deselective, note: if, he said, painters only knew "the influence of such pictures in perverting simple minds, they would hold their own works in horror and detestation."[35] He sounds exactly like Max Nordau (see chapter 7). Indeed the whole of the bonfire of the vanities could easily be interpreted as removing from the city its stock of attractive but degenerate reproductive goals.

Artists often chose their loved ones—their partners, offspring, and parents—to pose for Christ, the Madonna, and the saints. In some ways this practice was simply a continuation, or revival, of the frequent practice in antiquity in which, for example, the most beautiful girls in Croton were used as models by Zeuxis when he wanted to paint a portrait of Helen of Troy (Cicero, *Inv. Rhet.* 2.1.2–3).[36] In a similar spirit Andrea del Sarto painted his own wife, Lucrezia, every time he was asked to do a female saint. "Owing to this habit," writes Vasari, "all the women's heads which he did are alike."[37] And Andrea combined these real-life portrayals with flawless bodies.[38] The apparently unfaithful Lucrezia also posed, more fittingly, for the Magdalen.[39] Vasari lists many other occasions on which artists painted their relatives, and even themselves, as saints—as when Andrea included himself among the apostles in the 1526 Pitti *Assumption* (with Lucrezia as the Virgin).[40] Rubens and Francesco Albani also painted their wives, as did Alessandro Allori and Van Dyck their mistresses. Nor was it just a question of heads and faces. Domenichino's beautiful wife, Marsibilia Barbetti, reported after her husband's death that he hardly ever did a painting without studying her hands and feet.[41] Thus did the artists celebrate specific, prescriptive faces and bodies pictorially at the same time that as husbands or lovers they selected them sexually and, as fathers, reproduced them.

2.16.

Domenichino. The fresco of *Justice*, 1628–1630. Detail. Rome, San Carlo ai Catinari.

For instance, in figure 2.16—a detail from the Justice fresco in San Carlo ai Catinari, Rome, which dates from a couple of years after Domenichino's marriage to Marsibilia—the artist has given us two very similar allegorical women: twins. Their similarities extend from their wide, symmetrically oval faces, their round, shadowed eyes with large and prominent dark pupils, their ash-blond, tightly done hair, their long noses and narrow nostrils, their short, full, sharply etched lips, their soft, fleshy, small-boned limbs with heavily rounded joints, their wide waists and small, wide-set breasts, and so on, to their supple-fingered hands. Marsibilia, as a specific, unique face and body, is presented by her husband to the worshipers in San Carlo ai Catinari as a cynosure of virtue.

Christians were urged to imitate, to be, and, via art, even to look like images of the saints. Above all they were urged to imitate images of the Virgin and of Christ, the latter being the incarnate image of both man and God, and both of them fully susceptible to, and capable even of eliciting, human sexual urges (though on their part without sin). Often, representations of such holy persons were in turn modeled on selected men and women of the community. The process was mutually reinforcing: certain types were holy because they looked like preexisting holy pictures, and those pictures had in turn been based on local selectables.

3 Body Canons

3.1.
Venus of Willendorf, 21,000–30,000 BCE (Delporte's dating). Vienna, Museum of Natural History. From H. Delporte, *Image de la femme dans l'art préhistorique* (Paris, 1979).

3.2.
Lucian Freud. *Evening in the Studio*, 1993. Detail rotated 90 degrees. Private collection.

In this chapter, as in the others, I cannot hope to encompass the vast subject I take up. I shall have to continue my technique of choosing a few examples from a huge array. But the data I do present will at least serve to show how concerned people have been about this whole business, demonstrating that there has been a surprising amount of agreement, over a period of about 2,500 years, as to the quantitative contents of the body canon in art.

For most of the millennia leading up to the fifth century BCE, art had proposed male and female physiques that were considerably more varied than what we see in the "canonical" or post-Polykleitan period. The famous Willendorf Venus (3.1), with her goatish legs and superwide pelvis, her large stomach and gulflike vulva, has a body that I estimate at 6 heads high. Though her breasts and navel are at the 2-head and 3-head points, as was to become standard, her body as a whole must be compared with the Polykleitan ideal of 7 1/2 to 8 1/2 heads (see table 3.2), and, post-Michelangelo, with figures whose longer legs led to even higher measurements (see, e.g., fig. 3.8).

It is nonetheless true that these extremely wide variations do reappear in art from time to time, first in the Middle Ages and second since the advent of modernism, with its relative abandonment of Polykleitan models. The recumbent female in Lucian Freud's 1993 *Evening in the Studio* (3.2, rotated from its original position to make the comparison with the Willendorf Venus) is a case in

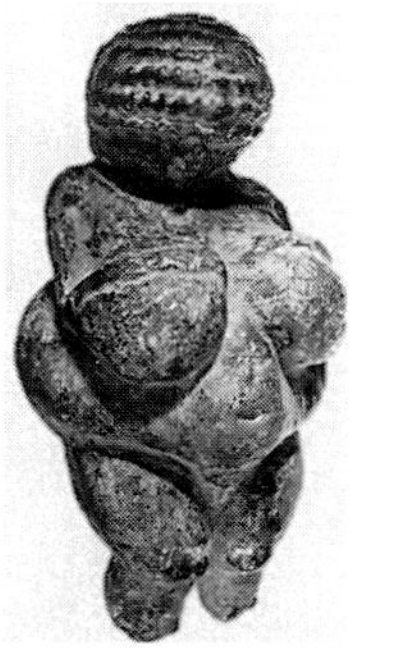

Table 3.1
Four Male Body Canons

	Egyptian*	Polykleitos Doryphoros	Leonardo	Michelangelo *David*
Nipples	2	2	2	2
Navel	3	3	3	3
Groin	4 1/2	4	4	4
Knee	5	5 1/2	5	5
Heel	7 1/2	7	7 1/2	7
				Canon of Integers

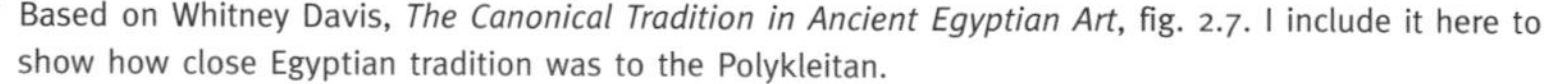

* Based on Whitney Davis, *The Canonical Tradition in Ancient Egyptian Art*, fig. 2.7. I include it here to show how close Egyptian tradition was to the Polykleitan.

3.3.

Los Caballos. Spain, Valltorta, Castellón. Mesolithic hunting scene. Copy by Douglas Masconowicz. From T. G. E. Powell, *Prehistoric Art* (New York, 1966).

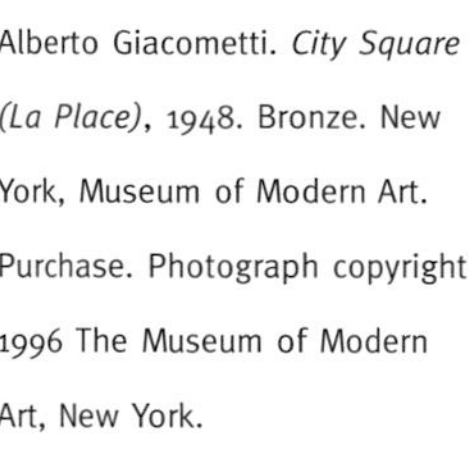

3.4.

Alberto Giacometti. *City Square (La Place)*, 1948. Bronze. New York, Museum of Modern Art. Purchase. Photograph copyright 1996 The Museum of Modern Art, New York.

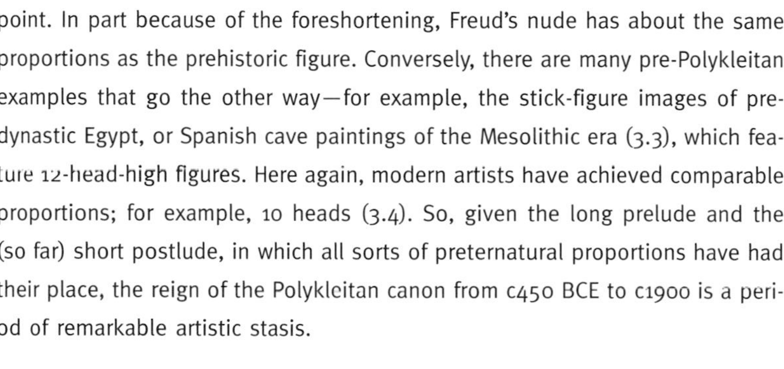

point. In part because of the foreshortening, Freud's nude has about the same proportions as the prehistoric figure. Conversely, there are many pre-Polykleitan examples that go the other way—for example, the stick-figure images of predynastic Egypt, or Spanish cave paintings of the Mesolithic era (3.3), which feature 12-head-high figures. Here again, modern artists have achieved comparable proportions; for example, 10 heads (3.4). So, given the long prelude and the (so far) short postlude, in which all sorts of preternatural proportions have had their place, the reign of the Polykleitan canon from c450 BCE to c1900 is a period of remarkable artistic stasis.

But what, first of all, *is* a body canon?[1] Originally the word "canon," in Greek κανῶν, meant a reed or canna marked off in equal spaces for use in measurement. By extension canons were also braces to preserve the shape of a leather shield, the weaver's rods to which alternate threads of the warp were attached, and lines rubbed with chalk to be snapped across a surface to mark it for cutting

Table 3.2

Three Female Canons (plus Michelango's Dying Slave)

	Sciarra Amazon	Mattei Amazon*	Medici Venus	Michelangelo *Dying Slave*
Nipples	2	2	2	2
Navel	3	3	3	3
Groin	4	4	4	4
Knee	5 1/2	5	5	6
Heel	7 1/2	7	8	8
		Canons of Integers		

* I have allowed for a smaller head than the oversize alien one now installed.

or coloring. Canons could also be various kinds of posts and rods, the pipes of a wind organ, window bars, and the monochord—a one-stringed instrument used to establish the geometric dimensions of musical pitch. In architecture the canon is the long molding that supports the lineup of triglyphs and metopes in the Doric entablature. The Latin word for this feature is *regula*, "ruler." In literature a canon is a grammatical rule, a scheme that shows all possible forms for a verse, a table of dates, or a generally specific set of rules for composition. These do not exhaust the word's meanings. Nowadays, in literature and other arts, a canon is a set list of key works that every educated person should know—classics against which other works (e.g., one's own) can be measured.

Inwardly, then, the word "canon" carries the notion of prescription, demarcation, proper preparation. In most cases it is a question of number and numerical measurement. The canon stiffens that which would be otherwise without structure. It is, in a sense, the grid against which the scorpion fly's symmetry is measured—or a person's. Not only have canonical human bodies traditionally populated works of Western art, but we also can measure ourselves and others against those very canons.[2]

Polykleitos, Praxiteles, and Vitruvius

The most influential human proportional system in Western fart has been that of the fifth-century Greek sculptor Polykleitos.[3] His masterpieces were a life-size bronze statue now called the Doryphoros (Spear Bearer)[4] and, for the female canon, a similar figure known as the Wounded Amazon. Polykleitos is said to have written a book about his Doryphoros, appropriately entitled the *Canon*, as was the statue itself. The book, it is claimed, was the first piece of writing known to us by an artist about an object he had made.[5] Unfortunately both the book and the originals of the Doryphoros and the Wounded Amazon are lost. However, ancient copies of the two statues remain.

Like so many of his contemporaries, Polykleitos believed that numbers ought to govern the human form because numbers and their rational sequences contain innate moral and perhaps magical powers. One word for this power was "symmetry." In antiquity that word meant not mirror reflection on either side of an axis, which is how we now think of it, but commensurability—a commensurability in which some built-in module in an object dictates its complete measurements in whole rational numbers.[6] This is what Galen means, for example, when he says that "the body's beauty consists of symmetry, not of its elements [i.e., of its chemical substances] but of its numbers." Elsewhere he repeats these phrases, explaining that as a result there are proper proportions for finger, hand, and arm "as set forth in the canon of Polykleitos."[7]

Generally in antiquity the numerical symmetries Galen mentions were not merely rational and whole, but numbers that comprised arithmetical, geometrical, harmonic, and other series. So Galen, I believe, meant two things in the quotation above. First, that an arm that can be measured out—for example, in its own hand-lengths—with a nonfractional result, is better than one that cannot be so measured. If your arm is exactly 3 of your own hands long it is ideal. If it is 3 1/2 or 2 1/2 of those hands long, it is disproportionate or, as the ancients would say, asymmetrical.[8] The second thing that Galen meant, I believe, is that the list of hand or arm measurements should constitute a rational number series. This would correspond to the rule Plutarch expresses, that the individual numerations within the body, of hands, heads, and so forth, must sum to a καιρός or "proper outcome."[9]

He was even perhaps saying that the surge of attraction we feel when we look at a beautiful physique is quantifiable, that its beauty is dependent on its numerical analysis. Modern echoes of this idea reverberate when we read the height, bust, waist, and hip measurements of a beauty queen or the measurements of a bodybuilder's bicep and chest diameters (see chapter 9). But it would probably be more Galenic to give those values all in the head-heights, hand-lengths, or even the thumbs (i.e., inches) of the particular body being measured, rather than using standard values. By concentrating on and repeating certain configurations of number and shape, and rejecting all others, artists soon created a steadily similar set of physiques that became canonical. This mensurational canon, I will demonstrate, has pressured the forces of sexual selection ever since.

There are several ancient copies of Polykleitos's lost original Doryphoros. Probably the best is a marble version now in the Museo Nazionale, Naples (3.5).[10] The youth is well muscled, thickly built through the chest. He saunters as he cradles his (missing) spear in his left arm. His face is calm but his body etched with readiness. There is a tradition that it is a portrait of Achilles (Servius on *Aeneid* 8.803).

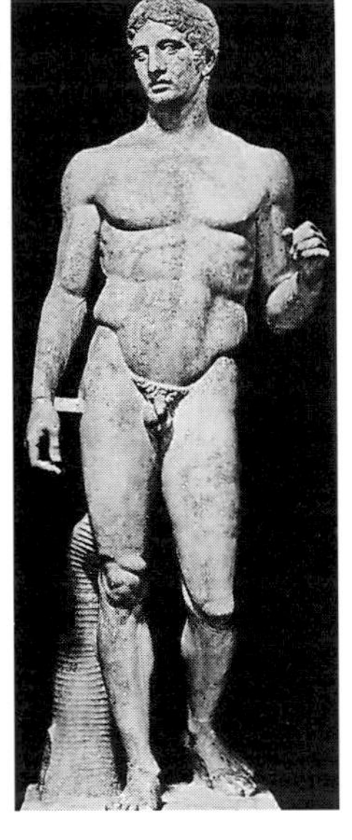

3.5.
Polykleitos. The Doryphoros (Spear Bearer), c450–440 BCE. Roman copy. Naples, Museo Nazionale dell'Arte Antica (6011).

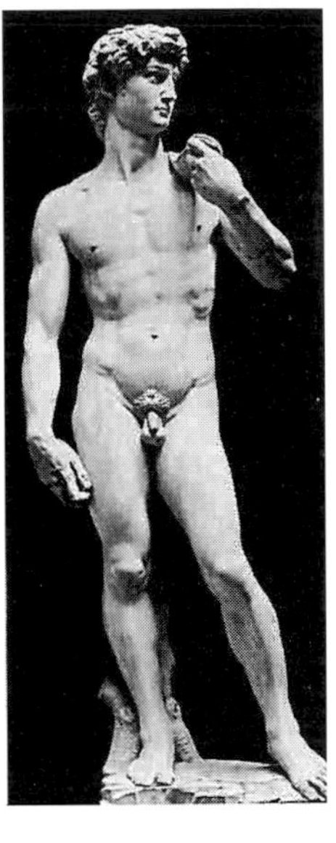

3.6.
Michelangelo. *David*, 1501–1504. Florence, Accademia. Photo Alinari/Art Resource, New York.

3.7.
After Polykleitos. Amazon (Sciarra type). Original c430 BCE. Roman Copy. Vatican (2252).

The Doryphoros and its ancient cousins have had enormous influence not only on the later canon but also on specific later statues. It was probably the prototype for the Primaporta Augustus, for example (see fig. 1.14), and, to move into the Renaissance, it has an uncanny resemblance to Michelangelo's *David* (3.6). The Naples copy of Polykleitos's statue was not found until the eighteenth century but other versions were known earlier—though they had not been identified as copies of the Doryphoros. But the pose, gesture, and effect of the original statue were described in classical texts and its actual proportions had been worked out by Leonardo in 1485–1490 (see fig. 3.9), twenty years or so before Michelangelo's *David*.

Polykleitos is also credited with a canonical female, identified as an Amazon, versions of which exist (3.7). These display more variety than do the Doryphoros variants. With a weary gesture, her right arm raised and bent over her head, the woman warrior sets her bow alongside the quiver of arrows slung at her left side. Her garment flows in hundreds of tiny ripples around the central parts of her body. The drapery serves to augment and frame the body's sexual centers. Off-center ovals form downward from the belt so as to emphasize the thigh and knee, while, above, long dropping loops mark the one breast that is covered. The statue may represent a type of victory prize given in women's games (e.g., at the Heraia at Olympia).

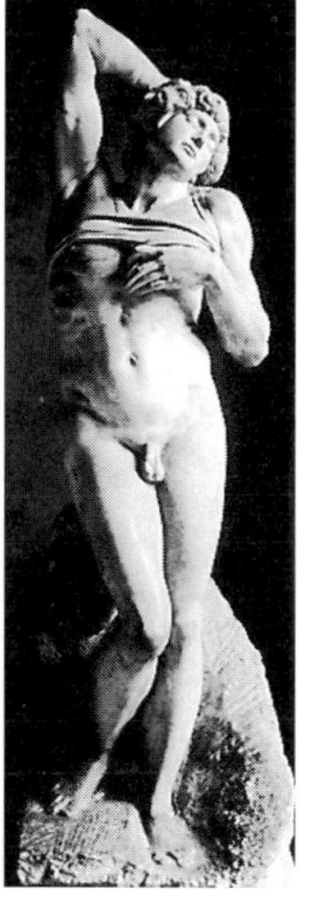

3.8.
Michelangelo. *Dying Slave*, begun 1513. Paris, Louvre. The image is flipped horizontally.

The Wounded Amazon type has been much discussed.[11] Michelangelo, who praised one specimen as "the most beautiful thing in Rome," seems to have translated its fairly mannish anatomy, along with its more feminine gestures, for the famous *Dying Slave* in the Louvre (3.8), begun in 1513 for the tomb of Julius II. Note that Michelangelo has transformed the gesture with which the archer adjusts her bow into the slave's attempt to relieve the pressure of the bonds on his neck. But he has preserved the original's air of fatigue touched with helpless languor. So the weariness of victory becomes that of defeat—an excellent *concetto*.

Polykleitos's Amazon belongs to a wider context of female images, especially those of his great contemporary, Praxiteles, creator of the Aphrodite of Cnidos. As I noted in the introduction, the main group of pre-Praxitelean females in Greek sculpture, the so-called korai, had adapted the proportions and square-cut muscularity of their male counterparts, the kouroi.[12] But the korai (unlike their male counterparts) are almost always clothed. With Praxiteles' nude Cnidian Aphrodite, however, something really new occurred—a definitive declaration of the female body: "a figure designed from start to finish," says Robertson, "in proportion, structure, pose, expression, to illustrate an ideal of the feminine principle."[13] Unfortunately the innumerable copies of Praxiteles' masterpiece, which was the most popular statue in antiquity, are a bit coarse. But the Medici Venus (see fig. 0.1) makes the point well enough.

Canons and Number: Alberti, Leonardo, Michelangelo, Dürer, and Lomazzo

All these general observations should, if we are to be true to the nature of the canons, be translated into specific values. Table 3.1 indicates the head-heights of Polykleitos's Doryphoros, to which I will also proleptically add Leonardo's interpretation of the latter figure, to be discussed in a moment, and Michelangelo's *David* (3.6). Despite this air of agreement as to the body's trunk and legs, the "Galenic symmetry"—for example, arm-and-hand commensurability—yields variation. The Naples Doryphoros has 2 $^1/_2$-head arms, the Leonardo 3 $^1/_2$, while *David* possesses truly huge hands, as long as his forearms. It is worth noting, too, that only Michelangelo's figure is commensurate in what I take to be the Galenic and Polykleitan sense, producing the whole-number sequence, in heads, all at natural demarcations: 2:3:4:5:7. I call this result an integral canon of all the body's demarcations in head measurements (since all numbers are integers). Even better would have been an arithmetic series, but the missing 6, which comes at the middle of the shin (not a natural demarcation), spoils this possibility.

These measurements also make clear the compatibility between the Doryphoros head-heights (table 3.1) and those of Polykleitos's female (table 3.2). The Medici Venus type, which I will call Praxitilean, moves toward fully rational numbers for the subdivisions by head, and toward a proportionally taller figure, just short of 8 heads high. Her shoulders, meanwhile, are slightly less than $1/4$ her total height, and, in terms of the developed Polykleitan tradition, her nipples, navel, and crotch come precisely and canonically at the 2-, 3-, and 4-head points. Michelangelo, going further still, with his *Captive* (3.8) has radically lengthened the whole lower body, and in somewhat different proportions than those by which he lengthened the *David*.

It is thought that some of the number values included in Polykleitos's lost book are preserved in Vitruvius's *De architectura*. In 3.1ff., Vitruvius describes what he calls the *homo bene figuratus*, "the well-shaped man," and gives him the proportions shown in table 3.3.[14]

Note, first of all, that the denominators of the fractions in the first panel (I give them in Vitruvius's order) form an arithmetical series, 10:8:6:4. The series is commensurable, since each number is formed by subtracting 2 from its predecessor. (Andrew Stewart has indicated, using different evidence, that the original Polykleitan canon applied comparable arithmetical series—namely, 1:2:3:4, 1:3:5:7, and 2:4:6:8—to body measurement.)[15] A proper face must be divisible into three horizontal thirds, and the body as a whole can be seen in detached fourths: from the bottom panel, forearm length and chest height or width, as well as the distance from midchest to crown of head. There are also the two detached sixths: throat to hair roots and foot length. According to Vitruvius, then, the well-knit male body must total all these interwoven commensurate or "symmetrical" measurements—measurements that, at least for the body proper if not for the face, echo and reecho with the numbers 4, 6, 8, and 10.

All of which makes crystal clear something that should have been obvious, but seems not to have been, to the many who have studied Vitruvius's Polykleitan man: *Vitruvius provides no canon for locating the main junctures of the body*

Table 3.3

Body Measurements from Vitruvius 3.1

	Proportion of Total Height
Face height	1/10
Hand length	1/10
Head height	1/8
Throat to hair roots	1/6
Midchest to crown of head	1/4
Chin to base of nose	1/3
Base of nose to brows	1/3
Brows to hairline	1/3
Forearm length	1/4
Breast width	1/4
Foot length	1/6

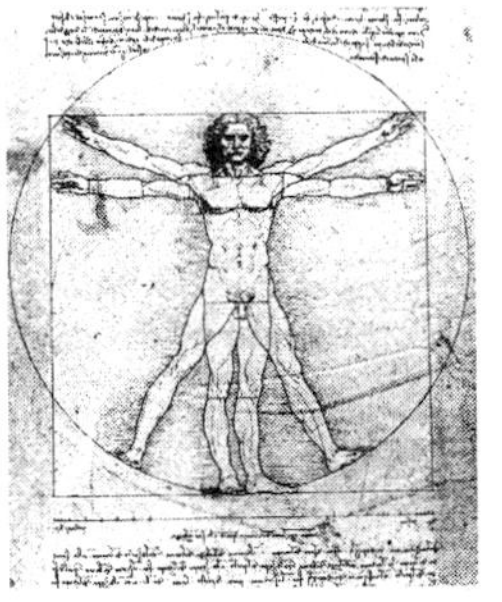

3.9.
Leonardo da Vinci. The Vitruvius-Polykleitan canon, c1485–1490. Venice, Accademia.

between its extremes. He does not tell us where the nipples, navel, groin, and knee come. Nor can this be extrapolated from the data he does give. While his values may well be Polykleitan, they are too incomplete actually to *construct* a *homo bene figuratus*. That is one reason why there has been so much activity, artistic and scholarly, in this area.

After the description of the well-shaped man comes an even more famous passage. Vitruvius adds that if this man lies down with slightly raised arms, and with his legs stretched so as to form an open triangle, a circle can be inscribed around the perimeter formed by his finger ends and feet. The man's navel will be at the circle's center. If the man then brings his legs together and extends his arms horizontally, a square should be inscribable around his outstretched limbs and head (3.9).[16]

So far as I know, the first person in the Renaissance seriously to revive these ideas about canonical bodies was Leone Battista Alberti.[17] He even designed and constructed machines to make detailed measurements of human models.

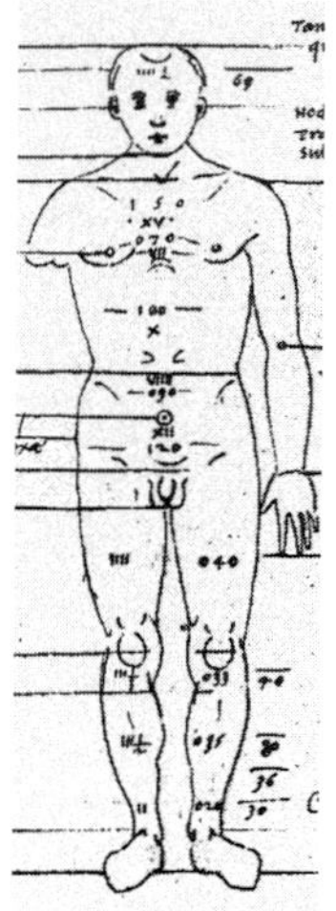

3.10.
Proportioned man copied from a lost manuscript of Alberti's *De statua*. In Album cod. canon. misc. 172, fol. 232v. Oxford, Bodleian Library.

His findings, which appear in his book *De statua* (written in the 1450s), have most recently been studied by Jane Andrews Aiken and Gustina Scaglia.[18] Scaglia has also published two old copies after the treatise's lost original illustrations of the canonical male (3.10). These supplement the engravings in Cosimo Bartoli's published version of Alberti's text.[19] The images give us anthropometric information that is far more useful for comparative purposes than is Alberti's text itself.[20] In table 3.4, I give Vitruvius's fractions, the corresponding measurements as they appear in the Albertian images, and those from Leonardo's drawing. In table 3.5, I compare the relevant values from the Doryphoros and Alberti.[21] The greatest disagreement is over the total height in heads, which is 7 in Polykleitos and Alberti, 8 in Vitruvius and Leonardo. As such a height of 8 is quite rare in the early Renaissance, the correspondence probably shows how closely Leonardo is following Vitruvius. Another anomaly is Vitruvius's very broad chest width of $1/4$, which tallies with none of the others.

Similarly, when the Doryphoros is paired with Alberti's figure (table 3.5) we get an even closer set of agreements. The variations among chest width, chest to crown, and foot length are all negligible, and all other measures, including total body height in heads, are the same. For a third pair among the four physiques, Doryphoros and Leonardo, that sort of unanimity is strikingly absent. Chest width, chest to crown, and heads of total height (7 as opposed to 8) are all disagreed upon. I conclude, then, that Vitruvius's system is a distinct variant of that expressed in the Doryphoros, while the Alberti man is very close to it.[22] And here, at the risk of seeming repetitive to the mathematically minded reader, I must interject that these correspondences lead to many others. That is, if

Table 3.4

Agreements between Vitruvius, Alberto, and Leonardo

	Vitruvius	Alberti	Leonardo
Chest width	1/4 height	‹1/4 height	›1/4 height
Forearm and hand	1/4 height	1/4 height	1/4 height
Chest to crown	1/4 height	1/4 height	1/4 height
Foot length	1/6 height	1/6 height	›1/6 height
Throat to crown	1/6 height	1/6 height	1/6 height
Head height	1/8 height	1/7 height	1/8 height
Hand length	1/10 height	1/10 height	1/10 height
Face height	1/10 height	1/10 height	1/10 height

agreement ‹ smaller than

rough agreement › larger than

disagreement

Table 3.5

Agreements between Doryphoros and Alberti

	Doryphoros	Alberti
Chest width	1/5 height	‹1/4 height
Forearm and hand	1/4 height	1/4 height
Chest to crown	›1/4 height	1/4 height
Foot length	‹1/6 height	1/6 height
Throat to crown	1/6 height	1/6 height
Head height	1/7 height	1/7 height
Hand length	1/10 height	1/10 height
Face height	1/10 height	1/10 height

3.11.

Albrecht Dürer. *Nemesis*, 1505/1502. Engraving B.77.

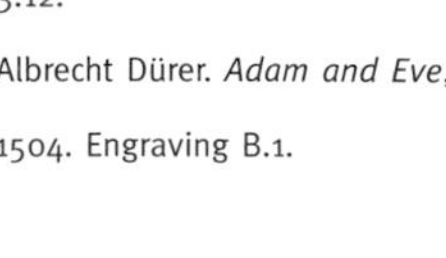

3.12.

Albrecht Dürer. *Adam and Eve*, 1504. Engraving B.1.

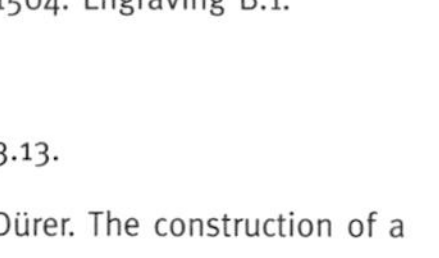
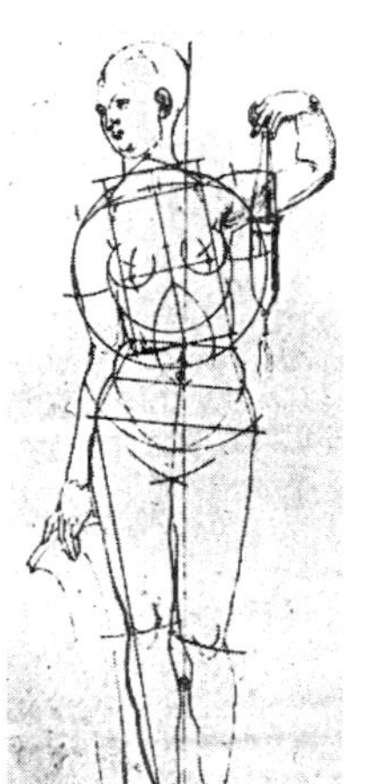

3.13.

Dürer. The construction of a woman's body, c1500. Drawing L38. Berlin, Kupferstichkabinett.

the forearm and hand of a figure are $1/4$ of that figure's height, then that figure has to be 4 forearm-and-hands high, no more and no less. The same applies to the other modules—that same body also *has to be* 5 chest-widths high, 8 foot-lengths high, 10 hands high, and 10 faces high. Finally: both Doryphoros and Leonardo, when they substitute a chest width of $1/5$ for $1/4$, lose Vitruvius's arithmetical series, 4:6:8:10.

All of which, allowing for the cited variants, will constitute my definition of the Polykleitan canon. It is strict within its parameters but allows for head-to-total-body ratios that range from 7:1 to 8:1.

Albrecht Dürer was fascinated by this canon and its progeny. One result, we are told, was the print of Nemesis known as the "Large Fortune" (3.11).[23] But the data do not match (table 3.6, column 1). However, the identical measurements for Dürer's *Adam and Eve*, done a year or so later (3.12), *do* match—they are in fact completely identical to those of Michelangelo's *Dying Slave* (table 3.2, column 4).

Dürer was interested in more than head measurements and Vitruvian fractions. He established the axes of the torso, pelvis, and legs by making geometric shapes, usually trapezoids, that were then developed into the body's organic members. Sometimes these shapes interpenetrated each other. Thus a large circle envelops the woman's upper body (3.13), and her breasts and abdomen are formed from arcs of smaller circles. (Note that most of the important body sites are established by the use of a pair of compasses, as in Renaissance architectural and mechanical drawing.) While it is Polykleitan, as Panofsky points out, Dürer's system also seems to have a debt to that employed by medieval draftsmen like Villard de Honnecourt.[24] But the classico-Renaissance "symmetries" we have been looking at are not found in Villard's figures.

Table 3.6

Three Dürer Canons

	Nemesis	Adam	Eve	Woman	Man
Nipples	1 3/4	2	2	2	2
Navel	2 3/4	3	3	3	3 1/4
Groin	3 1/2	4	4	4	4
Knee	5	6	6	6	6
Heel	7	8	8	8	8 1/2
		Canon of Integers			

Other diagrams subdivide the standing bodies of men and women into horizontal fractions like those Leonardo calls for in his Polykleitos drawing, but with the fractions marked out by horizontal lines. Many of Dürer's figures follow the Michelangelesque 2:3:4:6:8 sequence, though he was not wedded to it. Some illustrations for his planned treatise on human proportions utilize a 7 1/2-head-high figure. Normally in all of these the face is 1/10 of the body's total height and the shoulder width 1/4 of that height.

Leonardo's follower Gian Paolo Lomazzo, a Milanese Neoplatonist and painter, wrote treatises on art that speculated, rather more fantastically, about the numbered body.[25] Unfortunately Lomazzo went blind while he was preparing his illustrations and his formulas are full of mistakes. But he did make fascinating correspondences between human proportions and the ratios of musical intervals, and, more important, allowed for varieties of physiques that corresponded to the sex, temperament, and astrological nature of the individual. Lomazzo is the earliest art theorist I know of to make such equations and also to allow for considerable variations in human phenotype, with stars, gods, temperaments, and the like governing those variations. Thus Mars, Jupiter, Venus, the Moon, and so on all have characteristic types of body; the martial, or Mars-related, physique is a very lanky 10 1/2 faces high.

Lomazzo discusses women's bodies in as much detail as men's. There are the following possibilities: 10 faces high, 10 heads high, 9 faces high, 9 heads high, and 7 heads high. Of these, the second tallest, 10 faces high, is, he says, the

Table 3.7
Lomazzo's Body Measurements Matched with Gods, Temperament, Column Type, and Character

Height	God	Temperament	Column	Character
10 faces				
10 heads	Venus	sweet	Corinthian	Maiden
9 faces	Juno, Virgin Mary	grave	Ionic	Queen
9 heads	Minerva, Diana	fierce	Doric	Amazon
7 faces	Vesta			Mother Earth

most beautiful. More redoubtable female types, such as matrons, huntresses, and Amazons, should follow the larger-headed proportions, that is, having shorter bodies over all. Lomazzo does not elaborate on the very tall 10-face-high female physique. But he does liken several of these female body types to the architectural orders, which had always been read in terms of human analogies, female ones in particular. Lomazzo doesn't actually draw up a chart (called an affinity table by the Neoplatonists), but his text provides the basis for such a layout as table 3.7, showing the magical links between female body-type, temperament, relevant god or goddess, and suitable narrative psychology.

Lomazzo introduces another idea that will be endemic later on. Artists, he says, are influenced in their use of these planetary types by their own physiques and temperaments; Michelangelo alone transcends this weakness. For example, Raphael makes all his figures into variations of his own physique, which, Lomazzo claims, is 9 heads high. Leonardo does the same with his figures, he personally having been of solar build and hence constructed on an 8-head-high system. (Perhaps that's why he accepted Vitruvius's 8-head-high formula.) Mantegna, says Lomazzo, works with a mercurial and Titian with a lunar physique, these being 9 heads high. However, Lomazzo's measurements do not check out when applied to work by the artists mentioned. And I will add that he does not give the bodily points at which his head and face measurements should come, so that, in designing, say, a 10-head-high figure of Venus—sweet-tempered, maidenly, and associated with the Corinthian order though she may be—we have no idea where her nipples, navel, groin, and knees ought to be located.

Finally, Lomazzo, as Kretschmer and Sheldon will do in more recent times (see chapter 5), attaches specific temperaments to each type of physique. People with martial bodies, for example, are impetuous, choleric, cruel, bellicose, discordant, audacious, temerarious, and ripe for anger. This makes sense physiologically, adds Lomazzo, since martial people have large bones and their bodies are less fleshy than other people's. Fleshiness tends to soften anger, he thinks, which arises out of the bones. In art, martial people should be shown flaring their nostrils and other bodily openings—literally letting off the steam generated by their choler. Lomazzo's system applies not only to humans but to all sorts of superraces such as angels, daemons, gods and goddesses, and other bioprodigies.

One could list many other, mostly later, philosophers of bodily proportions. The same lists of tables of numbers, and sometimes the fantastic planetary relationships and links to the four elements or the four temperaments, reappear in works of Lorenzo Ghiberti, Petrus Bungus, Vincenzo Danti, Carel van Mander, Gérard Audran, Gérard de Lairesse, Gottfried Schadow, and a host of other writer-artists throughout the sixteenth and down through the nineteenth century. Most of the measurements are fairly consistent. The Polykleitan ideal is elaborated, not replaced.[26] One curious contribution to this lore is by the Scottish writer David Hay, author of several books on human proportion, including *The Natural Principles of Beauty in the Human Figure* (1852).[27] In one of his analyses of the female body, Hay makes use of a dense overlay of straight axes and interwoven ellipses to plot out, with considerably more detail than usual, such a body's geometrical beauties (3.14).

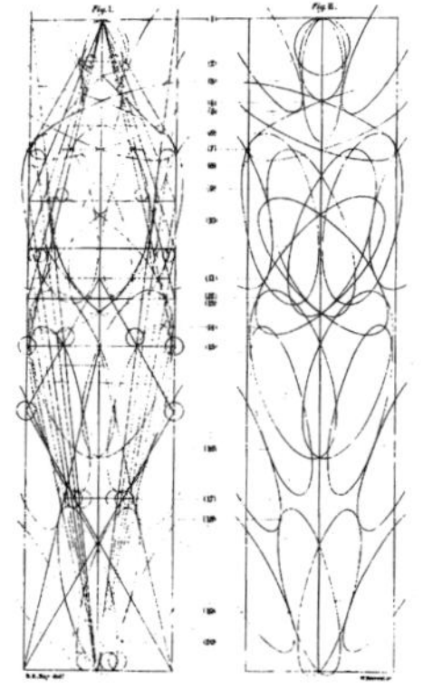

3.14.
David D. R. Hay. Ideal female figure. From Hay, *The Natural Principles of Beauty in the Human Figure* (London and Edinburgh, 1852). Photo courtesy of the Yale Center for British Art.

William Wetmore Story and the Seal of Solomon

Rather unexpectedly, a useful compendium of many of these earlier attempts at prescriptive body measurement is provided by the American sculptor William Wetmore Story. His book on the subject is a manual entitled *The Proportions of the Human Figure, According to a New Canon*, published in 1864.[28] The "new canon" is not a new shape or set of proportions but simply a new geometrical way of constructing the traditional Polykleitan physique. Much in the spirit of Lomazzo and other Neoplatonists, Story's system proposes that his formulas embody a priori mathematical ratios and mystical principles.

Or, as the author writes: "a new system is proposed, by which the measures of all its parts may be exactly ascertained and determined without reference to the Figure itself."[29] Among Story's main authorities are Alberti, Dürer, and Lavater.[30] Story juggles their formulas into comparative tables that differ from one another only in small details. (Just as artists repeated each other's proportions and poses, anthropometrists repeated each other's tables.) Like hundreds of other artist-anthropometers before him, Story also measured the Apollo Belvedere, the Vatican's colossal Antinoos, the Medici Venus, and the Venus de Milo. His data show that all are in accord with his "new canon."

Story prints three plates, two of the male and one of the female body (3.15, 3.16, 3.17). These show how his scheme, while built on the earlier ones and consequently derived from the old lists of fractions based on discrete features—heads, hands, feet, thumbs—can be reduced to a single geometrical figure: a circle with an inner inscribed square and equilateral triangle. This of course is Vitruvius's square-and-circle but with an added triangle. Leonardo's drawing, we recall, had actually put such a triangle between his figure's out-

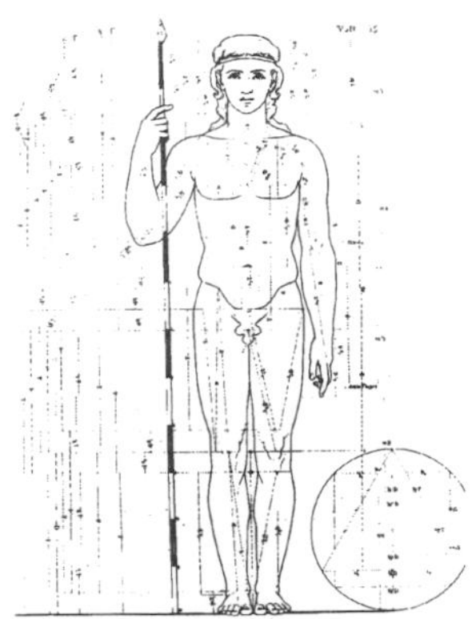

3.15.
William Wetmore Story. Male figure. From Story, *The Proportions of the Human Figure*, 1864. Yale Collection of American Literature, Beinecke Rare Book and Manuscript Library, Yale University.

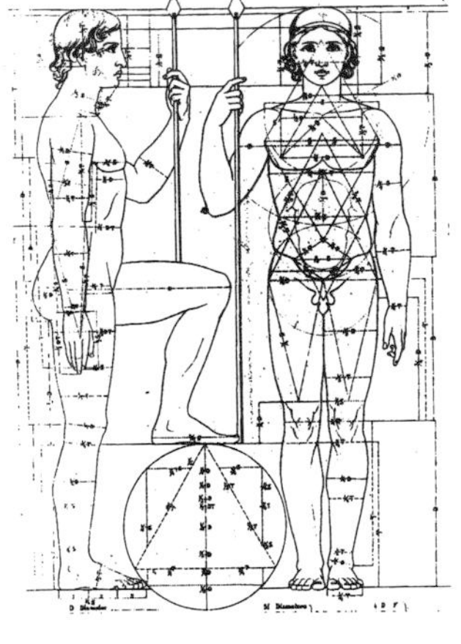

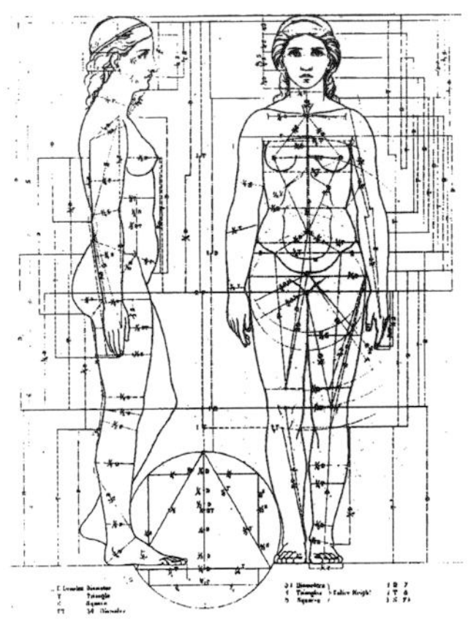

3.16.
William Wetmore Story. Second male figure. From Story, *The Proportions of the Human Figure.*

3.17.
William Wetmore Story. Female figure. From Story, *The Proportions of the Human Figure.*

spread legs, and Leonardo alludes to it in his text but does not draw it out. Story's idea, however, reverses the traditional one. It is not: the man makes the square and the circle; but: the square and the circle (plus the triangle) make the man. Thus far, then, Story is in the Dürer camp.

But there is more. Story identifies this diagram of an equilateral triangle inscribed in a circle with the seal of Solomon, God in the World, Man, and Christ the Perfect Man. By adding the circle's diameter to Solomon's seal, and then the outer square, the whole construction, he says, becomes the nearest possible thing to that unachievable mathematical goal, the squaring of the circle.[31] He goes on to list all the mystical appurtenances of the square in Pythagorean and biblical symbolism, telling how it is the foundation of things, how it represents the number and attributes of the cherubim in the temple of Jerusalem,

Table 3.8
Story's Body Canons

	FIRST MAN	SECOND MAN	WOMAN
Pectorals	2	2	2
Navel	3	3	3
Groin	4	4	4
Knee	6 1/2	6	6
Heel	7 1/2	8	8
		Canon of Integers	

and so on. Nor are Story's ideas unconnected with more recent phenomena, such as Le Corbusier's Modulor number mysticism and the beliefs of such early modern avant-garde groups as the Section d'Or.

Story's male (3.14), $7\,{}^{1}/_{2}$ heads high, corresponds well to the numbers in table 3.4. The circle-triangle-square of Solomon appears on each of Story's three plates. From this are derived the following values: *D* (diameter of circle), *T* (side of equilateral triangle), and *S* (side of square). The body's total height is then either $3\,{}^{1}/_{2}D$, $4T$, or $5S$. These three distances are then mapped out in a network all over the body—for example, from penis point to kneecap, top of kneecap to root of penis, root of penis to collarbone, and so on—always beginning and ending at important junctures of body parts. The distances often move along tilted axes, for example, from bottom of kneecap to inner anklebone (a distance of ${}^{3}/_{5}D$). To the left of the figure a large number of vertical axes are measured, from body point to body point—all of them conforming to rational series of *D*'s, *T*'s, and *S*'s, or in fractions thereof that are always ${}^{3}/_{5}$, ${}^{1}/_{2}$, or ${}^{1}/_{4}$.

A second male figure (3.15), shown both in front view and profile, illustrates two more principles. The profile figure on the left applies the data in the first illustration to the side view of the same male body and is mainly concerned with thickness (the diameter of the member, not its volume or circumference). Thus there are as many as eight thickness measurements on the leg and four on the arm. These distances, again, are always quoted as some fraction of *D*, *T*, or *S*, everything being derived from the seal of Solomon.

The front view then takes these same canonical modules and arranges them into networks of overlapping triangles. Some of these latter, as between nipples and chin, are equilateral, like the original triangle in the seal. Others comprise various types of lozenge and diaper patterns. The vertices of the shapes all lie at important body sites.

Story's female (3.16) is presented in much the same way. Like the second man she is 8 heads high. Her shoulders, however, are ${}^{2}/_{9}$ of her total height and her hips ${}^{4}/_{9}$, in which respects she departs from the other physiques we have been looking at.

Story's system yields rational values beyond those generated by any of the ancient number-series he analyzes. The woman's profile, for example, supplies lateral and thickness measurements—all, once again, in terms of *D*, *T*, and *S* and their allowed fractions. And the front view is constructed of, or at least encased in, Düreresque geometrical shapes like those imposed on the man. But in the case of the female body the circle, not the triangle, is emphasized. We saw the same thing in Dürer's female figure. Indeed the woman's whole body, in Story's engraving, is marked out with circles and arcs of circles, making a frame for the body's central area, and climaxing with smaller circles overlapping more densely in her pelvic region, just as the man's lozenges do in his. Thus here as so often, the canonical numerology of the human body analyzes it as a set of sexual proclamations translated into numerical and geometrical form. There are male and female geometrical forms and male and female numerical quantities.

Polykleitos and Praxiteles created body canons that have been repeated down the ages. The ideal may have faded out during the Middle Ages, but the Renaissance reestablished and elaborated it. We keep finding specific proportional reflections of the Doryphoros and the Amazon, and of Praxiteles' Cnidian goddess, down to our own time. They are reflected in art, and, of course, in life: a life that, I believe, more and more has selected its heroes and heroines, and its husbands and wives, with some regard to these canonical prototypes. We have noted cases where not merely the *idea* of such a mathematically expressed physique but the actual numbers, proportions, and commensurables that can, with variations, be generalized from it formed the key to the body canons.

Even today, in the mid-1990s, a century and more after modernism and the presumed overthrow of the Polykleitan tradition, when you take a class in life drawing, you will get lessons in the commensurate "symmetries" of the body, measuring its height in heads, hands, forearms, and the like. You will be asked to apply those formulas to the live model you are drawing. Often, you will be expected to "correct" the model's proportions—measuring them against the norms described in this chapter.

To return to the points raised at the beginning of this chapter: it would be interesting to know if science could measure the proportional variations of the people who created prehistoric art, with its enormous variety of proportions, to see if there was any correspondence between art and life. And similarly it would be instructive to see if, during the "Polykleitan" period, there had been any adjustment or adaptation of Western physiques toward that ideal. Indeed the overwhelming majority of the somatotypes published by Sheldon and his followers down to 1992 (see chapter 5) are Polykleitan.

Aryans and Semites

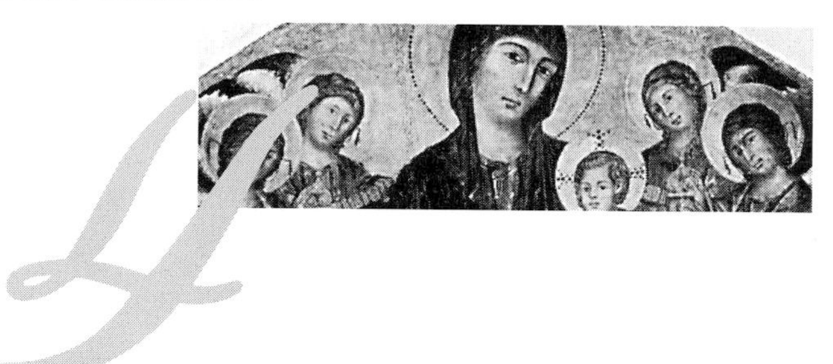

With William Wetmore Story we entered the period when modern physical anthropology was being born. In the following chapters I will be reemphasizing the wide extent of the real-life human variation that this science, along with kindred disciplines, studies. Unlike even the most flexible of the Polykleitan formulas, these sciences confront the human physique in all its discoverable variations. Yet we shall see that for all their objectivity the scientists, at least at the beginning, have often preferred Polykleitan to non-Polykleitan bodies. As to the moral, temperamental, and even magical qualities that have been attributed to different physiques, here too the physical anthropologists often follow unconsciously in Lomazzo's footsteps.

Aryanism

There have been many reasons for these still-continuing preferences. One of the most important was the cult of Aryanism, especially as it was preached and practiced over the years 1845–1945. Aryanism not only proposed parameters for ideal bodies and faces, it also advocated, more forcibly than did any Renaissance or baroque theory, that these ideals should serve as reproductive goals. "Aryanism" had several different meanings before Houston Stewart Chamberlain and his intellectual protégé, Hitler, made it the watchword of Nazi racism.[1] Rather than traveling this latter well-trodden way, in the present chapter I shall be focusing on Victorian ideas about Aryanism, for it was in Victorian Britain, I hold, that Aryanism first took artistic form and set up the sexual cynosures that came to populate Nazi art.

"Aryan" means "noble" in Sanskrit, and it is first of all an ancient Hindu name for a population that still exists in northern India. Short, dark-skinned, black-haired, today's Aryans, or *Arya* as they are called, are far from the Nazi Nordic ideal.[2] The word "Aryan" was also applied to what are more commonly known as the Indo-European languages. In other words all the major European linguistic groups—Sanskrit, Persian, Greek, Latin, Slavonic, Celtic, Teutonic, and hence all the Germanic and Romance languages—indeed, just about every tongue spoken in Europe except Hungarian, Basque, and Finnish, was supposed to have descended from an original Aryan language, now extinct, spoken millennia ago by the Arya of north India.

Nineteenth-century Aryanists believed that in the second millennium before Christ an attacking horde, emigrating from the shores of the Black Sea, swept through Mesopotamia and Asia Minor. In c1500 BCE they invaded India. They were said to have been tall and fair, a tough, nomadic people whose horse-drawn chariots galloped through mountain passes and descended on the hapless agriculturalists in the valleys below. Like most other conquerors, these original Aryans half-destroyed, half-absorbed the cultures they found in their way. Their style of life is hymned in the Vedas, the Hindu sacred texts first compiled in c1000 BCE.[3] These describe a society whose warrior class, of different and superior physical make than their fellows, specialized in hunting and conquest, leaving agriculture and servitude to the non-Aryan citizens they lived among. After conquering much of India these Vedic Aryans infiltrated most modern European stocks. It has been this class or race, an unproclaimed but omnipresent race-within-other-races, said the nineteenth-century experts, that has provided most of the great heroes and heroines, and engineered most of the great moments, of European history. This is the original ethnological essence of the Aryan theory: there is in our midst a race of heroes, a race that can be identified by certain key physical characteristics.

Some of the earliest writing on Aryanism was by Joseph-Arthur Comte de Gobineau, author of *Sur l'inégalité des races humaines* (1853). Gobineau linked the word "Aryan" to the Greek-derived words "Archaia" and "Argive," and to the German *Ehre*, "honor." He claimed that all races with dark skin, dark hair, or both have blond, white-skinned gods, which showed him that inferior physical types recognize the superiority of Aryans. Indeed, says Gobineau, the Olympians and the whole race of Greek mythological peoples are the greatest prototypes for the Aryans. And so are all other gods and goddesses. The miraculous deeds attributed to these beings, from whatever mythology they come, are simply ways of stating the superiority of a single Aryan race that has flourished in all periods of European history.[64]

Another early propagator of these ideas was the German historian Ernst Curtius.[5] He declared that the first great Aryan epiphany beyond the borders of India had been in Greece. Indeed, Greek culture did not take wing at all until the Aryans mingled with the local Balkan peoples and galvanized these lesser tribes. The resulting Aryan-Balkan peoples called themselves Hellenes after their legendary founder, Hellen. Curtius evokes them in almost Nietzschean terms. "Impulse and motion are first communicated [to Greek culture] by Hellen and his sons," he writes, "and with their arrival history commences." And the

Hellenes have continued their conquering march through the lands and cultures of lesser peoples. They "took the land way through the Hellespont's ancient portal of the nations: they passed through Thrace into the Alpine land of northern Greece, and there, in mountain cantons, they developed their peculiar life in social communities . . . under the [new] name of Dorians." Land possession, rule over lesser peoples by right of conquest, and the continual renaming of themselves seem to be among the chief Aryan traits.

Their great treasure was their language, which was by now Greek: "The whole language resembles the body of a trained athlete, in which every muscle, every sinew, is developed into full play, where there is no trace of fat or inert tissue, and all is power and life."[6] The living bodies and faces that that Greek language evokes, for Curtius, are themselves masterpieces of human biological reproduction. They can be found above all in the visual arts:

Apollo and Hermes, Achilles and Theseus, whether they stand before our eyes in stone or in paint, are simply transfigured Greeks, and the noble harmonies of their limbs, the simple gentle lines of their faces, their large eyes, their short chins, their straight noses, their fine mouths, belong to, and were the marks of, the people themselves. Moderateness is also a bodily characteristic. In height they seldom go beyond the norm. Equally rare are fat or fleshy bodies. The Hellenes were freer than other races of mortals from whatever hinders and blocks the motions of the spirit. They share with the other happy inhabitants of the southern lands the abundant gifts of the climate, free and fearless development of the body, and an easy transition from childhood to maturity. Near to Nature . . . their freer life in air and sunshine makes their lungs stronger and healthier, their limbs more elastic, their muscles more developed [than northern peoples'], and gives the whole organism a freer growth.[7]

Biological measures were taken to assure this preponderance of physical beauty. Whoever among the Hellenes was born crippled or with some other disability, says Curtius, had to abandon all inherited titles and honors. A true Aryan brain and personality may only exist in a noble body. (Blind Homer, pudgy Socrates, and Pericles with his deformed skull[8] were exceptions, presumably, though Curtius does not mention them here.) In ancient Greece, therefore, ugliness was as much the exception as is beauty in ordinary lands.[9] It is at this point that we can recall an earlier German effusion on the beauty of the Hellenic body—the epigraph from Lessing I used in chapter 1: "Beautiful statues fashioned from beautiful men reacted upon their creators, and the state was indebted for its beautiful men to beautiful statues."[10]

Hence, under definitions like Curtius's, the Aryans did not really constitute a race in today's sense. They were not a biological strain sharing statistically significant variations in hair, eye color, height, skin color, body types, blood types, and the like. The Aryans could be any color or shape. They could be short and black skinned, like the Arya of India, medium like Curtius's Hellenes, or tall like Gobineau's Aryans; they could have as much variety of physique and physiognomy as did the "Alpine" Pericles and Charlemagne, and the "Italic" or "Mediterranean" Caesar, Lorenzo de' Medici, and Napoleon—all of whom were Aryans, according to the theorist of Aryan art, Frederic Leighton.[11] Just to make things even more confusing, even biblical figures of heroic stature—for example, Moses—could be "Aryans." Gobineau claimed to have discovered African Aryans in Cameroon.[12] So the word "Aryan," though in many ways it overlapped with "Indo-European" and "Hellenic," also originally covered a wide slice of ethnological variation.

Futhermore Gobineau had written:

It is enough to compare the varied types spread over the globe to see from the more or less rudimentary facial construction of the Pelasgian and Pecherai [Petchenegs? Turkic peoples in South Russia] to the elevated design of noble proportions of Charlemagne, to the intelligent regularity of Napoleon's features, to the imposing majesty that breathes in the royal visage of Louis XIV, that there is a series of gradations by which the peoples not of white blood approach beauty, but do not attain it.[13]

Note that most of this information would have come to Gobineau via works of art. He adds that, after pure whites, the most beautiful people are those with black fathers and white mothers. Their beauty is of a much higher sort than that of the Russians and Hungarians, who are part white, part Oriental. And no Slav can have the beauty of a Rajput. Even among Aryan Europeans there are clear degrees of beauty. Thus are Italians more beautiful than Germans, Swiss, French, and Spanish. And English bodies are superior only to those of the lowly non-Aryan Slavs.

The lowest category, for Gobineau, is the Semitic. And it is a large category. To him most European cultures were Semitic—the Thracians, the Greek colonial civilizations, the Gauls, the Italiotes, Etruscans, and the original inhabitants of Rome. "Western Civilization," on the other hand, was composed of the Slavs and the "German Aryans" who invaded Rome and mixed with its native Semitic populations. The Spanish are part Semitic, part black African (*mélanienne*). This explains the great affinity between Spanish explorers and the native Americans, whom Gobineau like many others linked to African races.

We shall see that Leighton's ideas on Aryan versus Semitic art are Gobineau-like. But a more important figure than Gobineau for the Victorians was Friedrich Max Müller, an Oxford linguistics scholar.[14] Müller wrote a number of popular books on the Aryan language and its Indian context. Though he came to deny that Aryanism had any anthropological aspect whatever, his authority was often invoked by Aryanists like Carlyle and Carlyle's disciple James A. Froude.[15] Under Müller's direction, moreover, a series of translated Sanskrit texts was published to acquaint Victorians with Aryan thought.[16] These reflected certain characteristics of Victorian society, albeit in a strange light. Aryan law, for example, is mainly devoted to the intricate processes by which an elect male cultivates himself to attain a perfected maturity. To assist in this cultivation a complex of lesser social castes—the Abhisastas, the Sudras, and others—perform society's menial jobs.[17] At whatever level, each Aryan hero's life was given over to ordeals of purification, by which he might hope for a higher social position in a later incarnation. The culmination would be "birth in a distinguished family, beauty of form, beauty of complexion, strength, aptitude for learning, wisdom, wealth, and the gift of fulfilling the laws of his caste."[18] Enormous emphasis is placed on grooming and personal cleanliness. After many progressive (I am tempted to say evolutionary) incarnations comes ultimate rebirth as a true Arya. The parallels with the Victorian British and other European class systems are patent. Francis Galton's multiclass analysis of British society will turn out to be even more germane. Except for one difference: in the British systems there is no reincarnation and hence no posthumous upward mobility.

Probably the greatest British statement of Aryan ideals, however, does not use that word, instead preferring to speak of the Indo-Europeans and Curtius's Hellenes. I have in mind Matthew Arnold's *Culture and Anarchy* (1869) and its famous chapter, "Hellenism and Hebraism." Hellenism is to Arnold everything in life that is reasonable, artistic, beautiful, Apollonian, and, above all, truth seeking. But Hebraism, far from being bad, is the voice of conscience, duty, and the fear of God. "The uppermost idea with Hellenism," Arnold writes, "is to see things as they really are; the uppermost idea with Hebraism is conduct and obedience. Nothing can do away with this ineffaceable difference."[19] The Middle Ages, he goes on, were marked by the triumph of Hebraism. But then "in the sixteenth century . . . Hellenism re-entered the world, and again stood in the presence of Hebraism." Even so, "the Renascence, that great re-awakening of Hellenism, that irresistible return of humanity to nature and to seeing things as they are, which in art, in literature, and in physics, produced such splendid fruits, had, like the anterior Hellenism of the Pagan world, a side of moral weakness."[20] Hebraism, indeed, is always, in Arnold's view of history, having to rescue Hellenism from immorality, from its neglect of humanity's fallen nature. But, at the same time, Hebraism in its obsession with morality and law has ever to be corrected by Hellenism's art and science, by its passion for truth and excellence.

For Arnold, Victorian racial science is Hellenism's latest vehicle. It throws light on the very contrast he describes. "Science has now made visible to everybody the great and pregnant elements of difference which lie in race, and in how signal a manner they make the genius and history of an Indo-European people vary from those of a Semitic people. Hellenism is of Indo-European growth, Hebraism of Semitic growth; and we English, a nation of Indo-European stock, seem to belong naturally to the movement of Hellenism." Arnold concedes, however, that there is always a salutary strain of Hebraism in Anglo-Saxon life—witness the Puritans and their descendants, the mid-nineteenth-century Americans—though the latter, for Arnold, have badly over-Hebraized themselves.

Arnold seldom deals with the visual world, let alone with faces and bodies. But he does quote with approval Emile Bournouf, a French anthropologist and author of *La Science des religions*, who describes what he calls the Aryan (and what Arnold calls Indo-European or Hellenic) as opposed to other body types.[21] And Bournouf also deals with the physical anthropology of the Semites:

Those scholars who have studied anthropology almost all agree in placing the Semites between the Aryans and the yellow peoples; not that their distinctive traits betoken a medium condition between those of our race and those of eastern Asiatics; but notwithstanding their being far superior to the yellow races, they betray with regard to us such disparities as to prevent their being confounded with Indo-Europeans. A real Semite has smooth hair with curly ends, a strongly hooked nose, fleshy, projecting lips, massive extremities, thin calves, and flat feet. And what is more, he belongs to the occipital races; that is to say, those whose hinder part of the head is more developed than the front. His growth is very rapid, and at fifteen or sixteen it is over. At that age the divisions of his skull which contain the organs of intelligence are already joined, and in some cases even perfectly welded together. From that period the growth of the brain is arrested. In the Aryan races this phenomenon, or anything like it, never occurs, at any time of life, certainly not with the people of normal development. The internal organ is permitted to continue its evolution and transformation up till the last day of life by means of the never-changing flexibility of the skull bones.[22]

Thus the fontanels and sutures of these non-Aryan skulls seal over to prevent the lifelong brain expansion that produces Aryan superiority. No evidence for this claim, by the way, is offered either by Bournouf or Arnold. Nonetheless a vast amount of European anthropology, from Gobineau in the 1850s at least through World War II, has sanctioned this unproven claim.[23] Friedrich Engels, for example, makes highly Arnoldian distinctions between early Aryan and Semitic races—both of these latter, for him however, being biologically and culturally superior to other races.[24] Nazi writings about and illustrations of Aryan types (see below, chapter 8) are only a part of this larger picture.

Another Victorian Aryanist of note was Thomas Henry Huxley. His thoughts appear in a much-reprinted 1863 essay, "The Aryan Question and Prehistoric Man."[25] Making a distinction that other Aryanists avoided, Huxley believed that the Aryans were a race in the strictest biological sense. In other words they constituted a subdivision of a species, one with "characters distinct from those of the other members of the species, [and] which have a strong tendency to appear in the progeny."[26] Huxley goes on to propose that in prehistoric times this Aryan race had inhabited the land mass that is now Europe, as well as parts of Asia, and that these Aryans, like Gobineau's and Curtius's, were tall, longheaded, blue-eyed, and blond, a race of congenital conquerors who gradually extended their habitat from the shores of the North Sea and throughout central Asia. Huxley's is the earliest writing I have come across (including even Gobineau) that so clearly presages the Nazi concept of the Aryans. We note also that Huxley is the first writer we have encountered so far to make them specifically Nordic. He even supplies a prehistoric raison d'être for their relish for conquest: *Homo sapiens*'s driving the lesser human races (now called *Homo erectus* and *Homo habilis)* into extinction.[27] Thus did the modern human race originate in acts of genocide against other humans who were not *Homo sapiens.*

Yet even with all this, Huxley does not really embrace the ideal of racial purity. He is perfectly willing to believe, and other early Aryanists were in agreement, that the Aryans varied their genocides with intermarriage, and did so to the advantage of both races. (We just saw Gobineau praising the children of black-white marriages as biologically superior to pure marriages between inferior whites like Slavs and Britons.) This, says Huxley, explains the wide physical variations found among Aryan types, and shows why there is nothing strange about modern Hindus being as Aryan as are modern Englishmen.[28] The tall, blond, blue-eyed Aryan was the starting point and is a type that reappears, but it is not the only type.

The notion that an ultimate Aryan hero-race would come into being and eventually exterminate lesser human breeds was taken up and politicized by Sir Charles Wentworth Dilke. Unlike Gobineau he gave the highest place, among whites, to Britons. In the 1860s Dilke campaigned to establish what he called Greater Britain, a proposed Anglo-Saxon superstate or confederation that would include Britain itself, its settlement colonies, and the United States. He claimed that, in the wider spectrum of Aryanism as a whole, the Anglo-Saxons were the latest and most powerful subgroup. And they, too, who constitute one of what he calls the "dear races," will eliminate the "cheap races."

In America we have seen the struggle of the dear races against the cheap—the endeavors of the English to hold their own against the Irish and Chinese. In New Zealand, we found the stronger and more energetic race pushing from the earth the shrewd and laborious descendants of the Asian Malays. . . . Everywhere we have found the difficulties which impede the progress to universal domination of the English people lie in the conflict with the cheaper races.

He predicts a grand racial Armageddon when "Saxondom will rise triumphant from the doubtful struggle."[29]

Aryan Art: Frederic Leighton

I define "Aryan art" as art intended to channel its viewers' sexual choices in terms of the ideas just described. In doing this, Aryan art replaced the anthropological confusion of the literary and historical picture with considerable clarity. Books, in short, did not make it clear just what an Aryan was supposed to look like; art did.

In my view the most influential, and at the same time most articulate, of the artist-Aryanists was Frederic Leighton, whose paintings began to appear about 1855.[30] Leighton the racial theorist, meanwhile, is amusingly and fully described by Benjamin Disraeli in his novel *Lothair* (1870), where the painter appears as a character named Gaston Phoebus. Lothair, a young British nobleman, naive but in every sense exquisitely mannered, is tempted by, but then rejects, various false religions and ideologies. One of these is Aryanism as preached by Phoebus-Leighton.[31]

But *Lothair* is not the only source of insight into Leighton's beliefs. In 1879, looking back on an immensely successful career, Lord Leighton (who was raised to the peerage a few days before his death in 1896) began giving his presidential addresses at the Royal Academy. These were published as a book in 1893. The lectures propose nothing less than an Aryan history of art, an art that Leighton opposes, Arnold-fashion, to a surrounding mass of artistic production that is antithetical and Semitic—and inferior. For Arnold, Semitism had been the moral equal of Hellenism; for Leighton, Semitic art was far inferior to the Aryan-Hellenic. Furthermore, Semitic art was a huge category—almost all of Western art except for a tiny strain. And all this inferior art was made because its makers and users had biologically inferior physiques and faces.

Art, for Leighton, is indeed entirely a matter of race: but race understood in a rather peculiar sense. (Perhaps one can say that "race" is *always* understood in a rather peculiar sense.) An artist's ultimate race, says Leighton, beyond the biologists' taxa, is the individual himself. Leighton believed that we each look out on the world and see it as an enlarged self-image (*Addresses*, 16ff., 32ff.). The world outside ourselves, and especially the world of art, is nothing more than Narcissus's mirroring pool (14ff., 21, 22). Thus with Leighton does the concept of race become even more complicated and contradictory than it may have seemed so far. But the idea that humanity is divided into physiological types, and that an artist tends to depict all his characters as belonging to his own type—that idea, we saw, goes back at least to Lomazzo.

Leighton begins with Egypt, whose art is overwhelmingly Semitic. Egyptian "idols," he finds, though beautiful in possessing some few Aryan properties, are, in their "peculiarity and inertness," essentially Semitic. They express the Semitic Egyptian race's "narrow but tenacious spirit." The Chaldeans and Assyrians were even more Semitic and hence had worse art. The Jews of course were the most Semitic of all—utterly "void of the artistic impulse." This was partly because of the second commandment and partly because, living in the level and monotonous desert, they were without the vivid landscape features—the hills, brooks, and trees—that the Greeks were to turn into anthropomorphic beings, and that became a "joyous fellowship of gods and goddesses" that the Greeks then magnificently portrayed in sculpture and painting (78). Polytheism is the arch-ally, as monotheism is the archenemy, of Aryan beauty. Athens in the age of Pericles, by directly imitating the actions and forms of its gods, by making projections of their own human bodies and faces, produced the purest Aryanism that has yet existed (90). It is at this point in history, the Periclean point, that the "sluggish stream" of the earlier, Semitizing civilizations first gives way to the "upleaping of a living source, reflecting and scattering abroad the light of a new and a more joyous day: a spring at which men shall drink to the end of all days and not be sated"(85).

Roman art, on the other hand, while it represents a return to the Semitic, has a special saving grace. Though Italy, says Leighton, produced no important art either in antiquity or in the Middle Ages, nonetheless the people themselves, because of an Aryan heritage—Aryan but impurely so—remained biologically beautiful. "The well-knit, stately type which marked them, a noble vessel which had once contained Imperial souls, was preserved as we see it even in our own day; but, together with this bodily type endured also the old sterility in the things that concern the graphic Arts" (138f.). Roman ethicism, which had powerful Semitic components, drove out the aesthetic sense that the first Romans had probably acquired from their Greek brothers. Elsewhere in Europe all was Semitic. Aryan aesthetic sense is entirely absent from Spain, for example, and always has been (189).

And what of that pan-European phenomenon, unhappy Christendom? It was, is, and will remain fanatically antivisual, antibeauty, probably more Semitic even than Judaism itself. Christianity teaches that the enjoyment of the visual world is the enjoyment of a treacherous mirage. Christianity indeed reverses paganism: the gods of the Greeks become Christianity's devils. Pan, fun-loving pagan Pan, kept his historicity, along with his horns and hooves, and turned into

Satan. Only with the revival of humanism, Leighton continues, and with the renewed study of nature, the human physique, and classical art, will Aryanism ever triumph again. The Italian Renaissance was a recrudescence of all Aryanism's essentially Greek racial qualities, a "strange mixture of Attic subtlety and exquisiteness of taste, with a sombre fervour and a rude Pelasgic strength" (8). But this brief Aryan revival in Florence was swept away in turn (and here Leighton sounds more than ever like Arnold) by the Renaissance's Semitic wing—the Reformation.

Hence Leighton wanted a modern British art that was completely free of Semitic/Christian elements. I assume, also, that he wished to revise the currently popular (in some circles) reproductive models portrayed by artists like Holman Hunt and other Pre-Raphaelites. Certainly there was plenty of Semitic inertia and ungainliness to be found in it. And he wanted the artists themselves to look Aryan and Greek. Their own bodies had to correspond with the bodies they drew. The *Addresses* are full of adjurations to his listeners, who were mainly art students, to take up physical culture. Leighton wanted a nation, a population, of bodies that were Polykleitan, Praxitelean, Pheidian (95ff.). And he thought Britain would be an excellent breeding-ground. Indeed, he claims that such a new race is in the making even as he speaks: "a new ideal of balanced form wholly Aryan [is] found," he says to his listeners, "in the women of another Aryan race—your own" (89).

In *Lothair* Disraeli makes Leighton a eugenicist, eager to eliminate Semitic types more aggressively than merely by having Aryans outbreed them. Gaston Phoebus declares:

It is the first duty of a state to attend to the frame and health of the subject. The Spartans understood this. They permitted no marriage the probable consequences of which might be a feeble progeny; they even took measures to secure a vigorous one. The Romans doomed the deformed to immediate destruction. The union of the races concerns the welfare of the commonwealth much too nearly to be entrusted to individual arrangement. . . . Laws should be passed to secure all this, and some day they will be. But nothing can be done until the Aryan races are extricated from Semitism.[32]

Hearing Phoebus expound all this, Lothair regrets that he has for so long been ignorant of it. "'Do not regret it,' said Mr. Phoebus, 'What you call ignorance is your strength. By ignorance you mean a want of knowledge of books. Books are fatal.'" And he goes on to deplore the invention of the printing press, which has interfered with the truer, nobler instruction that is obtained via the hand, voice, ear, and eye—the body, in short—of a living teacher.

The essence of education [says Phoebus] is the education of the body. Beauty and health are the chief sources of happiness. Men should live in the air; their exercises should be regular, varied, scientific. To render the body strong and supple is the first duty of man. He should develop and completely master the whole muscular system. What I admire in the order to which you belong [Lothair is a British aristocrat] is that they do live in the air, that they excel in athletic sports; that they can only speak one language; and that they never read. This is not a complete education, but it is the highest education since the Greek.[33]

As a painter Leighton specialized in grand, bland scenes of ancient life featuring lordly young women and men in domestic episodes and mythological tales. The setting is almost always ancient Greece or Rome. The backgrounds consist of fresh, cold, Poussinesque skies and mountains. The rich colors of foreground fabric and foliage play against the sugary marble of temples, palaces, and pools. The nude, after a partial mid-Victorian eclipse, was in Leighton's generation emerging with a frequency and dominance never before seen in Britain. These "classical" Victorian figures, furthermore, had a monumentality and authority, a swagger, that had been found in earlier British art only in portraiture.[34] Aside from Leighton, the most prominent of these Hellenizing artists were Albert Moore, E. J. Poynter, Lawrence Alma-Tadema, Burne-Jones, and, in a special rather smudgy way, G. F. Watts. Continental parallels are found in Ingres, Ary Scheffer, Jean-Léon Gérôme, Alexandre Cabanel (the genre was known in France as *Néogrec*), and (important for Nazi art) Arnold Böcklin. So we are looking at a Europe-wide phenomenon. Not all of these artists can confidently be labeled conscious Aryanists. But some of them were perceived as such by those who *were* conscious Aryanists, as we shall see.

Leighton's own figures are filled with expectant inactivity, as if blossoming under the viewer's measured (and measuring) gaze. They are canonical in the sense that they present themselves as models. A woman reclines in sumptuous abandon by the warm waters of the sea. Salomé dances dreamily. An odalisque with a peacock fan confronts an interested swan. Clytemnestra watches stoically from the battlements of Argos. Venus disrobes. Nausicaa dreams of Odysseus. Ariadne, overcome by sleep and longing, reclines on the beach. Greek girls wind their skeins, play ball, search with balletic grace for pebbles, weep before a wreathed urn, sleep to the music of a flute player, draw water from a fountain. Andromeda, chained to a narrow steeple of rock jutting from the sea, her costume spilling from her, quails, but very self-consciously, beneath the monster's wing. Or the Hesperides, looking like lounging Parthenon goddesses, entwine with each other under a fruit tree, happily ensnared by a smiling python. The mood is always that of highly elaborated self-presentation, of anticipation, of the display of the intensely prepared body. This is true even of Hero, whose anxious desperation for her drowned lover is drenched in Leightonian narcissism.

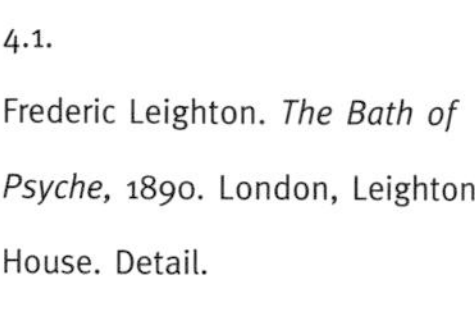

4.1.
Frederic Leighton. *The Bath of Psyche,* 1890. London, Leighton House. Detail.

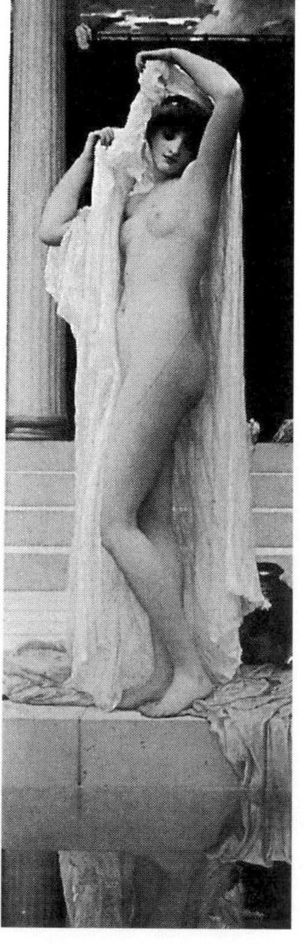

Frederic Leighton painted these Aryan types from Aryan models. Nor was he in any doubt that he himself was and looked admirably Aryan. He appears thus in *Lothair*—tall, lithe, athletic, "aquiline," his face being remarkable for its radiance. So fiery is his eye, indeed, and so lustrous his complexion and crest of chestnut curls, that onlookers can be dangerously dazzled.[35] Yet Phoebus is no mere mannequin. He is "nursed in the philosophy of our times," and his face is "weighted with deep and haughty thought." Like Leighton himself—and despite his condemnation of books—he is profoundly read in history, philosophy, and mythology. And he is a natural leader, the prince, the god, of an Aryan island in the Mediterranean. Leighton's self-portrait as president of the Royal Academy in his scarlet Oxford gown, which simultaneously portrays him as Zeus, deep-bearded and hyacinthine-curled, makes the same point.

The *Bath of Psyche* (4.1) can represent the corresponding female Aryan goal.[36] Near a clear pool rimmed by white marble steps, backed by elegant columns with gilded Ionic capitals, Psyche stands erect. Her face is warm and softly rose-colored, cradled by exquisite arms and the crystalline garment she lifts from her shoulders. An outer drapery, a light gold cloth, lies at the pool's edge and spreads its thousand crinkles into the mirroring water. Beside her feet, slightly behind her, is a gilt-bronze water jug. The typical classical Aphrodite-mood, of bodily preparation, of expectancy, is present.

Psyche's name, which means "soul," is also a trope of ψυχρός, fresh and cool—as with Leighton's pool, marble, and indigo sky. Psyche had attracted Aphrodite's hostility; but after an abortive affair with Eros she and Aphrodite

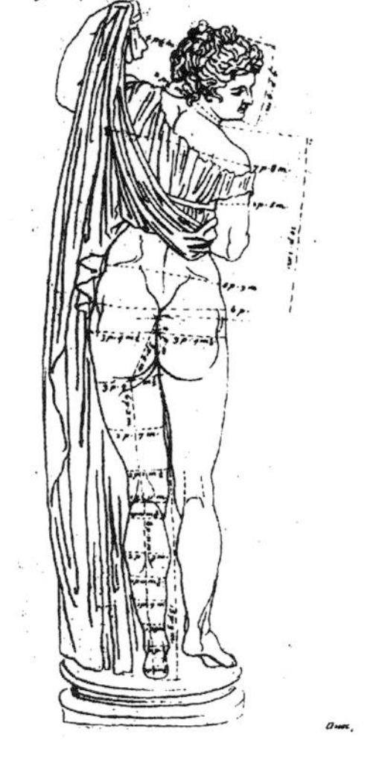

4.2.
Gérard Audran. Measured engraving of the Venus Callipygos. From Audran, *Les Proportions des corps humain mésurées sur les plus belles figures de l'antiquité* (1683).

were reconciled, and Psyche went to live in the goddess's dove-haunted palace where Leighton's scene is clearly set. Her toilet preparations, then, involve the soul's purgation and preparation for a new life in the service of the goddess of love and beauty.

In order to reaffirm this connection to Aphrodite, Leighton's figure makes use of a well-known classical pose, that of the Aphrodite Callipygos (4.2).[37] The ancient statue is said to illustrate a story in Athenaeus of two young Syracusan sisters who were discussing which of them had the better buttocks. Unable to decide, they stopped a passing young man and asked his opinion. "His choice," as Haskell and Penny put it, "was his reward."[38] But then the sister who had lost out approached a second young man. The comparison was made again, and the second young man conveniently chose the second young woman—*his* choice, of course, becoming *his* reward. The two couples got married and dedicated a temple to Aphrodite Callipygos. There, a version of the Naples statue was worshipped. Athenaeus's story, then, is about sexual selection on the basis of bodily charm, and of one particular pair of attractors, the buttocks; and it is the story of art as the record and reinforcement of that charm.

But what about the Aryan body as a canon? As the seventeenth-century artist and anthropometer Gérard Audran presents the Callipygos, based on a Naples specimen of the statue, she is a $7\frac{1}{2}$-head figure with nipples at 2, navel at 3, groin at 4, but knees at $5\frac{1}{2}$. Her "beautiful buttocks" are thus extremely long. The original statue is similar but with very short shins, considerably less than 2 heads long as opposed to a length of fully 2 heads in Audran. Leighton, in his turn, has lengthened the legs so as to make his Psyche an extremely tall $8\frac{1}{4}$-head figure. He has also shortened the arms (excluding hands) to a mere 2 heads (probably in line with the common belief that the shorter our arms and the longer our legs, the less apelike, and more evolved, we are: see chapter 6).

Note that Aphrodite Callipygos, meanwhile, is not only showing off her buttocks to us, but is admiring them herself. Or perhaps she is admiring our admiration. This can be set alongside Leighton's recension of this pose as the soul's act of self-perfecting, the body being a metaphor or vessel for the soul. Such an association, as well as Psyche's act of self-admiration, also accords with the Leighton doctrine that art and our whole view of the visual world are mirrors in which we really see only reflections of ourselves.

4.3.
Sarcophagus from Cerveteri, c520 BCE. Terracotta. Rome, Museo Nazionale di Villa Giulia.

Semitic Art: The Etruscans, Cimabue, and Michelangelo

Leighton found the Semitic qualities of Etruscan art particularly ugly. In the art of Chiusi, he writes, there is a dominant type of body with square head, "the jaw broad, the eyes are not oblique [like other Etruscan eyes], the nose . . . short—a type which has something of the Keltic character." He probably saw similar things in such works as this Cerveteri sarcophagus (4.3). "The obese and unattractive male personages who take their ease and toy with their prodigious necklaces, and not less the lolling ladies who lie lazily curled in their last slumber on the sepulchral urns . . . by no means belie in their suggestiveness the character bestowed on their prototypes by Greeks and Romans alike—the character of gluttons and of sluggards" (*Addresses*, 103ff.). Like the other races that Leighton feels have been tainted with Semitism's gloom and lack of talent, the Etruscans also have "an Assyrian edginess [i.e., insecurity] of touch" in their sculpture (109).

Even more, Leighton disapproved of what he called the Semitic Christian art of the Italian thirteenth century. He linked its lack of convincing perspective space to the authoritarianism and fear of innovation present in any culture that seeks to adopt biblical morality, especially as that morality was extended and narrowed by the Roman church (4.4). Above all Leighton read into medioeval art's extreme disregard of Polykleitan bodily proportions a fatal fear and loathing of the body itself.

Indeed, for Leighton, Christianity did not simply ignore but reversed the standards of Aryan beauty. It was not ignorant of Aryanism, as Etruscan art seems to have been, but actively destructive of this beautiful nemesis. The era of the Man of Sorrows, says Leighton, ushered in an art of "gaunt ungainliness" (143ff.) in portrayals of the human physique—that is, it did so on those rare occasions

4.4.
Cimabue. *Madonna Enthroned with Angels and Prophets*, c1280–1290. Detail. Tempera on wood. Florence, Uffizi.

4.5.
Albert Moore. *Dreamers*, 1882. Detail. Birmingham Museum and Art Gallery.

where the body was allowed to be visible at all. Early Italian painting, he adds, though expressive in line, is willfully ignorant, empty, and inaccurate.[39]

More to Leighton's taste would certainly have been the elegant seated blond lady in figure 4.5, whose pose by chance is somewhat similar to that of Cimabue's Madonna. So, for all its piety and genius, and looking at it now with our temporarily "Aryan" eyes, we have to add that Cimabue's Madonna is indeed dark-browed, long-nosed, and sloe-eyed, as Leighton has so damningly said; and, furthermore, that she seats herself on her throne with the utmost peculiarity. Indeed her body disappears completely somewhere around her waist and the entire lower half of her anatomy is replaced by a coruscating but flat swag of fabric. Albert Moore, on the other hand, and with typical late-Victorian outspokenness, has emphasized the outstretched lazy legs and haunches of his dreaming subject. She also has the requisite pale waxy skin, pink blossomy cheeks, abundant fair hair, hyperlong legs, long neck, and short upper arms of the Victorian-Aryan type. Like so many of her sisters, too, she sleeps in anticipation of an unspecified awakening.

Leighton's pictures often play intricate games with art history as well as with his ideas about Aryanism and Semitism. The famous *Flaming June* is such a work (4.6).[40] Dressed in the thinnest, most fluid of orange gowns, a girl lies before us, her haunches to the fore. It is an intricate pose. Her right leg is to the rear and twisted up to the forward curve of her upper body. The toes of her right leg project from under her bent left knee. Her arms are formed into a

4.6.

Frederic Leighton. *Flaming June*, 1895. Ponce, P.R., Museo de Arte.

4.7.

C. Bos. Engraving of the 1529–1530 *Leda* by Michelangelo. London, British Museum. Copyright British Museum.

similar helix, right elbow at thigh, drowsy head sunk back into an arm's embrace. Her face is a dreamy mask of sleep. Her skin melts into her brown hair, which in turn streams into another loop of drapery trailing along a marble rampart set with a porphyry panel and carved with simple scrolls. The wall separates the sleeping girl from the distant beach, where the midday sun makes a flat wash of hot white light on the motionless ocean, and forms a halo for the girl's head. Plants enliven the scene's upper right corner. Nothing could better evoke sleep, midsummer, midday—yet, as so often with Leighton's art, with every sort of expectant self-absorption.

I mentioned playing games with art history. Leighton is here quoting Michelangelo's *Leda* composition, restating the main ideas of that famous image but making them his own (4.7). He has reversed the figure left to right (though he may have been using a print, as shown here, that would already have incorporated the reversal). And he has eliminated the swan, which is the sinuous spine of Michelangelo's conception, as the bird, kissing Leda's lips, inserts his member into her groin. Leighton's picture, in fact, could even be portraying the aftermath of that sacred rape. Zeus has departed, leaving his partner, who has hardly bothered to move, asleep, her arms remembering the god's embrace.

Reproductively, great things will come of Leda's affair with Zeus. In some stories her children are Clytemnestra and Helen of Troy: here, if ever, are sexual selection and Darwin's law of battle! In other stories Leda's children include the Dioscuri, that is, the twins Castor and Polydeuces, who turn into the zodiac's

4.8.
Michelangelo. *Night,* from the Medici Chapel. Begun 1520. Florence, San Lorenzo.

Gemini. Among other things, since their constellation contains Venus, the morning and evening star, the Dioscouri symbolize the alternation of night and day.[41] Leda herself, moreover, is associated with the idea of night,[42] a fact Leighton may have known, or sensed, since he utilizes details from Michelangelo's own source for his *Leda*, namely his Medici Chapel *Night* (4.8). And that such a Leda, Leda as night, should now be sleeping at noon would then be one of Leighton's appropriate *concetti.*

In any event the girl in *June* is a typical Leighton Aryan. Yet here is another mystery: to Leighton, we saw, Michelangelo was not Aryan but Semitic. In the *Addresses*, Michelangelo is particularly contrasted with the Aryans Raphael and Leonardo (167ff.). For all their power, or perhaps because of it, Leighton held that Michelangelo's figures were Judeo-Christian in a way that prevented him from being truly of the Renaissance. Instead, says Leighton, Michelangelo is "the supreme type of the medieval [hence Hebraic] artist."

And so Leighton's young woman is an Aryanized recension of the *Leda* and the *Night*. Note how the legs and bones in Leighton's figure are far more delicate, the nose snub instead of driving and powerful, the ears smaller, the hair softer and finer. At the same time, in Leighton, the woman's jaw is rounder and deeper and her neck thicker and more columnar than in the two Michelangelo images.[43] *June* also displays those short, plump antisimian arms we almost always see in Leighton's women, and much less muscle than either of Michelangelo's figures.

Nonetheless Leighton has preserved a good deal of Michelangelo's version of the Polykleitan canon, Semitic or not. The *Night* is fully 8 heads high, the additional height being in the legs, which are as many as 4 heads long; and the legs in *June* are just as long. Both figures match Michelangelo's most extreme (in head-height) male and female figures. But the *Leda*, meanwhile, at least as given by the engraver Bos, has a contrastingly short torso, which only increases her legs' apparent length. The *June* figure is too foreshortened in this area for us to make further claims, but that very foreshortening means more apparent length for the legs.

Two Afro-Aryan Heroines

Leighton celebrates fair skins, fair hair. But we saw at the beginning of this chapter that for many experts Aryans could be dark-skinned. In fact, Gobineau found Aryans in sub-Saharan Africa. And at this point William Wetmore Story and Disraeli will reappear, this time in each other's company.

Disraeli introduces African Aryanism when Lothair visits Belmont, a stately house on the Thames near London whose art collections are entirely Aryan. Here he examines two marble statues, a *Cleopatra* and a *Sibyl*. These are by an American sculptor, identified by Disraeli's editor as Story. Lothair admires the statues' "mystical and fascinating beauty."[44] On the walls nearby, meanwhile, are canvases by Ingres, Delaroche, and Ary Scheffer—these too, it seems, Aryan.

Story's *Cleopatra* was indeed one of the most celebrated American statues of the nineteenth century. Along with the *Sibyl* it was shown with éclat at the 1862 World Exposition of Arts and Manufactures in London, and it was highly praised by Nathaniel Hawthorne and by Story's biographer Henry James.[45] In a poem by Story entitled "Cleopatra," often linked to the statue, the queen is dreaming of her absent Antony. Her dreams are Darwinian. Long before they evolved into humans the two had met as gorgeous tigers:

And we met, as two clouds in heaven
When the thunders before them fly.
We grappled and struggled together,
For his love like his rage was rude;
And his teeth in the swelling folds of my neck [sic]
At times, in our play, drew blood.

Now she summons Antony to her arms as the tiger's blood reasserts itself in her veins:

Come, as you came in the desert,
Ere we were women and men,
When the tiger passions were in us,
And love as you loved me then![46]

The *Cleopatra* appears again in Hawthorne's *Marble Faun* (1859), where, as a work by the novel's hero, Kenyon, it gets an ekphrastic chapter to itself.

By reading these images as "Aryan" in the sense that they portray heroines of their races, we can perhaps explain an oddity we have noted: that this and so much other Victorian-classical art looks both Victorian and "antique." Hitherto this hybrid quality—the Melpomenes who look like Mary Annes and the Artemises who look like Emilys—has been interpreted as a solecism. But if, indeed, Disraeli is correct, if Story was portraying members of a perennial master race, a race as capable of Africanness as of Anglo-Saxonness, such a combination of antiquity and modernity is a scientific or pseudo-scientific affirmation. In this reading the *Sibyl* and the *Cleopatra* should be, must be, Greco-African, and modern, too. Indeed Story makes this very claim in his letters.[47] And Henry James says something similar, affirming that the *Cleopatra*, as a type, is not quite English, not quite French, and not quite American, but partakes of them all.[48] The idea conjures up Huxley's notion of Aryans as varied racial mosaics.

Both the *Cleopatra* (4.9) and a *Libyan Sibyl* (4.11) vary the pose of the well-known Roman work known in Story's era as *Agrippina* (4.10). In the nineteenth century this was the model for a number of works dedicated to motherhood, ranging from Canova's portrait of Napoleon's mother at Chatsworth to Whistler's portrait of his own mother (*Arrangement in Grey and Black,* 1871), now in the Louvre. The *Agrippina,* as a portrait of Nero's mother, was described

4.9.
William Wetmore Story. *Cleopatra*, 1858, version of 1869. New York, Metropolitan Museum of Art.

4.10.
Helena, Mother of Constantine, c324–329 CE. Rome, Capitoline Museum.

4.11.
William Wetmore Story. *The Libyan Sibyl*, 1861. New York, Metropolitan Museum of Art.

by guidebooks as being filled with "pathetic, deep despair [shown] at the very moment her lunatic son doomed her to death."[49] Such a mood, of a mother betrayed and confronting a fearful future, is more than appropriate for Story's two sculptures and for our theme of human reproduction—for of course Cleopatra's unfortunate son, Caesarion, was as unfit in his way as was Agrippina's son. Cleopatra, indeed, marks the end of a line of Aryan rulers: reproductive failure, the last of the Nile Ptolemies.

Looking down at her lap and away from the viewer, Cleopatra's right arm rests on the back of her chair, cradling her head. The upper parts of her drapery are very like those on Polykleitos's Amazon. Note, too, the sweeping ovals of fabric across her lower body. Her haunches are well forward, her legs extended. She is the soul of careless but noble dejection. Her dress is classical yet has a scooped, off-the-shoulder Victorian neckline half uncovering what Disraeli, describing the statue in *Lothair*, called an "undulating breadth of one shoulder,"[50] not to mention her left breast. A loosely knotted sash trails over the back of her chair. Her face, with its longish squared-off nose, broad inset lips, and eloquently sightless eyes, is both Victorian and African, the latter effect being enhanced by a pharaonic veil and scarab circlet.[51]

To Hawthorne the work portrays an African rather than a Macedonian woman, black rather than white:

The face was a miraculous success. The sculptor had not shunned to give the full, Nubian lips, and other characteristics of the Egyptian physiognomy. His courage and integrity had been abundantly rewarded; for Cleopatra's beauty shone out richer, warmer, more triumphantly beyond comparison, than if, shrinking timidly from the truth, he had chosen the tame Grecian type. The expression was of profound, gloomy, heavily revolving thought; a glance into her past life and present emergencies, while her spirit gathered itself up for some new struggle, or was getting sternly reconciled to impending doom.[52]

Story's other "Aryan" effort, the *Libyan Sibyl* (4.11), has nothing to do with Michelangelo's Sistine version who prophesies the advent of Christianity.[53] Instead, like Cleopatra, the seer contemplates her Africanness and her race's future slavery.[54]

I have taken the pure Coptic head and figure, the great massive sphinx-face, full-lipped, long-eyed, low-browed and lowering, and the largely-developed limbs of the African. . . . It is a very massive figure, big-shouldered, large-bosomed, with nothing of Venus in it, but as far as I could make it, luxuriant and heroic. She is looking out of her black eyes into futurity and sees the terrible fate of her race. . . . I made her head as melancholy and severe as possible, not at all shirking the real African type.[55]

The generous barefoot woman, legs crossed,[56] sits forward on a rocky outcrop. Her legs are wrapped in a thick mantle, her upper body bare and bent forward as she cups her chin in her right hand, supporting her elbow on her knee. Her left arm descends along her side and her hand idly grasps a bundle of papers. Perhaps they are pages from the Sibylline Books. She wears a horned Amorite crest and a necklace with a Star of David—which recalls Story's use of the somewhat similar seal of Solomon as a device for proportioning the body (see chapter 3). Braids like the cornrows worn in ancient Egypt and modern Africa dangle down the back of her neck.

Both Cleopatra and the Libyan Sibyl appear in Story's statues as the sort of Aryans who are inner heroes in any race. Heroic or not, though, both women face not merely reproductive failure but the failure of their peoples, their nations; they lament Africa's enslavement. They contemplate, for those peoples, a future of suffering at the hands of white persecutors. As such they are works of tragedy. Story's African faces and bodies also combine a new interest in human biological diversity and new sorts of heroic types.

Story's two African images are hence a telling contrast to the Leighton beauties we looked at earlier. The latter belong to a biological master race of conquerors. They are the womenfolk of Dilke's "extirpating Anglo-Saxon Aryans." Leighton himself—whatever the Disraeli version of him thought—would not have permitted the possibility of such a Semitic Aryan. Leighton's ladies await their reproductive partners, concentrating on their faces, bodies, and ornaments. Their careful self-differentiation from Semitic phenotypes, as Cimabue from Michelangelo and Michelangelo from Leighton's version of him, embodies their creator's conception of the renewed long-legged, short-armed, blond, blue-eyed, willowy, hyperwhite physique that will constitute the "new ideal of balanced form wholly Aryan" (*Addresses*, 89).

We have looked, then, at an astonishingly wide set of definitions of just what, in the nineteenth century, an Aryan might be. To summarize, he or she could be (1) anyone who is Indo-European in language; (2) one of the Arya of India; (3) a tall blond warrior type who infiltrated prehistoric Greece; (4) a member of any heroic strain within a given population; (5) a member of a race devoted to reason and beauty, as opposed to conduct and obedience; (6) anyone who isn't a Semite—that term being applied to most of humanity; (7) an Anglo-Saxon set to conquer the earth; (8) a British aristocrat who doesn't read or know languages; (9) someone who looks like a Leighton painting; and (10) someone who looks like a Story statue. We shall take up this tangled theme again in chapter 8.

More Body Prescribers

5

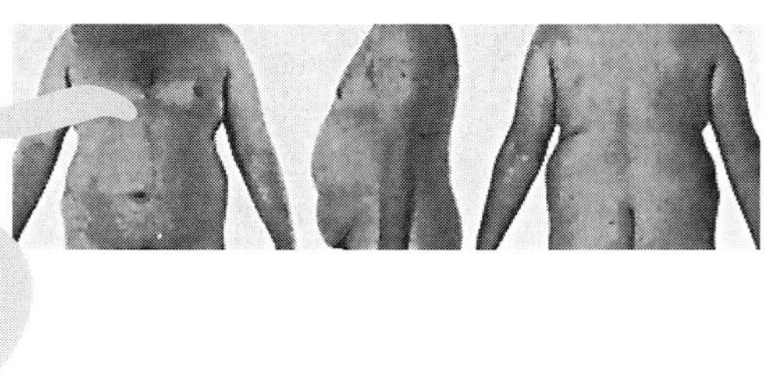

Selecting Scientifically: Lavater, Ammon, Virchow, and Kretschmer

The new methods of body measurement that came in with the rise of physical anthropology were ostensibly descriptive not prescriptive. In this the anthropologists differed from everybody discussed in the last few chapters. At the same time, *purely* descriptive, scientific body measurement was no novelty before the nineteenth century. Aristotle, Hippocrates, and Avicenna all took a crack at it, though only fragments of their observations have been preserved.[1] But this sort of measurement remained in abeyance during the Middle Ages and Renaissance. Even Vesalius's figures are highly idealized—Polykleitan—and, in physique and movement, part of the prescriptive artistic tradition, much as medical and artistic anatomical drawings have been ever since. This is simply another way of saying that the early social scientists involved in anthropometry usually had highly canonical ideas about what human beings ought to look like, and classed the people who did not measure up as in some way abnormal, if not pathological.

Body description has always been specially linked to the description of one major part of the body—the head and face. In this book I have tried to get away from that custom so as to focus on the body as a whole. But in the late eighteenth century, head description became a science unto itself—in fact several sciences. The practice was developed into craniometry, or skull measurement, which still has its practitioners. And there have also been the sciences, or arts, of physiognomy and phrenology. These were both based on the premise that the physical contours of the face and head express the personality harbored within. These ideas, in turn, were obviously related to earlier typologies of face and body as expressions of emotion: for example, in Charles Le Brun's treatise, *Méthode pour apprendre à dessiner les passions* (1698), and his earlier, heavily illustrated lectures on the likenesses between men's faces and those of animals, illustrated with a sheep-type man, a camel-type one, and so on.[2]

The most famous of all face-investigators was J. C. Lavater. And his findings (unlike those of Le Brun) had roots in sexual selection, since one of his titles can be translated *Physiognomic Fragments: On the Encouragement of the Knowledge of Human Nature and Love of Humanity* (1775–1778). The book consists of plates of male facial silhouettes, almost all of them considered by Lavater to be, in our terms, selectable, but all with individual patterns of excellence (5.1). Lavater, indeed, held that physiognomic expression was an older

5.1.

Silhouettes (by Johann Heinrich Lips?). From Lavater, *Fragmente*.

and richer language than the spoken word and that the face and head were primal, wrongly neglected indexes to the truths of our inner natures.[3]

Lavater's system for measuring profiles was geometric. A grid was generated by lines located at preset points in the profile—nose tip, chin tip, and so on (5.2), and the grid thus constructed, which would be unique to each individual, became an index of that individual's unique personality. Lavater's scheme for measuring profiles prefigures, and probably influenced, Francis Galton's plan to have every face in Britain diagrammed with a very similar triangular "isoscope" (see chapter 6).[4]

But the softer tissues, flesh and cartilage, told their stories too. Thus, writes Lavater, "persons with delicate, narrow, sharply drawn, angled noses, pointing somewhat down towards the lips, are rich in wit."[5] Lavater himself, we note, had such a nose (5.2). And so did Robert Fitz Roy, master of HMS *Beagle* and a disciple of Lavater (5.3). Fitz Roy, furthermore, considered that the young Charles Darwin's short, snubbed, flattened, very different nose "betokened indolence," as Darwin himself tells. "I think he was afterwards well satisfied that my nose had spoken falsely."[6]

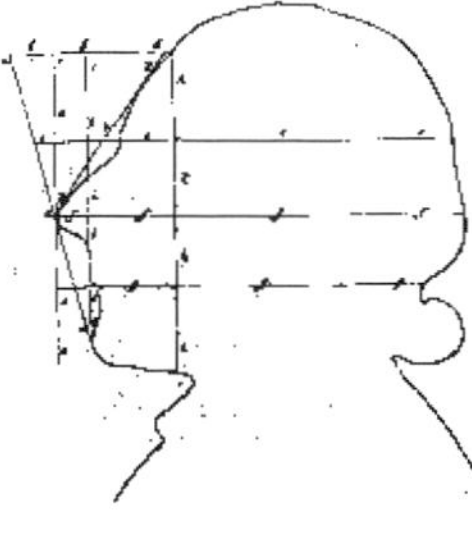

5.2.

Silhouette of the author. From Lavater, *Essai sur la Physiognomie*.

5.3.

Captain Robert Fitz Roy. From J. J. Parodiz, *Darwin in the New World* (Leiden, 1981).

5.4.
Head of Socrates. Roman copy of a Hellenistic original. Naples, Museo Nazionale.

5.5.
Unknown sculptor. Bust of Darwin in the collection of J. J. Parodiz. From Parodiz, *Darwin in the New World.*

A glance at the two noses in question confirms this. Captain Fitz Roy's nose is in fact even more gracefully noble than Lavater's. It rises gently but firmly from the brow, after only a slight and rounded indentation in the septum's long, slow arc, which prolongs itself somewhat beyond the plane of the nostrils. Darwin's nose, in contrast, is like the two snub noses in Lavater (5.1)—the second from the left in the top row and the second from the right in the bottom row. Its smallness, together with its wide-set prominent nostrils, not to mention the beard and bald pate, make Darwin's physiognomy a bit like Socrates' (5.4), whose satyrlike ugliness was legendary. Perhaps the sculptor of the Darwin bust I illustrate was making just this point (5.5).

Lavater and the other eighteenth-century physiognomists were less interested in the physique as a whole and seem to have had no interest in measuring human faces on a population-wide scale. They were interested in variation but not distribution. But in 1871, around the time Galton was beginning to publish his articles on population statistics and in the very year of Darwin's *Descent of Man*, Rudolf Virchow, whose most permanent scientific achievements are in the field of cell biology, was undertaking a physical survey of males in the German state of Baden. Originally this was to have been limited to skull measurements, but eventually it included height, hair, and eye color. By later standards Virchow's data remain rudimentary.[7] It is, however, worth noting that, like Charles Goring in later years, Virchow used his survey to cast doubt on any possible correlation between physique and temperament.[8] He even doubted the existence of such a thing as an Aryan physical type,[9] which made him in those days very much a lone voice.

Otto Ammon was more typical. He was the author of *Der Darwinismus gegen die Sozialdemocratie* (1891), which argued that democracy was a bad idea because it gives the vote to biologically inferior individuals. And how does one determine biological inferiority? A simple matter. Ammon categorized people by their having either long or short heads, that is, as being dolichocephalic or brachycephalic—categories that were already familiar in physical anthropology. He also subscribed to various theses about Aryanism, which he mixed together with ideas from Galton such as the chart of human biological classes (table 6.1).[10]

But few of Ammon's predecessors had dealt with the huge numbers of subjects he managed to corral. Between 1887 and 1894 he examined over 27,000 military recruits—again from Baden—assessing their racial characteristics for temperamental, intellectual, and spiritual content. He found all the correlations he was after. "Seek, and ye shall find" has been the motto of many social sciences, then and now. Long heads, says Ammon, predominate among academics and officials. Their skulls are marks of superior talent, capacity for hard work, and idealism. Heroes and leaders—for example, Bismarck and General von Moltke—almost invariably have long heads. Shortheaded people, in contrast, tend to lack heroic qualities. They are calculating, complacent, emotionally dependent, and hence tend either to be socialists or Roman Catholics.[11] So for Ammon brachycephalism is what Aryanism was for others—the mark of a superior, longheaded race living among a lesser, roundheaded one. Ammon is representative of much of the anthropometric analysis that was being carried on in Europe and the United States in these years. One unfortunate result was that the old categories of class, money, manners, education, and ethnos, which had historically always divided people into antagonistic groups, were now augmented by new scientific hierarchies based on head shape and body build.

The German-speaking lands continued to be important in these matters. Ernst Kretschmer was the author of the influential *Körperbau und Charakter* (1921).[12] As Sheldon was to do, Kretschmer built his theory out of three basic body types. His terms were "asthenic" (weak), "athletic," and "pyknic" (compact), with the athletic by all odds the best, though pyknic individuals could be impressive. Skull size and shape were important. Kretschmer's head types were related in turn to various face types, for example egg-shaped and shield-shaped. There were also gauges for skin texture and harmony of proportions. Sexuality was measured; men weak in it were called "eunuchoid." Certain combinations of characteristics were highly deselective. A midface region that is too narrow, for example, along with an undeveloped nose, short upper lip, and piercing gaze, is particularly bad. The phenomenon is called "hypoplasia" (smallness of make), that is, the symmetrical reduction in size of all measurements, vertical and horizontal.[13] When one's entire body is hypoplasic one is a dwarf.

These physical features are related to several categories of temperament. And the temperaments, in turn, are evolved from a distinction between cyclothymic and schizothymic individuals (*kuklos,* circle or cycle; *schizō*, I split; *thumos,* mind or heart). Every individual represents a combination of at least two of the five categories, one of them describing physique, the other temperament or personality. Cyclothymics have cycles of madness and sanity; schizothymics are insane all the time. However, these states are not always pronounced. It is only when they have the temperaments in extreme form that people are certifiable. Kretschmer's ultimate aim was to diagnose whole populations in state-mandated programs so as to improve German mating practices. It does not take many hours with his book to learn that there is a definite pecking order to his types, and that moderate cyclothymic athletes are the alphas of his world. These were to be selected for; the other types, with due intensity for each category, were to be selected against.

Kretschmer devotes many pages to the appearance of his types in art. But in doing so he substitutes historic for the legendary or imaginary personages that, hitherto, had usually served. And this led him into the unlovely actualities of human variation. Gottfried Keller (a nineteenth-century Swiss novelist), Tasso, Alexander von Humboldt, Locke, Mirabeau, and Calvin constitute his chief pantheon. He analyzes another gallery of great men (and a few women) in *Geniale Menschen* (1929). This time he does both Humboldts, Alexander and Wilhelm, plus Descartes, Locke, and Darwin. The book also has chapters on the Demonic (genius as a kind of sickness), Genius and Race, the Researcher, the Hero, the Inspirer, and the Prophet, all as scientifically established anthropological types with characteristic faces and figures.[14]

Endomorphs, Mesomorphs, Ectomorphs, and W. H. Sheldon

Both Kretschmer and the Italian anthropologist Cesare Lombroso had important American disciples. Among Lombroso's were N. Pende (1927),[15] G. Viola, F. W. Beneke, and A. Di Giovanni.[16] And there was also Sante Naccarati, ultimately based at Columbia University.[17] Lombroso himself was a prophet of doom and therefore belongs in chapter 6. But his disciples in America were more cheerful about our biological future and led on to the optimistic anthropometrist W. H. Sheldon. In 1921, Naccarati correlated the physical measurements with the IQs of a group of Columbia undergraduates and came up with a statistic that served as Sheldon's inspiration. "In one group of 75 male students," Sheldon writes, Naccarati "found the remarkably high correlation coefficient +0.36 between morphological index [physique] and intelligence test scores."[18] Proceeding forward from Naccarati's findings, Sheldon became the most significant figure in American body typology.

But Lombroso's greatest, most influential admirer in the United States was Earnest Albert Hooton, professor of anthropology at Harvard from 1930 until his death in 1954. Hooton taught a generation or more of distinguished anthropologists. Like almost all American social scientists of the time, he was a eugenicist.[19] A founding member of the Galton Society of New York,[20] his chief early scientific work consisted of neo-Lombrosan analyses of criminals *(The American Criminal,* 1939).[21] What governs the tables in *The American Criminal* is the correlation of particular crimes with particular builds. Thus in a given sample five individuals with short slender bodies committed first-degree murder but only one tall heavy man did so. This is out of a possible nine types of body and ten different offenses. The physiques are rearranged in all sorts of other ways and correlated with the number of previous convictions, age, marital state, occupation, and so forth.

Here are some of Hooton's results that could be reflected both in art and in sexual selection: Tattooing is commoner among criminals than among civilians. Criminals, compared to noncriminals, are apt to have thinner beard and body hair and thicker head hair, more straight and less curly hair, more red-brown hair and less gray and white; blue-gray and mixed eyes rather than dark or blue ones; speckled irises, thin eyebrows, eyefolds, low and sloping foreheads, high narrow nasal roots, high nasal bridges, undulating nasal profiles, nasal septa inclined upward and deflected laterally, extreme variations in thickness of the nasal tip, thin lips, and compressed jaw angles. However, marked overbites are rare in criminals. The ear of the criminal is more likely than an honest man's ear to have a slightly rolled helix and a perceptible Darwin's point (i.e., a pointed top). More extreme variations of ear protrusion are found in criminals than in civilians, though the criminal ear itself tends to be small.[22] One purpose of Hooton's book is to counteract Charles Goring, whose *British Criminal* (1913) had sought to prove, with what is now held to be considerable success, that there was *no* correlation between body type and crime.[23] But note also that Hooton, in the Lavater tradition, is mainly interested in the head and face.

Finally, and more perhaps than any of the investigators we have discussed in this chapter, Hooton was interested in race. Thus he presents data showing that, in the two populations he studied, namely of 167 noncriminals ("civilians," he calls them) and 299 criminals, 42% of the noncriminals were of English stock as opposed to only 20% of the criminals. However, 37% of that same noncriminal population was of Irish background, as were 33% of the criminals.[24] Hence—and here the extrapolation is mine—a given man of Irish background has a 13% greater chance of being a criminal than does a given man of English background. Hooton advocated new immigration and eugenics laws to take account of these findings—both those involving the greater genetic criminality of the Irish and those involving the facial and other phenotypic markers that betoken criminality in people of whatever race. Hooton gives short shrift to the idea that a different sampling might have yielded different results.

The last chapter of Hooton's book *Why Men Behave Like Apes and Vice Versa* (1940) is a fanfare for an anointed successor. The purpose of physical anthropology, says Hooton, must be "to relate group and individual variation in anatomy and physiology to psychology and social behavior."[25] But before that can be done, the existing varieties of the human body must be properly mapped and measured.[26] This great beginning had been made by Lombroso, who gets a remarkable accolade: "he alone can contest with Darwin the honor of being acclaimed the greatest anthropologist of all." And Sheldon will be Lombroso's continuator.[27] Sheldon did indeed concoct a far more detailed scheme for body measurement than any of his predecessors, and he probed more deeply than they into the personality housed within that body. But Sheldon's relative lack of interest in the mechanics of inheritance, along with his paradoxical belief in biological determinism, brought severe criticism from his fellow professionals on both sides of the nurture/nature controversy.[28] Sheldon, however, never fell silent, and indeed his system, purely as a way of describing physiques and minus the correlations to temperament, is still used.

William H. Sheldon was born in rural Rhode Island. His father, appropriately, was a breeder of prize poultry and dogs.[29] His earliest book, on heroic leaders, bears the Nietzschean title *Psychology and the Promethean Will* (1936).[30] Humanity is divided into the many who are after-thinkers—maintainers of tradition and the status quo, like Prometheus's brother Epimetheus—and the few godlike people who think forward (*pro-mētheus*), reach for the impossible, bring fire to humanity, and are its bold but sometimes criminal leaders, saints, and heroes. Among Sheldon's more prominent Prometheans are Giordano Bruno, H. G. Wells, H. L. Mencken, and John B. Watson, founder of behaviorist psychology.[31] One recognizes in the list the outlines of the Victorian Aryanism that posited a race-within-the-race of superior aggressive types.

Early results of studies that Sheldon did of 4,000 incoming college freshmen were published in *The Varieties of Human Physique: An Introduction to Constitutional Psychology* (1940).[32] The group was limited to white males of European background. Sheldon discerned three basic types of body. The first was called the endomorph. Evolutionally the endomorph is the most primitive of the three, says Sheldon, since his body is constructed around the most ancient forms on the evolutionary scale of animals—reptilian and lower.[33] Endomorphic bodies are dominated by the digestive system and organs for food assimilation. Such people have longer and heavier intestines than normal. The second body type is the mesomorph, dominated by the muscle or intermediate body layer, which also includes the heart, connective tissue, and blood vessels. Mesomorphs have some of the characters of Lombroso's ape-throwbacks, or as Sheldon writes: "the head shows heavy supraorbital ridges, prominent and massive cheek-bones, and heavy, square jaws."[34] Yet despite his apelike aspect, the mesomorph is the most heroic of the three types. People with dominating mesomorphy are biologically superior. We are about to see that their evolutionary backwardness, unless overdone, is a blessing in disguise.

The *most* evolved of the three types is the ectomorph. With him, skeleton, outer organs, and skin predominate—in his body and his life. A large proportion of his anatomical mass is given over to surface organs and nerves. Touch, temperature, sound, sight, and atmosphere play larger roles in his sensory experience than they do with endomorphs and mesomorphs. But in fact ectomorphs are supersensitive. They cannot stand extreme temperatures and constantly require protection and buffering from the environment. They are relatively uninterested in such endomorphic activities as eating and drinking and abhor the exercise that mesomorphs love. Even their greater degree of evolution is hardly an advantage: they are in fact overevolved.[35] Ectomorphs, accordingly, are common among aristocrats and the overbred. They do not flourish in the struggle for existence, in city life, or in dangerous occupations, and they require special protection if they are to survive.[36] They lose out in the competition for mates.

There are no absolutely pure examples of any of these types in nature, says Sheldon. Every individual combines something of all three—and to a precisely measurable extent that can be expressed in a three-digit code. This code becomes the person's "somatotype." The first number measures endomorphy, the second mesomorphy, and the third ectomorphy, with 1 the minimum and 7 the maximum for each of the three categories. Thus a somatotype of 117 (1 in endomorphy, 1 in mesomorphy and 7 in ectomorphy) is abnormally lacking in visceralness and muscularity and is overendowed with surface and skin elements.

Sheldon further divided the body into five zones, each with its own somatotype code. Each zone could have normal or abnormal correspondences with the others. The first zone is the head, face, and neck; the second is the area of the thorax; the third consists of the arms, shoulders, and hands; the fourth is the abdominal trunk; and the fifth is the legs and feet.[37] If one region of the body differs from another, against the norm, that person suffers from dysplasia (*plasis*, molding, conformation). Each body has a dysplasia quotient or value, predicated on the somatotypic sameness or difference of one body area to another. Thus a person with a 117 pair of legs and a 711 abdomen would have a great deal of dysplasia; someone with 711 in both, none.[38] Men have less dysplasia than women, and the 3,500 male psychotics that Sheldon studied had greater dysplasia than did the 4,000 college males.[39] So dysplasia, or at least extreme dysplasia, especially in males, could well be an index of deselectability.

Sheldon's most criticized belief was that physique is linked to temperament, a belief that forms the subject of his *Varieties of Temperament: A Psychology of Constitutional Differences*, which appeared in 1942. This book analyzes the somatotypes of 2,000 nude photos of college men and then posits a system of three basic temperaments that correspond to the endomorphic, mesomorphic, and ectomorphic body types. The endomorphic temperament is called "viscerotonia" (stomach tendency). Viscerotonics concentrate on their primeval reptilian or selacious (from *Selacii*, the order to which sharks belong) selves. They love comfort, ingestion, and cuddling. They are infantile, as underevolved in personality as in body. "Somatotonia," in contrast, which is the mesomorphic temper, leads to exertion, vigorous self-expression, and exercise. Somatotonics are evolved to just the right degree. The third temperamental character is "cerebrotonia," brain-centeredness, linked to the overevolved ectomorphs.[40] Cerebrotonics are brainy, obviously; but if their cerebrotonia is extreme it leads to all kinds of ailments.

A person's temperament and physique may have different scores. Thus the man with the 117 somatotype, mentioned earlier as an extreme endomorph, has a temperamental score of 216. This means that mentally or psychically he is a bit stronger in endomorphy; thus he has more visceral characteristics, though still very few, and maintains his 1 in mesomorphy, that is, has the least muscular kind of body and also, so to speak, the least "muscular" spirit.[41]

Readings of people's bodies, Sheldon confides, could be taken anywhere—Jones Beach, Coney Island, and so on. He produces scatter charts proving among other things that ectomorphic endomorphs and endomorphic ectomorphs (low on muscle and high, respectively, in boniness and fat) were more apt to be at Jones Beach than at Coney Island where, in contrast, mesomorphs prevailed.[42] (In those days Jones Beach was considered middle class and Coney Island plebeian.)

The highest rank in Sheldon's race of mesomorphic heroes is the somatotype of 172, who is a bit like Gobineau's or Curtius's Aryan:

The 172 is probably the masculine ideal which, in heroic moments, rides in the romantic imagination of both men and women. As an ideal, it carries supreme strength and masculine ruggedness with no trace of softness or weakness, yet it also carries a secondary note of ectomorphic linearity and sharpness of outline and feature. This is the legendary ideal of nearly all combative and dominating peoples. The perfect hero for the serial action-thriller of the cinema or of the newspaper cartoon is the 172. "Tarzan," "Dick Tracy," "Smilin' Jack," "Li'l Abner," "Superman" and so on, all are fine 172's.[43]

The temperamental qualities that go with such bodies reinforce their superiority. These men are claustrophobic. But this is no pathological condition; it is a saving liberation from confinement. Mesomorphs like space. They put their desks in the center of the room. “They love life on the grand scale. . . . They prefer houses on a hill or in a conspicuous, commanding position. They dislike restraining clothing.”[44] Mesomorphic claustrophobes also have an excellent sense of geography, space, and sound. They are well able, that is, to command the environments their bodies so forcefully occupy.[45] They are humanity's alpha males, who come out on top in the struggle for survival. They are Prometheans rather than Epimetheans. According to Sheldon, even Hercules and Zeus were only 271s, that is, behind Superman in mesomorphy and with a greater endowment of unevolved fat.[46]

But Sheldon warns that these heroes can be dangerous. American society favors them too much. So subject to the reign of mesomorphy is the American educational system, for example, that a humane eugenics program, with appropriate niches for a variety of somatotypes, will probably never be put into effect. America in 1942 has cast off the bonds of cerebrotonic and ectomorphic Christianity and embraced the permissive religion of Freud, a religion that is overmesomorphic. It leads to the (undesirable) notion of the master race.[47] But, sexual selection being what it currently is, nothing at present will prevent the mesomorphs' eventual reproductive success.[48] America's people will evolve toward the reproductive goal of the 172. Some day, says Sheldon, we will all look like Superman and Wonder Woman.

I illustrate Sheldon's three extreme body types from the *Atlas of Men* (1954): the mesomorph (5.6), the ectomorph (5.8), and the endomorph (5.9). How do these men line up in terms of the Polykleitan canon (table 4.1)? The mesomorph, like the Doryphoros and Alberti's man, is 7 heads high and has the Doryphoros's chest

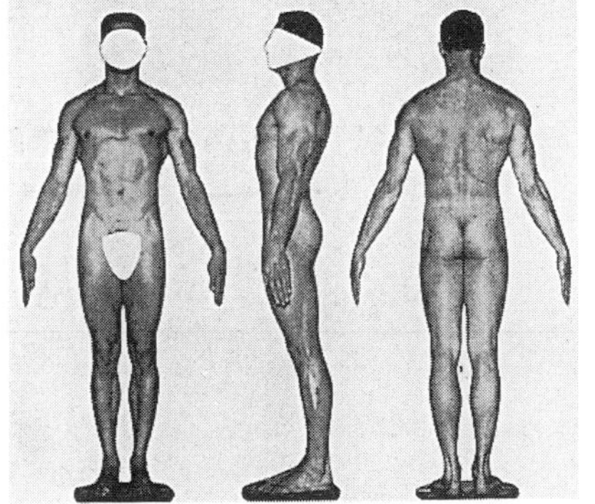

5.6.
A 172 somatotype. Extreme mesomorph. From Sheldon, *Atlas of Men*.

5.7.
Batman in 1970. Copyright © SPP, 1976. From M. L. Fleisher and J. E. Lincoln, *Encyclopedia of Comic Book Heroes*, vol. 1, *Batman* (New York, 1976).

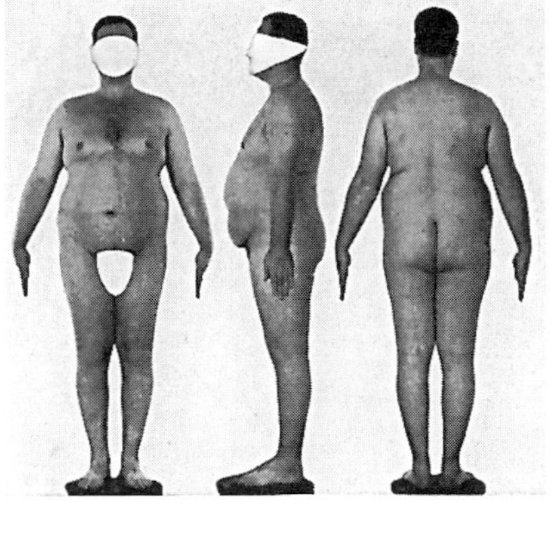

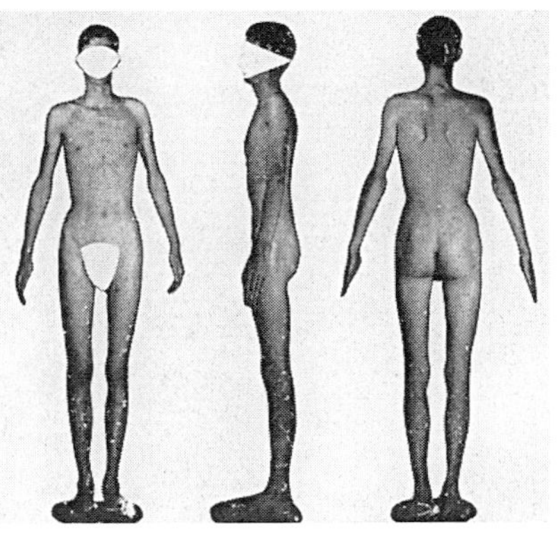

5.8.
A 117 somatotype. Extreme ectomorph. From Sheldon, *Atlas of Men*.

5.9.
A 732 somatotype. Extreme endomorph. From Sheldon, *Atlas of Men*.

width of 1/5. His forearm and hand are an equally canonical 1/4, hand length and face height each a proper 1/10. The ectomorph fares less well: he is 8 1/2 heads tall, a Lomazzan proportion, but his chest is a mere 1/6 of his body height. None of the Polykleitan authorities permit that. However, his forearm-and-hand, hand, and face measurements are all correct. The endomorph is 7 heads high and his chest is 1/4 his height: so far so good; and his hand and face measures are correct at 1/10. But his arm-and-hand measurement—as opposed to the forearm-and-hand distance—is too short. All three men have feet that are 1/8 their total height, as opposed to the 1/6 called for in table 4.3. So of the three Sheldon types illustrated, only the mesomorph measures up perfectly. Note that Batman (5.7) is clearly a 172 or close to it, though compared to Sheldon's figure Batman has extremely long legs—a variation that we have seen as both Michelangelesque and Aryan. And his head is narrow, giving him the Kretschmerian "shield-shaped" face that the Nazis were taking up with (see chapter 8).

Sheldon had a Neoplatonic streak. In his book on temperament and elsewhere he prints what he calls "a schematic two-dimensional projection of the theoretical spatial relationships among the known somatotypes" (5.10). This is an equilateral spherical triangle (its sides are outward-curving arcs, as if it had been inscribed on a sphere). Around its edges are arranged the seventy-six different somatotypes found in nature (out of a possible 343, i.e., 7 × 7 × 7). Each of the three corners is a pure, not necessarily existent type: ectomorph (117), mesomorph (171), or endomorph (711). In between, like the intermediate points on a compass, are the mixed types: the ectomorphic endomorphs, the endomorphic ectomorphs, the mesomorphic ectomorphs, and so on.

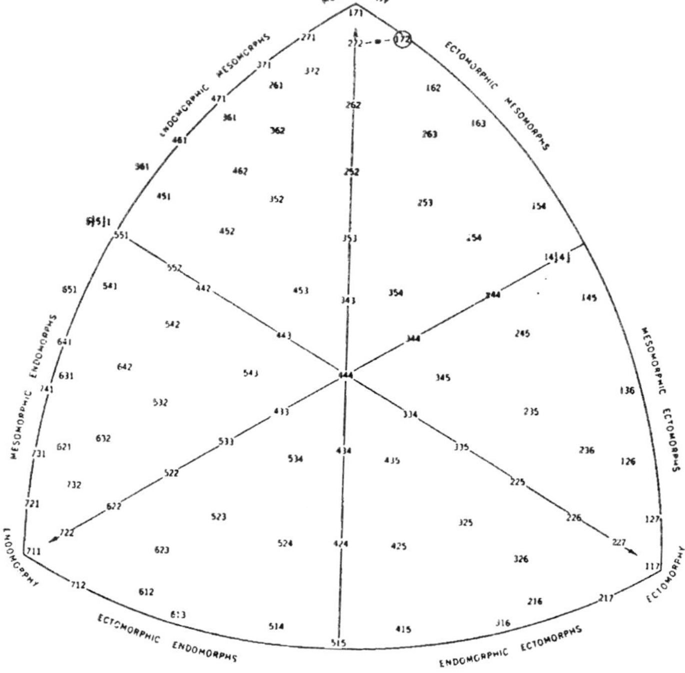

5.10.
Sheldon's diagram of existing somatotypes. From Sheldon, *Atlas of Men*.

The axis of each side is mapped so that all three axes meet at the center of the triangle. Along these inner axes further mixtures occur. The pure mesomorphic code, 171, and the axis on which it occurs run up and down vertically to bisect the triangle's base at 515. In between, top to bottom, runs the series 262, 252, 353, 343, 444 (which latter is the center of all three axes), 434, and 424. Other mixtures are scattered regularly in the areas between the axes and the sides of the triangle.

This triangle becomes, for Sheldon, a mystical country, a continent. He talks about Northeasterners, Southwesterners, and so forth, and those who dwell at the poles, the vertices, and of the "center-meaning people" (i.e., those near the central means). Yet all this is only an approximation of what Sheldon really has in mind:

The somatotypes can be considered as distributed within a three-dimensional section of a sphere. Depth, or polar diameter, is present as well as an East-West and a North-South dimension. The 4-4-4 sits atop the somatotype edifice and defines the pinnacle of it. The other somatotypes totaling 12 are in the upper surface of the somatotype edifice. Those totaling less than 12 are at the lower levels, with the three polar extremes, 7-1-1, 1-7-1 and 1-1-7 (all totaling 9)—defining the lowest level of the somatotype edifice and falling at the surface of the sphere. At the North Pole would be the hypothetical 7-7-7—impossible in organic life but theologically postulable as Mr. G, or God. At the South Pole would be the hypothetical 1-1-1, which organically is absolute nothingness. Other points on the surface of the sphere would be the hypothetical (but organically impossible) somatotypes 7-1-7, 7-7-1, and 1-1-7. We see then that any combination of the three numerals which includes one or more 7's will fall at the surface of the sphere, while all the other combinations will fall inside.[49]

Now he sounds like Buckminster Fuller—or like Cornelius Agrippa, though the Renaissance Neoplatonists did not venture into spherical trigonometry. The sphere of which Sheldon's triangle is a surface portion would in fact be a palace of bodies, a globe, a world of partly nonexistent but "postulable" physiques, comparable to the Neoplatonists' worlds of visible and invisible beings—a world we glimpsed in Lomazzo's system with its superhuman races of gods, angels, daemons, and so on. And note that the 171 mesomorph rises to the central summit of the "edifice," a nonexistent king with a real-life 172, son to the father, at his side.[50]

With this chapter modern science enters our story. Lavater in the eighteenth century and then German-speaking anthropometrists throughout the following century undertook the descriptive rather than prescriptive definition of the face and body, eventually increasing their field of study from selected types to whole populations. Yet, sub rosa, their characterizations often continued the selective prescriptions inherited from earlier centuries. The bodies studied all cluster around hierarchies running from good to bad—in our terms, selectable to deselectable. Inspired by the work of Lombroso, Kretschmer, and Hooton, Sheldon also continued the Renaissance and baroque practice of equating the body's features, proportions, and measurements with temperament and intellect. This habit, precisely, is what has continued to tempt the anthropometrists into value judgments right down to our own time. That Batman, as late as 1970, was still a Sheldonian mesomorph is proof that Sheldon's insight (or act of selection) was still alive. Chapter 9, indeed, will deal with what I am calling the hypermesomorph.

But meanwhile I have devoted the last three chapters to what might be called the canon of selectability—the *homo bene figuratus*, the Aryan hero and heroine, the Promethean mesomorph. Now we will deal with the reproductive fates of what the anthropologists of the late nineteenth century were calling the "undesirables"—Ammon's brachycephalics, Kretschmer's schizothymics, Sheldon's ectomorphs, and the like—those whose existence and reproduction were, in the opinion of a very large number of leading scientists and intellectuals, pushing sexual selection off course.

6 Galton and Lombroso

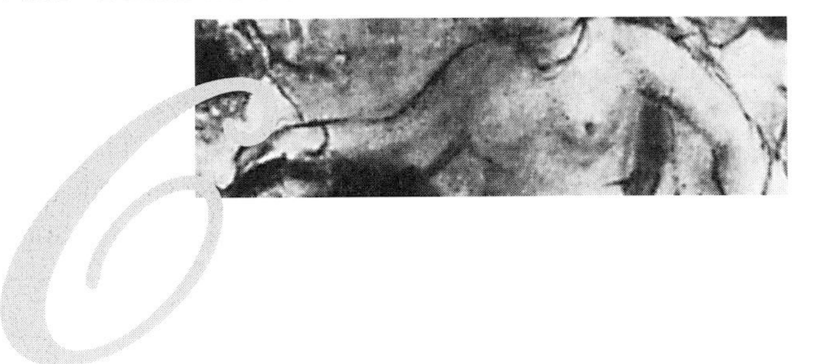

Worse and Better Faces

We turn, then, from optimism to pessimism, from the hope that with the help of science humanity can breed up, to the fear that the species is deteriorating and may even descend from *Homo sapiens* to something lower—possibly much lower.[1] Here, once more, art plays its role in what might be called the saga of deselectability.

The idea of biological decay is actually old—older than that of evolution itself. Its classic form was given by Plato in the *Timaeus* (91Dff.), which roundly declares that birds are biologically descended from men and women who were "harmless but light-minded and always watching the skies; that the four-footed animals are degenerated humans who paid no attention to philosophy, stared at the ground rather than the heavens, and finally drooped so far that they started dragging their hands along to assist themselves in walking." Meanwhile the Carthaginian writer Hanno the Navigator (c500 BCE) took the apes he saw at the mouth of the Gabon River in West Africa for degenerate humans.[2] Similarly, when the greatest of the Renaissance anatomists, Vesalius, was reviled for disagreeing with Galen, one ingenious critic surmised that bodily features that Galen had described, but that were not found in modern bodies, had atrophied and disappeared as a result of the long, slow biological degeneration of the human species.[3]

Such beliefs seem endemic. Thus in 1847 Dr. Thomas S. Savage, an American medical missionary, published a paper on primate behavior on the coast of West Central Africa.[4] His account became famous: it is one of the bases for Freud's theory of totemism and was cited by Darwin in *The Descent of Man*. Savage lived for a time near the Mpongwe people, who shared their habitat with troops of *Verus* chimpanzees. The Mpongwe, says Savage, identified the chimps as degenerate humans who had once been like themselves. Neighboring peoples seem to have subscribed to this theory, for they commonly called the apes "Pongoes," a word clearly similar to the human community's own name for itself. (In the same way "orangutan" comes from a Malay expression meaning "*man* of the forest.")

Judeo-Christianity, with its biblical God who often threatens to wipe out humanity, and who every once in a while almost does so, also fed this mood of pessimism. But it was only in the later nineteenth century that such thoughts, boosted by Darwinism, added up to a clear and present doubt as to our species' future. One other (non-Darwinian) contemporary theory that also increased this fear was called orthogenesis. Orthogenesists believed that the decay of species was fixed and immutable, pointing out (which was perfectly true) that 99% of all the species that had ever existed were already extinct; so why not *Homo sapiens?*[5] Engels, meanwhile, in an 1876 essay that became Marxist gospel, declared that existing groups of "the lowest savages . . . [are regressing] to a more animal-like condition."[6] As late as 1974 *Pravda* was condemning Alexander Solzhenitsyn thus: "He can be described in one word: degenerate."[7]

Many liberal and radical thinkers feared this degeneracy and held that the needs of intelligent human breeding far outweighed the unpredictable, often incomprehensible vagaries of mate choice as currently practiced by young people when left to their own devices. Their acts, it was now becoming clear from the writings of Westermarck, McLennan, and others, were at best random and at worst biologically dangerous.[8] Thus was the possibility of prescribed sexual pairing, as in many "primitive" societies, revived. It became one of the keystones of a new science—eugenics.

Led by Darwin's cousin, Francis Galton, the eugenicists proposed a compromise in which marriages would still take place but only if predicted to be reproductively positive. In line with Galton's idea of restricting marriage to acceptable couples, Westermarck pointed out that in many societies prospective bridegrooms had to pass public tests of financial means, endurance, and physical courage; and these ordeals, he said, were nothing more than age-old forms of eugenic testing.[9] For Galton, moreover, the great need was not only to prohibit the reproduction of inferior human types but also to counteract Britain's tendency to underproduce selectables. As one measure against this, he planned what he called a Beauty-Map of the British Isles, which would rate the selectability of British women by region and city, using a numerical scale. This would aid the state in bringing together suitable couples. As a start, Galton gathered preliminary data by walking the streets of a chosen town, clicking off the good-looking, medium-looking, and ugly girls on a counting machine discreetly hidden in his pocket.[10]

Thus to a great extent the selectability of the new elite depended on their physical appearance. Excellence in the activities Galton most valued—art, mathematics, football (i.e., soccer), and management—was determined by visual examination along with other tests. Thus do the visual cues for excellence in these activities become the most selectable kinds of attractors. This led him to pioneer a photographic method of studying physiognomy.[11] His photographs were made by successively projecting lightly exposed facial images of different people onto the same plate. For members of the same family the result was what might be called a family face, one in which the transient or uncharacteristic features of single individuals came out underexposed while the dominant traits, which reappeared in face after face, showed up in exact repetition and thus achieved firm contrast. Theoretically there could be such a normative face for a whole population. Galton also made composite photographs of ancient coins and medals with results that, to his own satisfaction, screened out the transiently seen features and emphasized the permanent definitive faces of such individuals as Alexander the Great and Cleopatra.

But composite family or racial physiognomies, says Galton, do not remain constant over long periods. And within a given family the composite face can change as it is determined by, for example, a dominance of male or female members, or by emphasis on one bloodline over others. Equally the British face, as a national characteristic, has not always been the same. Visiting the National Portrait Gallery, Galton observes that in Holbein's time the average Englishman had high cheekbones, a long upper lip, thin eyebrows, and lank dark hair. This, he says, was obviously no longer true: the basic British face had changed in 300 years.[12] Quite clearly selection—natural, sexual, or both—had been at work. Racial type also varies with political and religious beliefs, Galton finds: the Puritans had more than the normal number of dark-haired adherents, "for there is a prevalence of dark hair among men of atrabilious and sour temperament."[13]

Differences of social class are also markedly present in Galton's composite faces (6.1, 6.2). He does not say this in words but his photographs make the claim: note the sharper definition of the officer face, which shows that men who are well-born, talented, and intelligent have faces that tend to be similar. Their eyes are more brilliant and direct, and they have greater unanimity of ear size and placement and a firmer bone structure.[14] Composite photographs can be also used, says Galton, to identify the biologically determined physiognomies of criminals and the congenitally ill.[15] The pronounced brow ridges, deep-set eyes,

6.1.

Francis Galton. Composite faces of 12 officers of the Royal Engineers (left) and of 11 privates (right). From Pearson, *Life, Letters, and Labours of Francis Galton.*

6.2.

Francis Galton. Composite photographs of criminal types: 9 individuals (left), 5 individuals (right), composite of left and right photographs (center; 14 individuals in all). From Pearson, *Life, Letters, and Labours of Francis Galton.*

balding foreheads, compound-curved nasal septa, short upper lips, and large projecting ears of the fourteen faces of these convicts (6.2) only show their true colors, and therefore their biological meaning, when repeated over and over in the faces of men who have in common a record of violent crime.

With similar composite photographs Galton claims to reveal a typically "phthisic" face. Such faces are determined by the way in which the hollows are organized, the depth of the eyes, and a dozen other things. By generalizing from many particular cases, Galton's composite photographs are a visual application of his pioneering statistical techniques (Galton invented or developed the laws of regression, standard deviation, and variance).[16] He made similar photographs of all sorts of other categories of people, concentrating on the "unfit": prostitutes, sufferers from venereal disease, idiots, and various kinds of criminals. The impact of his ideas on Hooton and Sheldon was considerable.

One mode of sharpening the British people's sense of the possibilities for degeneration, Galton suggests, would be to create national catalogues of the physical characteristics of all British faces—good, bad, and indifferent.[17] The catalogues would also contain each individual's fingerprints (another practice that Galton pioneered) and composite photographs. There would also be geometrical indexes, not too different from Lavater's diagrams, of each individual's facial profile (6.3). In a paper titled "On the Measurement of Resemblance,"

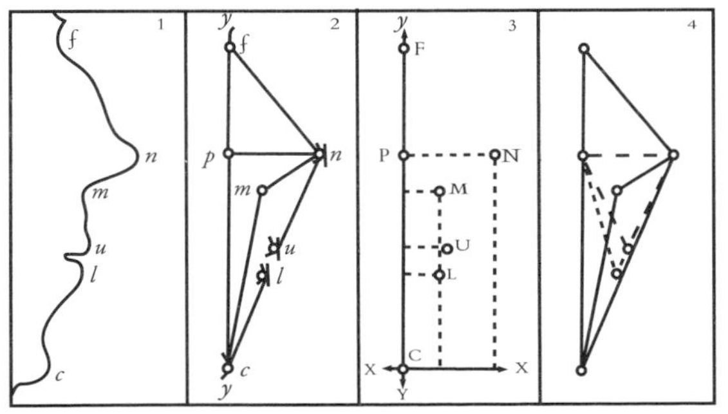

6.3.

Chart for indexing and numeralizing faces. From Pearson, *Life, Letters, and Labours of Francis Galton.*

Galton outlined these profiles in the form of measured diagrams or "isoscopes."[18] From hundreds of noses and chins he constructed mean noses and chins of various types that would be numbered. "A new profile might be described as having Forehead No. 3, Nose No. 31, Lips No. 26 and Chin No.8," explains Karl Pearson, Galton's pupil and editor. Thus could the precise likeness of a person be reduced to a six-word code. Profiles of Britons were also recorded and analyzed by social classes, as well as for non-British races—Copts, Arabs, and Negroes.[19]

The diagram in figure 6.3 illustrates how a naturalistically drawn profile can be turned into a diagram that will be different for each individual. If a police officer is trying to identify a suspect and the isoscope of, say, a known murderer is available, the police can measure the suspect's face and see if it matches the isoscope. Galton thinks that the isoscope will be as unique to an individual as his or her fingerprints. The key points in the face are *f*, *m*, *n*, *u*, *l*, and *c*. Tangents are drawn from these points on the geometrical diagram, *P*, *Y*, and *X* (two middle diagrams). Meanwhile *f*, *c*, *m*, *u*, *l*, and *n* are accommodated to a scale in which *c–f*, the height of the whole face, equals 100 units. The places where these points lie within that scale would sufficiently measure the precise uniqueness of any profile.

Breeding Baroque Bodies: Guido Reni

Galton wrote an unpublished novel about a eugenic utopia. *Kantsaywhere* details the physical nature of the new breed of women and men that will emerge once the science of eugenics is brought to bear on humanity. The girls of Kantsaywhere remind the novel's hero

of . . . the "Hours" in the engraving of the famous picture of 'Aurora' by Guido in Rome [illustrated in Pearson's book]. It is a favourite picture of mine and I recall it clearly. The girls have the same massive forms, short of heaviness, and seem promising mothers of a noble race. The simple way of gathering the hair in a small knot at the back of the head, shown in the dancing 'Hours,' is the fashion at Kantsaywhere. So is the general effect of their dresses, only they are here more decorously buttoned or fastened, than are the fly-away garments of the picture. As for the men, they are well-built, practised both in military drill and in athletics, very courteous, but with a resolute look that suggests fighting qualities of a high order. Both sexes are true to themselves,

the women being thoroughly feminine, and I may add, mammalian, and the men being as thoroughly virile.[20]

6.4.
Guido Reni. *Aurora*, 1614. Fresco. Rome, Palazzo Pallavicini-Rospigliosi, Salone dell'Aurora.

Guido Reni's Hours (6.4) are majestic, big-bosomed, soft, their hair plaited and braided into a thousand patterns (not the simple bun that Galton remembered). Their arms and legs are thick and creamy yet strong. They have round rosy faces, red bow-lips, long throats, and submissive heads.

The story in Guido's picture also has relevance here. On the right, Aurora strews dew-drenched roses and crocuses, bringing dawn to the cities of the world. Her dancelike flight is followed by Apollo in his chariot, surrounded by seven dancing Hours. The god rides out of the darkness of night, a great burnished cloud of golden sun as his background.[21] Apollo certainly fits Galton's description of the men of Kantsaywhere.[22] As to the Hours, they were frequently represented in wedding scenes, symbolizing not only the hours of the day but the seasons of the year, and indeed any sort of time-measuring cycle.[23] They bring freshness, youth, and abundance to humanity and represent maturation and ripening. They thus made excellent eugenic goals. Gods and goddesses were almost unbelievably fecund and their progeny were usually of the highest physical and mental order. The whole sense of the picture probably evoked, for Galton, the dawn of a new and better race.[24]

A word should also be said about the anthropometry of Reni's picture, or rather its gynecometry. Reni had a colossal reputation in the Victorian age. And his female figure types were widely popular, though there was increasing competition from the leaner, taller, more austere bodies of neoclassicism. Artists like

6.5.
William Mulready. *Bathers Surprised*, c1852–1853. Dublin, National Gallery.

6.6.
Guido Reni. *The Rape of Europa*, 1638–1640. Detail. London, coll. Denis Mahon.

William Etty and William Mulready (6.5) were important purveyors of the Reni ideal to the generation in which Galton grew up. These figures, with their softer, rounder bodies dominated by ovals, their short, fine-boned arms and legs with dimpled joints, and their exceedingly broad pelvises, are quite a contrast to the commanding, grandiosely classical, mesomorphic women that were Leighton's specialty. Reni's female faces, in particular, were extremely brachycephalic, smoothed into almost globular skulls, with large damp eyes, slender nasal septa projecting without break from the brow, and soft, small thick lips (6.6).

The late Victorians could remake and harden Galton's ideas as well as his reproductive goals. George Bernard Shaw announced at one unspecified eugenics meeting: if, from the eugenic standpoint, a marriage is truly successful—that is, if the husband has a sufficient degree of potency to assure the transmission of his desirable traits to a large progeny—"it seems a national loss to limit the husband's progenitive capacity to the breeding capacity of one woman."[25] I infer from this that society should appoint such superior males as the community's master breeders. This sort of breeding, let us recall, would be a return, of sorts, to "nature," for it would introduce or reintroduce into British society the practices of those communities, both human and otherwise, where a single male, or a small group of them, does all the impregnating. We could thereafter expect, if Shaw's plan were to be adopted, the appearance of a superrace. Shaw's *Man and Superman* (1905) discusses the same point. Such prophets

Table 6.1

Galton's System of Eugenic Classes

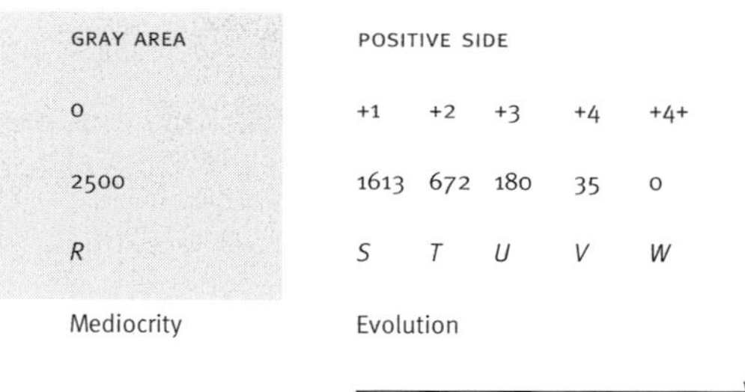
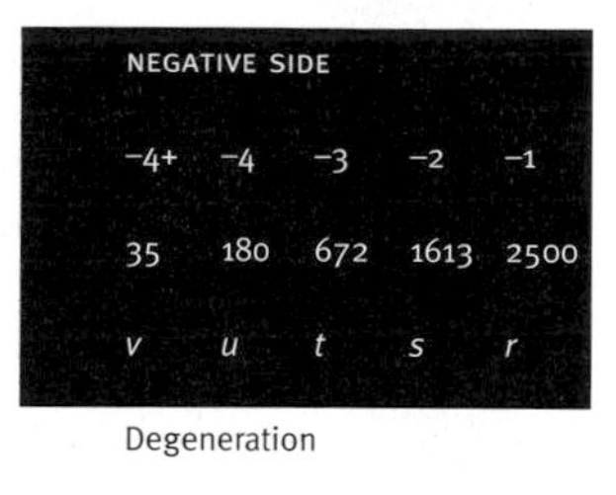

	Negative Side					Gray Area	Positive Side				
	−4+	−4	−3	−2	−1	0	+1	+2	+3	+4	+4+
Number of People	35	180	672	1613	2500	2500	1613	672	180	35	0
Eugenic Class	*v*	*u*	*t*	*s*	*r*	*R*	*S*	*T*	*U*	*V*	*W*
	Degeneration ←					Mediocrity	Evolution →				

found support in Darwin's *Descent of Man*, which, as I did not mention earlier, also advocated state-planned sexual selection, the elimination of undesirables, and the conscious breeding of a superrace.[26]

Galtonian eugenics is based on a complex system of social and intellectual classes. It was not entirely unrelated to the traditional British class system or, for that matter, to Aryan theories with their complex class structures. But rather than dividing society up into nobles, bourgeoisie, working class, paupers, and criminals, Galton ranked his populations by beauty, health, ability, and reproductive potential.[27] The ten classes, with their alphabetical designations, are shown in table 6.1.

This table represents Galton's future projection, not a record of observed fact. It shows how a representative sample of 10,000 British men would subdivide statistically into ten graded physico-intellectual classes. *R* is the mean, and the classes above it (to the right) are, in order, *S*, *T*, *U*, *V*. There is a space for a class *W*, but in Galton's imaginary population it has no members. The descending classes of degenerates occupy, in order, *v* through *r* (moving leftward). I have already mentioned the four talent areas—art, mathematics, management, and football. If you possess a "negative talent," you have marked *disabilities* in that endeavor. Thus someone in class *v*, the lowest, belongs there by being particularly bad at all of the four activities. These deselectable classes of people all occupy the left side of the chart. If you are neither negative nor positive for talent in these four areas you are in class *R*, which I have dubbed the Gray Area. If you *do* possess positive talents you have them respectively in one, two, three, and four areas, running from classes *S* up through *V*, and on to the unoccupied class, *W*.

Groups *v* and *V*, respectively consisting of the least and most talented, consist of only 53 and 35 persons respectively out of the 10,000 total, and groups *r* and *R*, the two central ones, who each respectively have one major disability and one major talent, contain 2,500 each. The presently empty class *W*, comprising superpeople who are good at the four diagnostic activities plus others, will fill up as *V*-class people breed with each other and produce supertalented children.

Galton then calculates how many of these *V*-class children can be expected from the matings that take place across this distribution. A new generation will produce, from its 35 original *V*-class members, 34 or 35 sons, 6 of them coming from pure *V* parentage. But another ten *V*-class children can be expected from among the *U*-class people, 10 more from the *T*'s, another 5 from the *S*'s, and another 3 from the *R*'s. The lower—that is, lower-case—classes will produce no *V*'s at all. In short, the lower a positively talented class is, the rarer will be its *V*-class offspring.[28] One particular reason why it is important to breed from *V*-class people born of *V*-class parents, rather than *V*-class people born of lower-class parents, is that the offspring of the latter type of *V*-class person, when they in turn breed, will regress to the normative type for their grandparents' class (this is Galton's statistical Law of Regression at work).[29] The aim, in short, must be to create whole, multigeneration families of *V*-class people. Galton ignored Mendelian genetics, which might well yield different distributions. But this could only happen once the genes or gene sequences for art, mathematics, management, and football had been identified, which has so far not occurred.

How is all this to be put into effect? Elsewhere, Galton predicts that if women of the upper classes normally marry at the age of seventeen, rather than at between twenty-two and twenty-seven, as now, they will have on average six rather than, respectively, five and four children.[30] This leads to the notion that sexual selection should concentrate on a tiny minority of superior families who constantly breed. Corresponding hindrances to marriage (which may become complete prohibitions) are invoked for the submediocre families. And, as Karl Pearson points out in elaborating Galton's argument, this concentration of all of society's breeding functions among a few individuals is already the case in Britain. Pearson calculates that a mere 10% of the population produces half of each succeeding generation of inhabitants. The only problem, he notes, is that it is very much the wrong 10%.[31]

Aside from adjusting, intensifying, and purifying this concentration, then, the other purpose of eugenics must be to eliminate, through natural and assisted attrition, all members of classes *t*, *u*, and *v*. To this end every individual in the nation will be given a "diploma" declaring his or her eugenic status. The diploma would correspond to the data in a national databank of eugenically approved families that was to be known as the *Golden Book of Thriving Families*.[32] Holders of positive diplomas, known as VHTs (Valid for Hereditary Transmission), will write those initials after their names.[33] VHTs are strongly encouraged, but not forced, to marry each other. Their weddings, for example, will be public pageants attended by celebrities. People without VHTs would not procreate.

The most appalling part of Galton's program appears when we start thinking about how these rules would be enforced. This makes the whole business a clear prophecy of Hitler's laws for racial hygiene. Let us therefore note that per 10,000 in Galton's *t*, *u*, and *v* classes, the total number of people who are slated for reproductive prohibition is 905. Multiply this ratio by the typical population figure for a major twentieth-century European country of the 1930s, say 40,000,000, and you get a total of 3,620,000 people who must be eliminated by attrition. Individuals in these classes, says Galton, are to be gradually prevented from emigrating into Europe from other continents, and any foreigner wishing to reside in Britain must take eugenic tests to assure that he or she is not in one of the prohibited classes. The tests involve not only art, mathematics, management, and football but knowledge of one's own genealogy going back several generations. Galton instances, as excellent models for British imitation, the quotas on Chinese immigration to the United States and Australia, as well as the deportation of Jews from Europe.[34] He notes with equal approval the power that socialist countries will possess, once they come into existence, to enforce these laws through large-scale social engineering.

But migration control will not be enough. Britain will have to expel all her native-born misfits. For the time being, Galton suggests, these people should be put into special institutions and camps. "Many who are familiar with the habits of these people do not hesitate to say that it would be an economy and a great benefit to the country if all habitual criminals were resolutely segregated under merciful surveillance and peremptorily denied opportunities for producing offspring. It would abolish a source of suffering and misery to a future generation, and would cause no unwarrantable hardship in this."[35] As we shall see, the eugenicists' definition of "criminal" was a wide one, including not only those who committed statutory crimes but also those who were mentally retarded or physically deformed. And, as we are about to see, those deformities could consist of features we hardly consider to be such—for example, big ears, high cheekbones, long arms, black hair, and dimples.

Galton developed his ideas from the 1860s well into the twentieth century (he died, still active, in 1911 at the age of 89). The carnage of World War I brought home to his followers the fact that humankind seemed newly intent on destroying rather than propagating its elites. The war exacerbated fears of biological degeneration. Eugenic ideas therefore flourished particularly in the postwar period. By 1930 there were eugenics institutes in England, the United States, Sweden, Norway, Russia, Switzerland, Germany, and Poland. A good number of these organizations—for example, the Cold Spring Harbor (Long Island) Laboratory, founded as the Eugenics Records Institute—still exist today, though with changed names and programs. In many countries popular magazines and scientific journals devoted to eugenics were also published.[36] Some of these, as well, exist today under different names. Not all eugenics theory was pseudo-science. R. A. Fisher, who may be said to have founded modern genetics by marrying Darwin's theories about selection to Mendel's discoveries about what came to be called genes, published his first findings in the *Eugenics Review*.[37]

While, in the end, applied eugenics was to become mainly a Nazi obsession, most pre-1930 scientific intellectuals though that eugenics would combine with socialism. All governments, worldwide, were to compile Golden Books filled with the fingerprints, isoscopes, and composite photographs of selectable citizens, issue genetic diplomas, and establish camps or labor colonies in which the undesirables would gradually vanish.

The Monsters among Us

Cesare Lombroso was a strange, wild, original thinker.[38] If Galton reminds us of Shaw's Professor Higgins, Lombroso is more like Du Maurier's Svengali. We have already met Lombroso briefly as Hooton's hero, who with Darwin was "the greatest anthropologist of all." But Lombroso does not truly belong with the more or less optimistic Americans. Like Galton, and indeed far more than Galton, Lombroso had violent, tragic prophecies to make about humankind's biological future. In many ways he stands at the core of this book, a pungent and permeating force. Lombroso reinterpreted Galton's "undesirables" into a well-defined class of born criminals whose personalities could be analyzed through their physical appearance, their dress and careers, their tastes, and their artifacts. In short, without using Richard Dawkins's expression, he posits an "extended phenotype" for criminals.[39] As with Galton, on identification such individuals were to be incarcerated and prevented from reproducing.

In other words, Lombroso gave new impetus to the idea that there were secret populations whose antievolutionary inheritance threatened to bring about humanity's extinction. Thanks to Lombroso's research these antievolutionary types could easily be spotted. They appeared not only in the streets and byways but, as Lombroso shows, in art. Indeed art provides an index of their existence in two ways—first, it shows how healthy artists portray these criminal types, and second, when the criminal types are themselves artists, it shows how they unconsciously portray their own degenerate bodies and faces in the guise of desirable-looking individuals.

Lombroso's "atavists," as he calls them, meaning evolutionary throwbacks, reproduced in their persons the ferocious instincts of primitive humanity and of the inferior animals who lie behind them in the evolutionary cladogram. Thus did Lombroso explain the "enormous jaws, high cheek bones, prominent superciliary arches, solitary lines in the palms, extreme size of the orbits, [and] handle-shaped ears found in criminals, savages and apes." The extended phenotype that went with these features included "insensibility to pain, extremely acute sight, tattooing, excessive idleness, love of orgies, and the irresponsible craving for evil for its own sake, the desire not only to extinguish life in the victim, but to mutilate the corpse, tear its flesh and drink its blood."[40] These fearsome individuals in our midst, then, are a kind of satanic pendant to the hidden race of Aryans, discussed in chapter 4, who prophesy our heroic future.[41]

A throwback's symptoms, Lombroso assures us, do not have to be pronounced in order to assure a proper diagnosis. It was not necessary to have a strong physiological resemblance to an ape or a Neandertal. It was enough that one's characteristics should point ever so slightly that way. Simply possessing *slightly* long arms or *slightly* handle-shaped ears was enough to make one atavistic. It is in the same spirit that Leighton, as we saw, gave long legs and short arms to his heroes and heroines, most of whom were created as Lombroso's early work was appearing. It was a question less of one's general physical appearance than of where one stood on an anthropometric chart. Count Dracula was just such a Lombrosan atavist. And we recall that Dracula intended to breed an atavistic population in London so as to swamp and eventually eliminate the positively evolving natives.

All this makes Lombroso's tone more urgent than Galton's. Lombroso transformed what, for Galton, had been merely a desirable goal into a dire necessity.[42] Accordingly, Lombroso's books are full of stern suggestions for revision of the criminal codes, the imprisonment or shipment overseas of atavistic types, and mass sterilizations. Foreign colonies like Italy's Eritrea, he adds, make excellent dumping grounds for Europe's undesirables.

How does Lombroso make his case? One key book, *L'Uomo criminale*, first appeared in 1876. In this we learn that atavism can be statistically analyzed. To us Lombroso's statistical methods are almost comically weak, but not by the basically pre-Galton standards of his day. Table 6.2 gives an example: he is proving that hair color is a determinant of moral character, and presents these figures based on studies of 500 normal and 500 criminal males.[43] This table proves, to Lombroso's satisfaction, that black-haired men have far greater frequencies of criminality (43% as opposed to only 27% noncriminal) than do blond men (the percentage ratio is 30:13), while redheads have only the most minuscule chances of being criminal. Most of Lombroso's statistical proofs are of this ilk (he might have learned better from Galton, but didn't). As noted, he seriously proposes that such figures, which are amplified by many similar charts, tables, and surveys, be used by the state in making its decisions and

Table 6.2

Hair Color and Criminality

Hair Color	Normal	Criminal
Black	27%	43%
Brown	39%	43%
Blond	30%	13%
Red	3%	0.7%

fashioning its criminal code. If, all other things being equal, a black-haired individual has a 60% greater chance of being a criminal than his blond competitor for an administrative post, who would hesitate to appoint the latter? The chart also proves to Lombroso that black-haired men are more atavistic than are blonds and redheads. (It was this sort of thing that inspired Hooton's analyses of Irish Americans.)

But while Lombroso comments on the similarities between contemporary degenerates, children, women, the insane, and "primitives," on the one hand, and prehistoric humans on the other, he does not simply lump them all together as was the fashion of the time. He makes distinctions, bringing to bear his love of medical jargon. Primitives, he points out, do not have the facial asymmetry, strabismus (being cross-eyed or having a squint), dyschromatopsia (color blindness), and unilateral paresis (paralysis on one side) that characterize modern urban degenerates. They also lack the civilized criminal's "desire to do evil for its own sake, and that sinister gaiety that is to be remarked in the argot of criminals, and which, alternating with a certain religiosity, is found also among epileptics."[44] Modern criminal types, indeed, have a higher degree of skeletal malformation than any other category of human being. Of 79 juvenile delinquents that Lombroso studied, 30 had goose ears, 21 had low foreheads, 19 were plagiocephalic (asymmetrical or twisted upper skulls), 16 had projecting cheekbones, 15 a raised coronal suture in the skull, and 14 had prominent (i.e., simian) jaws. There were 34 other such bodily anomalies among them.[45]

For Lombroso, particular criminal characteristics are attuned to particular types of crime and to the particular lower organisms toward which the criminals have evolved. Thus murderers have the bloodshot eyes and large mandibles of tigers.[46] A large-jawed human, in fact, is a natural predator. This reminds us of Story's *Cleopatra* who, we recall, dreamed of her and Mark Antony's prehuman life together as a pair of tigers. It also reminds us of the physiognomical theorists like Le Brun, whose *Methode pour apprendre à dessiner les passions*, mentioned earlier, likened human and animal faces.

Genius and Madness (1882) is the title of another important Lombroso book, its title page graced by a portrait of Schopenhauer. A first section discusses the anatomical similarities between madmen and geniuses. These are precocious baldness, early onset of gray hair, and painful thinness of body with little evidence of muscular or sexual ("genesic") activity. Like the madman, the genius is born and dies alone, cold and insensible to family affections and social conventions. Thus Michelangelo, Lombroso tells us, often explained that he had no wife by saying: "I have too much of a wife in this art." (I should add, however, that Michelangelo did not suffer from precocious baldness or painful thinness of body.) Goethe, Heine, Byron, Benvenuto Cellini, Napoleon, and Newton, Lombroso inaccurately adds, were the same.[47] Ironically, some of the very people whom the Aryanists were identifying as their principal heroes, Lombroso defines as being mad and atavistic.

Women, Ornament, and Degeneration

Most of what has been said has to do with sexually deselectable males. *La donna delinquente*, first published by Lombroso and G. Ferrero in 1893, deals with sexual selection from a potential husband's viewpoint. The authors' purpose is to establish that women are biologically inferior to men, and that this must be taken into account whenever sexual selection, or rejection, occur. One argument for female inferiority has to do with the relative rate of biological development between the sexes. The authors follow St. Augustine in proposing that, in all species, the mature female is equivalent to a partially grown male. Hence, say Lombroso and Ferrero, she is ipso facto less evolved. The more evolved males are, the authors further reason, the more they tend to develop or transform their secondary sex characteristics—for example, their voices change or they grow bald.[48] Females have fewer such changes. Furthermore, the lower in the evolutionary ladder a species is, the less dominant are its males, and vice versa; so that male dominance is, again, the sign of humanity's more evolved state.

The authors also cite Darwin and the French biologist Milne Edwards to the effect that in the higher species the "atavistic force," that is, the conservative tendency to keep things as they are and avoid progress, is stronger in females than in males. That is why women dress in fashions borrowed from the past while men prefer modern, unornamented clothes. Women's liking for such fashions is in fact a pathological condition—"misoneism," hatred of the new. And the fact that women ornament themselves—wear necklaces, rings, tiaras, and the like, dress their hair elaborately, and strut around in extravagant clothes—all this, to Lombroso, symbolizes not only their essential atavism but also the atavism of ornament and, for that matter, the atavism of art itself.

These things can be proved through the statistical analysis of body parts. Women's infantilism is demonstrated through their shorter bones and lighter body organs. The comparisons also include data on the incidence of left-handedness—this being particularly atavistic and female. Lombroso and Ferrero measure the cranial capacities, the orbital indexes, the weight of the mandibles, of body after body and for page after page, finding all kinds of subsidiary correspondences depending on whether the women thus measured are normal or degenerate, atavistic or evolving, born prostitutes, born murderesses, or born normal. The findings of other scientists are incorporated. An investigator named Mme. Tarnowsky shows that the hands of Russian prostitutes are longer than those of peasant women (*La donna delinquente*, 307). Contradicting his claim published elsewhere and just noted, that blonds are more evolved than brunettes, Lombroso here claims that prostitutes are more apt to be blond than are healthy women. They also have more abundant hair (320). Pubic hair is a particular key: healthy females have less of it than atavistic ones, and never have it in a male pattern (i.e., growing in a thin line up toward the umbilicus). Another telltale sign of atavism, in women, is the prehensile foot (323).

Lombroso and his coauthor are fond of circular arguments. Any supposedly good moral quality, if associated more with women than with men, turns out actually to be bad. Women, for example, are more sympathetic to the sufferings of others than are men, a fact, say Lombroso and Ferrero, observable in females throughout the animal kingdom (79ff.). But this is precisely because pity is atavistic. Indeed it is close to being pathological and, together with generosity, is a symptom of a disease the authors identify as hysterical altruism. The proof that pity and generosity are bad is that they tend to coexist, in the same women, right along with savage cruelty, impulsiveness, and other bad qualities. But sexual selection, as currently practiced, offers hope: cruelty and impulsiveness are gradually being bred out of human females because men, as they evolve, tend to choose ever tenderer, sweeter mates (111). Thus does the male instinct select for kindliness. (And yet women's kindliness is nothing to their credit, for it has come about entirely through male selection!) For these reasons it remains natural and right that women, like dogs and other domestic animals, should be subject to male domination. The women themselves deeply desire this; those who do not are criminally atavistic (129ff.).

We saw that, for Lombroso, sexual characteristics start out among lower animals by being less varied among males than among females, and that among upper animals the reverse is true. Thus, over the centuries, men have worn less and less ornament and women more and more (140ff.). Indeed ornament is basically a sexual attractor for lower forms of life, for example, birds and women. Furthermore, ornament is not merely atavistic; it is in essence a form of self-mutilation, even self-imprisonment. The authors describe ancient Hebrew maenads who "at night, deep in a sacred wood, cut themselves with knife blows, covering themselves with shallow wounds and cuts, drunk with wine and music, at last to fall down covered with blood" (225). This self-wounding is the primal act of ornamentation. In this and similar ancient practices lie the origins of modern females' love of bracelets, rings, and the like. Bracelets and rings are the descendants of wounds, or of the weapons that inflicted those wounds, or of the chains and shackles that women wore. After all, what does jewelry do to the body? It locks itself around the arms, legs, and neck (164ff.). It seems some modern advertisers agree (6.7, 6.8). The woman on the left wears nothing but a gorgeous manacle that shackles her wrists; the word "Jaïpur" is written above. That is the city, famed for its jewelry, whose maharajahs in legend seized the princesses of nearby Udaipuras as their "honored captives." The woman on the right has confined her shoulders in chains of pearls.

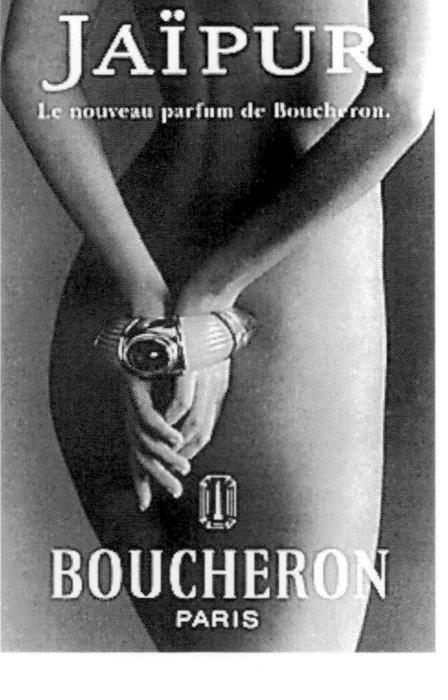

6.7.
Advertisement for Boucheron Perfumes from the *New Yorker*, 8 May 1995.

6.8.
Advertisement for Macy's from the *New York Times*, 4 May 1995.

Lombroso and Ferrero particularly emphasize ear piercing as a form of antievolutionary self-wounding. But the pain inflicted by women on themselves is far less than would be the case with a man piercing his ears. For, our authorities tell us, women are less sensitive to pain than men. Why? Because they are more atavistic. "One must remember that the greater resistance to wounds and operations in women accords with the greater resistance to wounds and illnesses among inferior animals (46ff.).

Ornament, fashion, and pronounced femininity bring us to that most female of professions, prostitution. *La donna delinquente*, as one might imagine, is largely about this. Prostitution is called the oldest profession for good reason, and prostitutes are in fact the key to understanding women in general. They were other women's original role models, because the actions and appearance of prostitutes are a relic of the original lack of sexual restraints that all women enjoyed (258ff.). It is for this reason that prostitutes have so many more atavistic deformities in skull shape, foot and hand articulation, hair, and so on, compared to more evolved women.

Yet prostitutes, as opposed to other female delinquents, normally lack certain of the more obvious signs of atavistic deformity, such as wrinkles, large lower jaw muscles, flatheadedness, deviated nose, and facial asymmetry. But—and here Lombroso and Ferrero take us on another of their syllogistic merry-go-rounds—such women only lack these things because such features would make them less physically attractive, hence less successful in their profession. In other words prostitution is a sphere of life that self-selects for attractiveness, but self-selection here only disguises the profession's underlying atavism. Prostitutes' good looks, their *apparent* accord with the healthy norms, can paradoxically be a sign that they are in actual fact atavistic. In any event, prostitutes are not really all that attractive. They frequently suffer from warts, swollen lower lips, a "virile larynx" (i.e., husky voices), exaggerated development of the bones of the cheek and jaw, and "anomalous teeth" (334ff.). Further, they have "greater tactile and gustatory insensitivity and more frequent tattooing" (359). And masculine, hence atavistic, handwriting; Ninon de Lenclos and Catherine de Médicis are instanced as famous prostitutes (381).

Very well. Let us, trying to look at all this through Lombroso's eyes, briefly illustrate with two portrait figures Catherine de Médicis commissioned for her tomb

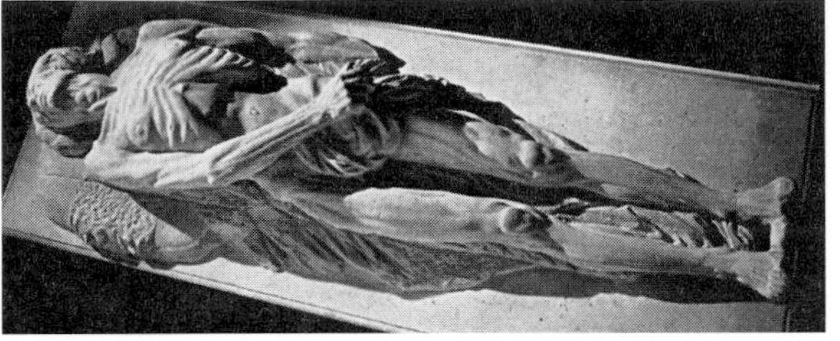

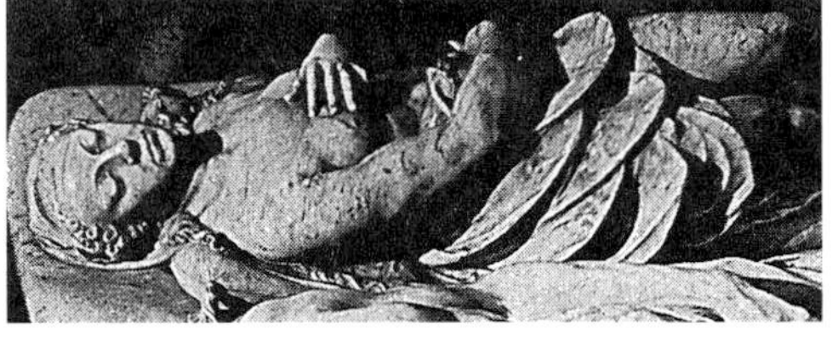

6.9.
Girolamo Della Robbia. Model for *transi* figure of Catherine de Médicis, c1562. Paris, Louvre.

6.10.
Germain Pilon. Gisant of Catherine de Médicis. Tomb of Henry II, 1563–1570. Paris, St.-Denis.

(6.9, 6.10). Originally Girolamo Della Robbia was asked to make a model (6.9). This was in 1562 or so, when Catherine was about 43, long before her death in 1589. The commission, however, stipulated that the queen was to be represented as she would have looked several days after her death had it been in that year.[49] Girolamo complied with a will. The queen lies almost nude, her winding cloth cast aside and her head thrown back as if in a postinterment spasm. Her skeleton and long lean muscle fibers show sharply through her withered skin. The notion behind such figures, which were called *transi*, was that the person had been stripped of all the earthly symbols and signs of power and lay in utter humiliation awaiting the summons to judgment. In some transi we see worms and other creatures actually eating away at the corpse's flesh.

Girolamo's model was rejected, presumably for being too grisly. Germain Pilon, who succeeded to the commission, created one of Catherine's most famous portraits (6.10). She is still a naked corpse but at the same time a handsome, sensuous Venus Pudica, her winding sheet now a great blossom of vectored ovals over her groin. The notion of dust-to-dust, of decomposition, is replaced by the older pagan conception of the queen becoming a goddess: postmortem apotheosis. Her husband, Henri II, lies beside her in the pose of a dead Christ, which is appropriate from the viewpoint of Pilon's *concetto* if not from that of Christian decorum.

By a strange fluke, then, taken together, Girolamo Della Robbia's rejected model and Pilon's finished effigy match Lombroso's vision of the attractive prostitute whose inner self is decayed and repulsive. Note especially the emphasis that Della Robbia has put on the queen's throat, larynx, and jaw. And by an even

stranger fluke—though perhaps it is no fluke—the isolated muscles and almost total absence of body fat (e.g., in the rudimentary breasts) in Della Robbia's queen make her a somatic match for a modern female bodybuilder like Kristy Ramsey (see fig. 9.8). Thus, and not for the first time, does a look of intended decadence, of bodily rot, much later reappear transformed into attractiveness.

Whether or not Catherine de Médicis was truly *una donna delinquente* is pretty moot. That is not the case with Lombroso's main exhibit, however, Messalina, the notorious wife of the Roman emperor Claudius I.[50] One notes that the empress (6.11) does indeed possess a heavy jaw and thick curly hair, Lombrosan indexes of atavism. She also has a low brow with a pronounced ridge, strong cheekbones, a full lower lip, large asymmetrical eyes, and deeply curved surfaces between nose and cheek. Her neck is long and widens at the base. Her head is flattish—platicephalic, as Lombroso would say. The intricate, ordered swarms of curls and ringlets in her hair are also delinquent, as is the rictus or dimple (cf. also Minos, in fig. 6.12).

To sum up, delinquent women exaggerate the characteristics of all women. Atavistic women are greater lovers of dress and ornament, are more sentimental, more dissipated, less maternal, and often more intelligent than the normal. And then there is the authors' parting shot: "like male delinquents, and the majority of male degenerates, prostitutes are very religious." Here, as so often, Lombroso, Galton, and company find religion a bad influence. Not only is Christianity basically cannibalism, it preserves unhealthy atavistic customs and enshrines criminal acts (crucifixion?). How do we know all this? Because an inordinate number of criminals are religious (*La donna delinquente*, 552).

6.11.
Marble bust of Messallina (d. 48 CE). Rome, Capitoline Museum.

6.12.
Michelangelo. *Last Judgment*, 1535–1541. Detail of Minos. Vatican, Sistine Chapel.

While females may seem to take the cake for atavism, males can be just as bad. Atavism, in its pure form, is seen in Giotto's *Massacre of the Innocents* (Padova, Arena Chapel), where the main killer has a flat head, dark abundant hair and beard, and a low brow. His eyes are mere slits on either side of his long sharp nose. The other soldiers, adds Lombroso, also have narrow heads and thick lips: they suffer from maxillary prognathism—more atavism. Mantegna, Raphael, Rubens, Ribera, and Titian are other artists who have instinctively portrayed criminal types. Lombroso declares that Veronese, in his *Crucifixion* (?) and *Jesus Bearing His Cross* (probably the *Andata al Calvario* in the Gemäldegalerie, Dresden, of 1570–1572) shows torturers with asymmetrical faces and scraggly beards, their upper skulls too large for their lower skulls, and with zygomatic apophyses (protuberant cheekbones).

Other degenerate types, Negro and Mongol, appear among the damned in Michelangelo's *Last Judgment* (6.12). Lombroso mentions their pointed, horn-shaped ears; for example, those of Minos, Hell's gatekeeper.[51] The pop-eyed faces and powerful brow ridges of the figures behind Minos are also atavistic. But I will note Minos himself, with his furrowed cheeks, prognathous jaw, deep-set eyes, and S-curved nose.

Even worse were geniuses: Galton may have wanted to breed more of them, but Lombroso clearly wants them eliminated. Charles J. Guiteau, the assassin of President Garfield (6.13), was a typical Lombrosan criminal genius. Guiteau was a polymath and religious maniac.[52] He possessed a number of physical atavisms: tall stature, asymmetrical macrocephalic head with a circumference of 619 millimeters (measured by Lombroso from the woodcut?). And he has a plagiocephalic skull (i.e., having a slanted axis), along with depression and flattening

6.13.
Charles Guiteau. From Lombroso, *Genio e Follia* (1876 ed.)

along the right-hand side, abundant dark hair, small, wide-set eyes set into deep sockets, and enormous jug-ears. Guiteau's biological inheritance is proved by his father's madness (he gave his other sons the insane names of Luther and Calvin) and by that of two of his sisters, who died in delirium, while a third became a religious fanatic at fifteen. A fourth sister had a deformed head. Finally, Guiteau's nephew was also a genius, a musician, and died mad.

Lombroso's art criticism is fascinatingly offbeat. His hatred of ornament, especially, would be communicated to Max Nordau and Adolf Loos, and through them to Gropius, Mies van der Rohe, and Le Corbusier, in whom it became a watchword of modern architecture. But Lombroso found criminal degrees of ornamentation even in wild nature. The abundant, lushly ornate vegetation of the tropics, for him, is composed of "criminal plants." To create ornament from the poisonous parts of these organisms, from their skins, arteries, teeth, leaves, and flowers, to glorify and exploit such sinuous tendrils, powerful ductile leaves, shining surfaces, and intoxicating blossoms (which is precisely what the Art Nouveau artists of Lombroso's time were doing), was nothing less than to celebrate crime. Such art praised and urged onward nature's vices and immoralities. It was poisoning European civilization.[53] Other criminal elements in art and literature are "exaggerated minuteness of detail, the abuse of symbols, inscriptions, or accessories, a preference for some one particular color. . . . [These things] may approach the morbid symptoms of mattoidism [criminal madness]." Criminal persons, indeed, are much more frequently color blind—or else they are hypersensitive to color, which is equally bad. They also have distorted visual fields, which means that they do not see in proper perspective; or else the field of vision will palpitate, distend, or wobble before their eyes.[54] Max Nordau will apply these insights directly to painters like Cézanne and Renoir and find their art a reflection of their optical and sensory handicaps (see chapter 7).

Anthea Callen has recently claimed that Degas, in some of his images of female dancers, was attempting to express these Lombrosan characteristics.[55] Thus the dancers, for her, have low, sloping brows, long arms, short legs, and the galvanic motions that Lombroso equates with throwbacks. She may be right; however, the Degas dancers I have seen are all constructed along principles that Lombroso held to be positive, though occasionally they have sloping foreheads. But the dancer in figure 6.14 is a canonical 7 heads high. Moreover, as far as one can tell, given the back view, her vertical body articulation measured in

6.14.
Edgar Degas. *The Dance Lesson*, 1874–1876. Detail. Paris, Musée d'Orsay.

6.15.
Edgar Degas. *The Party for Madame's Name-Day*, 1878–1879. Detail. Paris, Louvre.

heads is a canonical 2, 3, 4, 5, 7, respectively, for nipples, navel, groin, knees, and heels. These canonical demarcations are even established in this back view by the shoulder blades and the top and bottom of waist bow. The dancer's upper and lower arms, omitting hands, are each exactly one head in length.

In contrast, the same artist's prostitute (6.15) just as clearly *does* fit Lombroso's formulas for atavism. Like a gorilla or baboon she is just over 5 heads high; none of her important articulations come at the proper points, in part because her thighs are so extraordinarily short and her trunk so large. She has jug-handle ears and a deep jaw, and her mouth and nose are too close together, producing the effect Kretschmer was to call hypoplasia. (However, her arms are quite short, and complete atavism would have them long.)

Morelli and Lombrosan Connoisseurship

One of Lombroso's most curious and influential disciples, Giovanni Morelli, created what might be called a Lombrosan method of art historical connoisseurship. It is still evoked, though almost always the scholar who invokes it says that he or she is not being Morellian.[56] Morelli used anatomical analysis to identify not criminal types but an artist's personal styles. "The basic [human] form," he writes, "the hand, and the ear, among all independent masters, are characteristic and hence significant in assaying their works, just as their so-called whims *(Schnörkeln)* serve most usefully to distinguish their work from that of artists of little individuality."[57] In other words a great master supplied his madonnas and saints with ears, noses, and hands that are personally characteristic of that master. We have seen Lomazzo saying much the same thing, though Lomazzo goes further and plainly says that these features are self-portraits. And Morelli, too, has usually been taken to mean that great artists portray themselves. When art historians talk about seeing an artist's "hand" in his or her work they speak more truly than they know.

The essays in Morelli's book are illustrated by small sketches of hands, ears, and eyes as executed by Sebastiano del Piombo, Fra Filippo Lippi, Filippino Lippi, Signorelli, Bramantino, Mantegna, Giovanni Bellini, Bonifazio Veronese, Botticelli, and others. Morelli's system, however, is not based merely on the correspondence of small body parts. Borrowing from the great French naturalist Cuvier, Morelli claims that by thoroughly understanding a given finger, ear, or eye one understands the entire system of which that detail is a part, since the system dictates the complete nature of each of its components.[58] Just as paleontologists claimed to be able to reconstruct Neandertals from their jaws and toe bones, so a painted thumb, for Morelli, entails an entire painted figure.[59]

But intriguing as the sketches are, Morelli steers clear of analyzing a given body part in detail as Lombroso would have done. One has to supply one's own analysis, which, just for fun, I will do. One notes, looking at Morelli's line drawings, that Fra Filippo Lippi's hands (6.16, 6.17) are wide, unarticulated, with short fingers and thumbs that seemingly lack the joints, metacarpals, tendons, flexors, and the other articulations of the hand that other artists delighted in (6.18).

6.16.

Giovanni Morelli. Hand after Fra Filippo Lippi. From Morelli, *Kunstkritische Studien.*

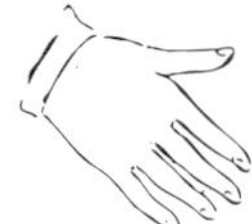

6.17.

Giovanni Morelli. Ear after Fra Filippo Lippi. From Morelli, *Kunstkritische Studien.*

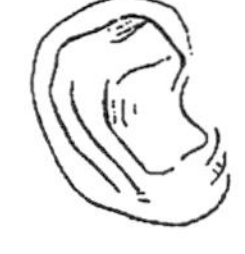

6.18.

Fra Filippo Lippi. *Madonna Enthroned,* 1437. Detail. Rome, Palazzo Barberini.

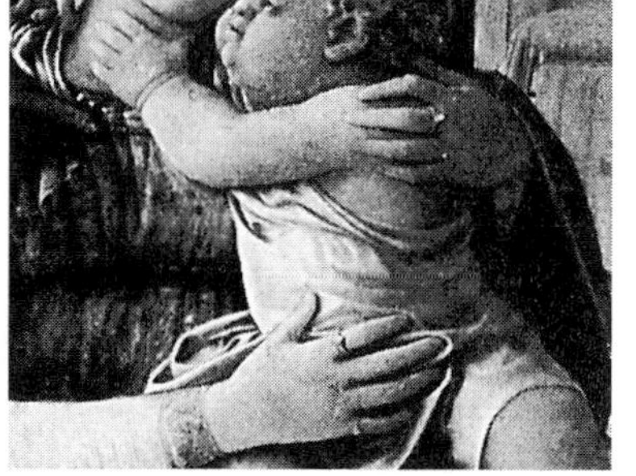

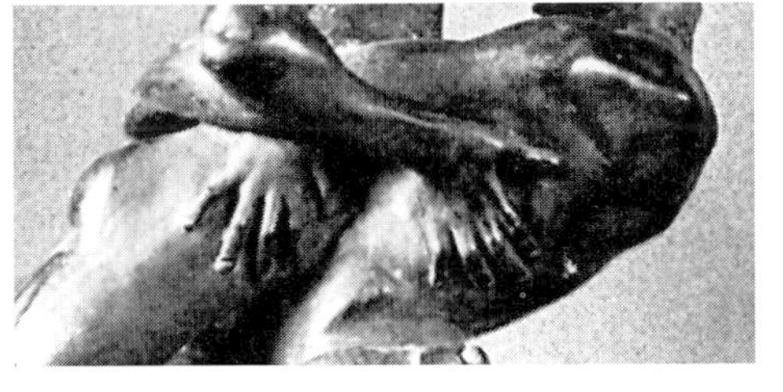

6.19.
Antonio Pollaiuolo. *Herakles and Antaeus*, c1475. Detail. Florence, Bargello.

6.20.
Hand after Pollaiuolo. From Morelli, *Kunstkritische Studien.*

6.21.
Sandro Botticelli. Portrait of a young man, late fifteenth century. Private collection, England.

6.22.
Two hands after Botticelli. From Morelli, *Kunstkritische Studien.*

On the other hand (so to speak), Antonio Pollaiuolo, as rendered by Morelli (6.19, 6.20), greatly emphasizes the second main finger joint, the one at the base of the proximal phalanx, while the other phalanges or upper finger bones seem to have been fused into a single bone. The little finger is meanwhile bowed outward and abnormally short. One must also observe that the hands in Filippo's paintings do indeed have something of the undifferentiated, inarticulate tubularity—the palms having a broad, geometric quality—that we see in Morelli's sketch. The hands (and ear) in the Pollaiuolo's *Herakles and Antaeus* (6.19) are good examples. Pollaiuolo's hands frequently, though not exclusively, have the twisting curled fingers of Morelli's drawing (6.20).

In contrast to Filippo's and Pollaiuolo's, Botticelli's hand appears to have been fatty, flexible, and seemingly boneless (6.21), though with softly projecting joints, practically invisible tendons, long, slender abductors for the thumbs, and rounded fingertips with deeply trimmed nails. The axes of individual finger bones—phalanges, metacarpals, and trapezoids—tend to zigzag slightly. These things pretty well match Morelli's drawing (6.22).

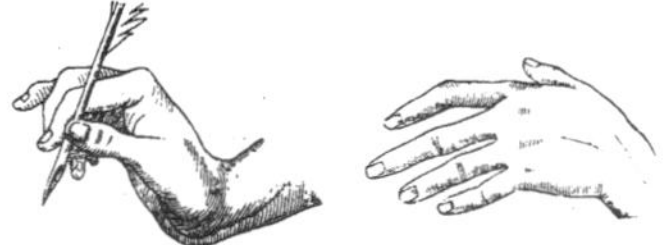

I have found no hints in Lombroso, however, that would help to identify any of Morelli's ear and hand shapes as either particularly criminal or particularly healthy. Morelli, in short, comes to no conclusions as to the selectability or evolutionary status of the artists he studies, or of their painted figures. He is a describer, not a diagnostician. Nonetheless—or perhaps because he is no Darwinian and did not invoke Lombroso's moral judgments—Morelli's anatomical details were taken up by other connoisseurs and do reinforce art's role within the sort of judgmental physical anthropology that Galton, Lombroso, and Max Nordau (discussed in the next chapter) were advocating.

Our first look at the fear of extinction has concentrated on Galton and Lombroso. Galton raised the possibility that Europe was on the brink of biological decline. Lombroso claimed, from a thousand physiological signs in the people around him, that the process had actually begun. Both men dedicated themselves to identifying the genetic malefactors in their midst who, in their works, their marriages, and their very faces and bodies, were aiding the devolution. As we follow the Galton-Lombroso arc we are carried from thoughts of immigration barriers, concentration camps for deselectables, and *V*-class mating programs to Lombroso's even darker world of asylums, beast-faces, and prehensile hands and feet, a world of prehistoric woundings and blood drinking that have been fossilized into modern life.

Lombroso's ideas influenced Morelli and hence art historiography and connoisseurship. And that in turn allowed Morelli's many followers to read art in a Lombrosan way—looking (as Morelli himself did not do) for selectable and deselectable human types. There is much more to be said on this point, especially about art that is called biologically decadent. For this the first spokesman will be Max Nordau.

Max Nordau

7

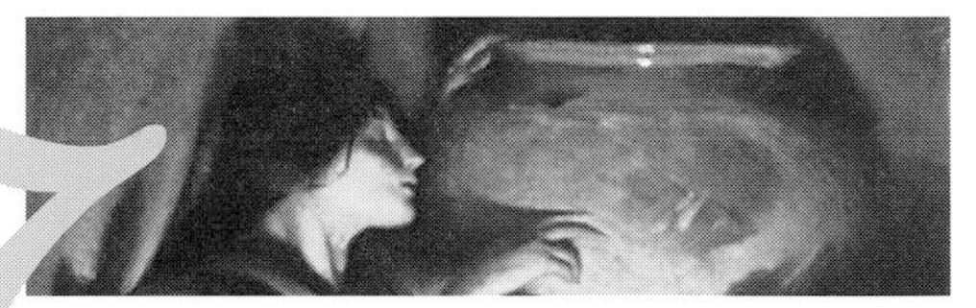

More Degeneration

The pessimistic streak we spotted in Galton, and which acquired such impressive force in Lombroso, was by the 1890s a river of dread. It came to be called the Great Fear.[1] In art criticism the greatest and fiercest fearer, by far, was Max Nordau. His predictions of an art-induced biological disaster centered around a popular scientific slogan of the time—that ontogeny recapitulates phylogeny.[2] This means that the development of the embryo in the womb reflects, in miniature and in the growth stages of one organism, the evolutionary elaboration, over time, of the different species from single-celled organisms all the way up to mammals. The belief was also known as the recapitulation theory.[3] I can well remember being taught it when I was in high school in the 1940s.

Nordau and others extended the idea from biology to culture. They believed that not just individuals but whole societies evolve in evolutionary stages. There are reptilian phases for cultures as well as for individuals and for species, and these can develop on through selacious (fish) stages to mammalian ones, and then to a maturity that is at last fully human. In devolution, meanwhile, an individual, a society, or a species may propel itself, or be propelled, in just the opposite direction. That is what Nordau, more sophisticated biologically than Galton and Lombroso (but equally wrong), so greatly feared. I have tried to diagram this principle in table 7.1.

Table 7.1

Biocultural Recapitulation

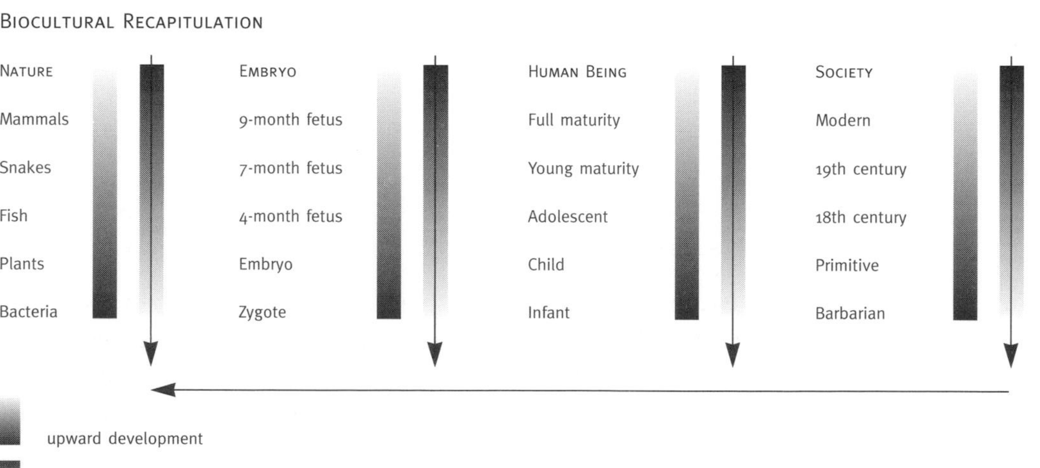

The chart embodies and harmonizes ideas I have culled from Nordau and also from Adolf Loos, a disciple of Nordau and Lombroso. In 1908 Loos wrote an article called "Ornament and Crime," which is probably the most influential article on architecture ever written. It condemned *all* architectural ornament as atavistic, as a survival among supposedly civilized humans of the tattooing impulse and other primal, even prehuman, practices. These ideas were mainly adapted from Lombroso. The article is credited with having banished ornament from the International Style.[4]

But let us examine the cultural version of ontogeny-phylogeny.[5] What was particularly galling to Nordau was that while most people agreed that degeneration could thus occur, and dreaded the prospect, others perversely welcomed it. Among these latter were Nietzsche, who envisioned a biological cataclysm to be followed by the emergence of the master race—superman and superwoman.[6] In a similar mood, and earlier, in the 1850s Wagner was describing Siegfried as the man of the future, free of low cunning and moralistic restraints, who could come into existence only through the immolation of humanity as then constituted. The music dramas, Wagner felt, when studied and experienced thus as prophecies of this annihilation followed by rebirth, would assist the process and make us more accepting of the cleansing cataclysm.[7] (Hence, presumably, does *Götterdämmerung* have a happy ending.)

Later on, furthermore, decadence was embraced in and of itself—for example, the aesthetic cults represented by Huysmans's *A Rebours* (1884) and Wilde's *Salomé* (1893). Decadence, seen thus as positive—dancing just before the deluge—was an important part of the art nouveau and various related movements that particularly earned the wrath of Nordau and Loos.[8] It was with this sort of decadence, too, that Nordau chiefly concerned himself—with the sensuous, mildly criminal, willfully perverse thoughts, witticisms, and works of art that, he felt, were heralding and assisting the fall of the European race, breeding new populations who perversely exulted in their atavism. Unlike Nietzsche and Wagner, Nordau did not believe in a purifying cataclysm from which a new race or human species would emerge: for him the cataclysm would be the end of everything.

Max Nordau was born in Budapest, practiced medicine in Paris, and wrote his books in German.[9] Today, at least as an art critic, he is almost unknown. But from 1883 until World War I he was world-famous: a journalist, a thinker, a novelist, a social theorist, and a pioneer Zionist. His theories on Darwinian progress in the arts, on sexually selective art and biocultural survival, and on the links between an artist's style and his or her physical appearance and condition were discussed everywhere.[10] His key book is *Degeneration* (1892), a blistering attack on the French literary decadents and their English and German allies. His criticisms of contemporary artists are found in his articles, many of which were collected in *On Art and Artists* (1907).

Being a doctor, Nordau often discusses specific physical signs of degeneration in the Lombroso mode. But he is more detailed. Lombroso had simply condemned jug ears. Nordau goes further: when the ear protrudes from the head like a jug handle, and its lobe is either lacking or else adheres to the head, while at the same time its helix is not involuted—*this* is the proper description of degenerate ears. Also degenerate are "squint-eyes, harelips, irregularities in the form and position of the teeth, pointed or flat palates, webbed or supernumerary fingers."[11] When such details are found in portraits and other works of art, they fatally encourage us to admire them.

Nordau's prose bristles with what might be called biopoeticism. "The disease of degeneracy," he writes,

> *consists precisely in the fact that the degenerate organism has not the power to mount to the height of evolution already attained by the species, but stops on the way at an earlier or later point.*[12] *The relapse of the degenerate may reach to the most stupendous depth. As, in reverting to the cleavage of the superior maxillary peculiar to insects with sextuple lips, he sinks somatically to the level of fishes, nay to that of Arthropoda [crabs, centipedes, insects, etc.], or even further, to that of rhizopods [one-celled animals] not yet sexually differentiated; as by the fistulae [tubular growths] of the neck he reverts to the brachiae [armlike protuberances] of the lowest fishes, the selacious; or by excess in the number of fingers (polydactylia) to the multiple-rayed fins of fishes, perhaps even to the bristles of worms; or, by hermaphroditism, to the asexuality of rhizopods—so in the most favorable case, as a higher degenerate, he renews intellectually the type of the primitive man of the most remote Stone Age; or, in the worst case, as an idiot, that of an animal anterior to man.*[13]

As Nordau explains elsewhere, if you have such physical defects your offspring will further devolve, physically, in a premammalian direction (as you yourself are already doing) and you will also have, at best, a Stone Age brain. Any sort of growth or tumor on your body is a sign of this decadence. Nordau links the origins of ornament not just to wounds, shackles, and the attractors used by lower organisms, as Lombroso had done, but also to the growths and deformities of this more clinical decadence.

And, let us recall, Lombroso, in all his generalizations, would have been talking about mental patients and the occupants of jails. Nordau is talking about Baudelaire, Verlaine, Mallarmé, Rossetti, Tolstoy, Maeterlinck, Wagner, Huysmans, Ibsen, Nietzsche (yes, though Nordau owed much to Nietzsche), and Zola. *Degeneration* is devoted to the demolition of these men and their works. It does so in large part by attacking the appearance of their faces and bodies.

Though he is mainly Lombroso's disciple, Nordau also took ideas from B. A. Morel, whose *Traité des dégénérescences physiques, intellectuelles, et morales* had appeared in Paris as early as 1857, well before Lombroso got going—and, for that matter, two years before *The Origin of Species*.[14] Morel, as Darwin, Lombroso, and Nordau himself were to do, had claimed that degeneration can begin with the smallest deviations from the healthy type. "This deviation," he declares, "even if, at the outset, it was ever so slight, contained transmissible elements of such a nature that anyone bearing in himself its germs becomes more and more incapable of fulfilling his functions in the world; and mental progress, already checked in his own person, finds itself menaced also in his descendants."[15] Quoting this passage, Nordau adds that the deviant's offspring will actually begin to form a degenerating subspecies. Such strains soon end in sterility and die out. Were they not to, they would keep on degenerating until they reached the lowest level of life. The process is a little like runaway evolution. But instead of peacocks' plumage rapidly getting longer and longer because only long-tailed males achieved copulations, in this case humans' brains, for example, would rapidly get smaller and smaller because potential wives were seized by a fatal preference for husbands with the smallest possible brains.

Erotomania: Verlaine and Rodin

The particular degenerative disease afflicting most artists and intellectuals, says Nordau, is erotomania. This develops when the spinal cord and the area of the brain known as the medulla oblongata are malformed. Since these are among the body's sexual centers, all kinds of visions and stimuli that in reality have nothing to do with sex are given a sexual interpretation by sufferers from this condition. For example, these people can get an erotic charge out of a railway train or a newspaper headline. A grand piano may bristle with malignant libidinal energy. Erotomania is in fact the principal form of degeneration in modernist art. It affects the artists, the sitters, and the viewers. It is most apparent in paintings of young females, which, far from representing healthy reproductive goals, mask an inner criminal atavism with the surface glitter of sexual fascination. Though they themselves are eminently deselectable, these women nonetheless project profound sexuality. Their sickness is part of their allure.

There are men like this, too. An example is the poet Paul Verlaine. "In this man," writes Nordau,

we find, in astonishing completeness, all the physical and mental marks of degeneration, and no author known to me answers so exactly, trait for trait, to the descriptions of the degenerate given by the clinicists—his personal appearance, the history of his life, his intellect, his world of ideas and modes of expression. M. Jules Huret gives the following account of Verlaine's physical appearance: "His face, like that of a wicked angel grown old, with a thin, untrimmed beard, and abrupt nose; his bushy, bristling eyebrows, resembling bearded wheat, hiding deep-set green eyes; his wholly bald and huge long skull, misshapen by enigmatic bumps—all these give to his physiognomy a contradictory appearance of stubborn asceticism and cyclopean appetites."

"Look," says Nordau, without reproducing it, "at the painting of Verlaine by Eugène Carrière." And indeed the Carrière portrait (7.1) does partly agree with Huret. The poet's face emerges like an unwelcome apparition from a thick mass of darkness, the thin whiskers wide and unkempt like those of a mustachioed

7.1.
Eugène Carrière. Portrait of Paul Verlaine. Detail. Paris, Musée d'Orsay.

cat, while the spotlit forehead makes the skull look like a planet spinning dangerously close. Carrière's paint swirls around the nose, intent on the highlight on its bridge and its rum-blossom. But this vortex of pigment serves at the same time to suggest a skin malady (rosacea?). The eyes, meanwhile, in accordance with Lombroso's test for mental instability, are asymmetrical in size and placement.[16]

Portraits of Verlaine, continues Nordau, also bring out the asymmetry of his skull and display his Mongolian (hence atavistic) attributes—for example, the thin beard and slightly slanted eyes. The biological degeneration of the poet's skull, moreover, is expressed through "multiple and stunted growths of the first line of asymmetry, unequal development of the two halves of the cranium, then imperfection in the development of the external ear, which is conspicuous for its enormous size." These observations are corroborated by extensive quotations from the poems. Verlaine's verse suffers from all sorts of pathologies such as repetition, echolalia (meaningless homonyms), concentration on mood rather than intellect, and the vain desire to achieve beauty with words that make no sense.[17]

But the most criminal of all contemporary erotomaniacs was Auguste Rodin.[18] Rodin carries the disease beyond all possible and impossible boundaries. His sexual passions are satanic, catastrophic. His women do not bother to screen their diseased but fascinating bodies with fashionable clothes. The *Gate of Hell,* Nordau writes, "exhibits rows of naked women in all the situations and occupations of the witches' Sabbath, when it is most devilish. Fits of hysteria shake and twist these bodies, every motion of which betrays shocking aberration and eager Sadism."

Rodin's degeneracy appears not only in his art but in his choice of models, and in the man himself. Madmen and madwomen pose for him. And "the patients of the Salpêtrière or the atlas of pictures edited in [Charcot's] clinic *(Iconographie de la Salpêtrière)* evidently deserved him."[19] Rodin is thus, to Nordau, curiously like Lombroso, who haunted the asylums of his native province for his subjects. But unlike Lombroso Rodin admired his mad models and was a lot like them. Nor did Rodin accept only models, however mad or bad, who exhibited the Polykleitan ideal. He also portrays wrecked and raddled bodies wreathed in fat, for example the infamous *Balzac* of 1893. Rodin's nude Balzac is bulging, goitered, swollen with protuberances that could be found,

7.2.
Auguste Rodin. *The Thinker,* 1879–1889. Detail. New York, Metropolitan Museum of Art.

7.3.
Auguste Rodin. *The Thinker,* 1879–1889. New York, Metropolitan Museum of Art.

says Nordau, on no true human. It is a loathsomeness, however, that remains highly and fatally charged with sex.[20] Somehow, Nordau thinks, Rodin makes us perversely want to mate with such individuals; and, if steps are not taken, we will!

More traditionally selectable, perhaps, is the *Thinker* (7.2, 7.3) his heavy and cruel thoughts clearly weighting him down.[21] But to Nordau the *Thinker* is the most unthinking of creatures, the purest of animals and the lowest.

The flayed man sits crouching, with a distinctly crooked lump, on a sharp-edged block of stone. His toes claw convulsively into the ground. He holds a clenched fist before his mouth, and seems to bite it fiercely. His bestial countenance, with its bloated, contracted forehead, gazes as threateningly dark as midnight. He who has to interpret the figure without the help of a title will, from the back view, conclude it is someone writhing in agony on the rack; and from the front view, a criminal meditating over some foul deed. . . . The last thing which one would think of would be to look for a mind working behind this bulgy forehead or to imagine that thought was supreme in this body seized by a spasm of rigidity in all its muscles."[22]

Meanwhile the whole of the *Gate of Hell* is "an illustration of hystero-epilepsy and feminine Sadism."[23]

Brain Decay: Whistler, Boldini, and J. W. Alexander

The chief symptom of degeneration in painting, says Nordau, is impressionism.

The curious style of certain recent painters—"impressionists," "stipplers," or "mosaists," "papilloteurs" or "quiverers," "roaring" colourists, dyers in gray and faded tints—becomes at once intelligible to us if we keep in view the researches of the Charcot school of the visual derangements in degeneration and hysteria. The painters who assure us that they are sincere, and reproduce nature as they see it, speak the truth. The degenerate artist who suffers from nystagmus, or trembling of the eyeball, will, in fact, perceive the phenomena of nature trembling, restless, devoid of firm outline.[24]

This accounts for Monet. Other forms of degeneration cause people to see nature in spots and blotches. This accounts for Seurat.

But far worse than Monet or Seurat was Whistler. He combined the optical diseases of the impressionists with Rodin's erotomania. And here I might remark that Whistler could also have fulfilled Nordau's formulas for personal physical decadence in that he was both short and dandified. Anyone who modeled his dress and deportment, not to say his conversation, on Baudelaire's, and got his ideas on art from Théophile Gautier ("art for art's sake"); who suffered chronically from rheumatic fever; and who poisoned himself (temporarily) with the white lead used in painting the *White Girl* (1862; National Gallery, Washington) would fulfill more than a few of Nordau's devolutionary diagnostics.[25]

Whistler the man was bad enough. But it was his female portraits that were his chief crimes (7.4, 7.5):

The intensity with which he feels young, high-bred, nervous women has quite an uncanny effect on me. I think of his "Lady Meux" and other capricious femininities, which were exhibited, in the last fifteen years, in the Paris salons and in London. He plants his model before us in some wonderful position. One stands with its back towards us, but turns its head, as if in a sudden caprice, to us. Another shows us its full face, and looks fascinatingly at us with a pinched mouth and impenetrable eyes that think troublous thoughts. These perverted, whimsical beauties wear remarkable and personal toilettes which, except the face and often the hands, reveal not a finger's breadth of skin, yet, in spite of the interposition of silk and lace, cry out for the fig leaf. They are

bundles of sick nerves that, from the crowns of their heads to the tips of their fingers, seem to thrill with Sadic excitement. It is as though they wanted to entice men [into] wild attempts, and at the same time held their claws ready to tear, with a loud cry of pleasure, the flesh of the daring ones.[26]

7.4.
James Abbott McNeill Whistler. *Valérie, Lady Meux,* 1881. New York, The Frick Collection.

7.5.
Detail of Lady Meux's face.

Lady Meux, then, is an evolutionary throwback, a quality in the sitter that it is hard for us to see today.[27] Nordau also calls the picture an "explosion of color." Yet as we look at the painting everything is cool, gray, whitish, and a very soft pink. Nordau's memory, overcharged with pain, has played him tricks. And is this woman, for us, "a bundle of sick nerves" who thrills with sadism? It is a narrow, fashionably tall picture in which the lady stands erect, almost but not quite in a swagger, her body facing to the viewer's right, her face turned and looking directly outward. Behind her a lush but simple gray fabric hangs three-quarters of the way down. The rest of the background is taken up by the warm brown floor.

So far the picture seems to lack the savagery Nordau sees in it. But, returning to the discussion in chapter 1, we see that Lady Meux does wear sexually selective clothing—a rounded satiny dress with tight sleeves and mauvish bodice, the latter being stiffened into a protuberance that frames the pubic area in a dramatic arch. An equally dramatic train of coruscating satin swerves up from the base of the skirt to her rump, from which it falls back toward the floor in a cascade of silk, lace, and perhaps lawn. She holds this fountain of fabric back from us gracefully with her right arm. Down the middle of her generous bust, meanwhile, a row of tiny buttons goes through the splash of darkness under her breasts. Her head is neatly nested in lace. She wears a cavernous straw hat with a wide brim, snapped upward in front, and a bunch of dark red flowers or laces on the crown. Therefore despite the sitter's leanly fashionable body, her clothed image is almost that of a Paleolithic Venus or bulbous early goddess. I believe it is the clothes in this picture, not the color, that troubled Nordau.

Her face, that fateful face (7.5), is strong, serenely symmetrical, with a deep oval chin. She has long, dark elliptical eyes and eyebrows that melt together in shadow (recall Nordau's "impenetrable eyes that think troublous thoughts"), an elegant thin nose, and neat nostrils. Her rather narrow lips do, it is true, have a slight suggestion of impatience. Lombroso would undoubtedly find the joined-together eyebrows atavistic. But she does not seem to have the pronounced browridge, asymmetry of cheek and skull, low brow, or other deformities that Lombroso and Nordau were defining as criminal. Still, we recall, Lombroso had also said that "delinquent women" often lacked these outward attributes, and that their very lack of them was a mark of their antievolutionary tendencies.

Whatever such marks Lady Meux has, she also has those of the painter's brush. These are strongly apparent across the picture—in the lush diagonal hatchings of the hat brim and in soft brilliant flakes over breasts, shoulders, stomach, hat, and hips. The painting process has obviously been very much a performance. Whistler's flashing strokes and succulent veils of subdued greyish color all record the actions of his hands and arms, even his movements around the picture, and perhaps around the sitter. Indeed, a contemporary writes of Whistler painting Lady Meux in just this way: "In action, he was like a wary fencer; he would approach the canvas, crouching a little, as a panther creeps towards its prey, his eyes on the lady, yet with side glances at the canvas. Arrived within arm's reach of the goal, he would deliver one touch, light but sure, snatching the brush back again. . . ."[28] In the lower right corner, dark against the lighter backcloth, the famous butterfly signature completes the picture like a kiss. The scene comes close to Nordau's vision of the male predator being enticed, by a fatal woman, into an attack.

Having indulged his fascinated abhorrence for Whistler, Nordau turns to another victim of erotomania and brain decay, Giovanni Boldini.[29] To Nordau, Boldini's women are not so much disdainful or neurotic as feral. Their accouterments become animal attributes—snakes' skins, lions' manes and claws, peacocks' plumes. Ornament is no longer a mere fossil but actively recreates our primal savagery. Boldini, Nordau writes,

is one of the most remarkable painters of female portraits in our time. In these he makes himself most solicitous to unite together the helical axes of [John White] Alexander's demoniacs, twisting in hysterical convulsions, and [Anders] Zorn's bold, sunbeam dances. Hardly anyone among his contemporaries possesses this uncommonly skillful Italian's talent for tumult. His pictures seem to fly up as from a bursting bomb. Every fibre in his women palpitates and throbs. One of his women sits half-naked on a lion's skin, just as if she had torn, in a rage, the clothes off her body, and he has made the head and skin of this common floor-rug bristle with such cruel savageness that you jump back in terror from the expected spring of the bloodthirsty monster. Another woman wears on her arm and shoulders a feather boa with wonderful convolutions, which seems to rustle from her in excitement like an eagle. A third lady stands in a door frame—she seems to be about to spring forward with the leap of a tiger. She wears one of those very modern, low-cut evening dresses, which are fastened over the shoulders only by a tiny chain; her bust looks as if it were laid bare because her dress was torn from her body in a brutal struggle with a satyr. There is an atmosphere about this woman of all hysterical convulsions, St. Vitus's dance, or defence with teeth and claws against lawless attempts.[30]

Plenty of atavism here. Looking at Boldini through the lens of Nordau's words, we can almost see the bird-headed women, the snake-bodied or lion-bodied goddesses, of antiquity. And, like Whistler and Verlaine, Boldini was degenerate of person. Squat, fat, and physically disabled, he was the painter equivalent of the ugly pug dog that the beautiful woman carries with her to increase her own beauty through contrast. The caricaturists made much of the difference between the dwarfish painter and his stupendous models with their long, lean limbs, broad bony shoulders, and harshly perfect, huge-eyed faces.[31]

Here is Boldini's portrait of Consuelo, Duchess of Marlborough (née Vanderbilt) with her son, Lord Ivor Spencer-Churchill, painted in 1906 (7.6, 7.7).[32] Boldini

7.6.

Giovanni Boldini. *Consuelo Vanderbilt, Duchess of Marlborough*, 1906. New York, Metropolitan Museum of Art.

7.7.

Detail of the Duchess's face.

is a more slashingly linear painter than Whistler. But his brush strokes are still manipulations by the artist's hand of the woman's clothes and body. The flash of his brush summons from the canvas a spidery, black-gowned sensuous lady, bold and pink, her face soft and her bright lips set hard with smiling lascivious disdain. She explodes with a beautiful shimmer, much as Nordau says, from a background of darker fireworks. Her clothes are a mere scribbled carapace for her flesh. (A closeup of some of Boldini's brushwork would look a bit like Franz Kline.) The little boy, meanwhile, is a knicker-clad Eros, his sweet-mouthed head nuzzling Venus-mother's bosom. His right hand spreads its little white fingers on her leg while his own leg has been dragged across the satin seat of a Louis XV settee from which he seems to have suddenly lunged into his mother's lap.

John White Alexander, equally decadent in Nordau's estimation,[33] was the artist of *Isabella, or the Pot of Basil* (1897), now in the Boston Museum of Fine Arts (7.8, 7.9). A tall graceful picture of a tall graceful young woman, it is carried out in muted tones of white, black, and tawny gold. She wears a long, full white gown falling in heavy loose folds to her feet. One corner of it is caught up across a bare shoulder. The sinuous black scarf around her neck, almost like a priest's stole, gives the picture a ritual quality. A group of thin black laces, in loops or hanging free, also descends along the front of Isabella's white gown and mingles with strands of her dark hair. Her face, eyes closed, thoughtful,

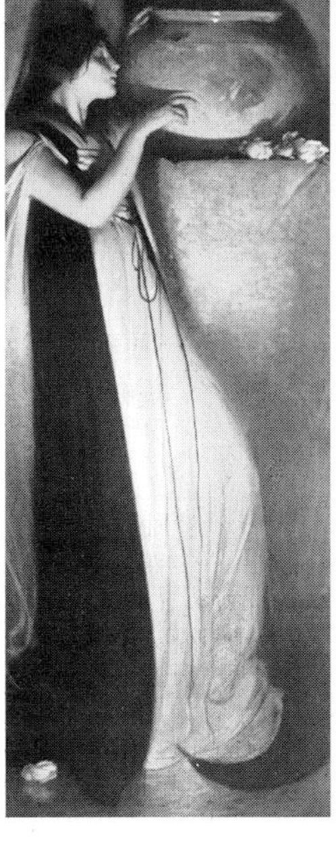

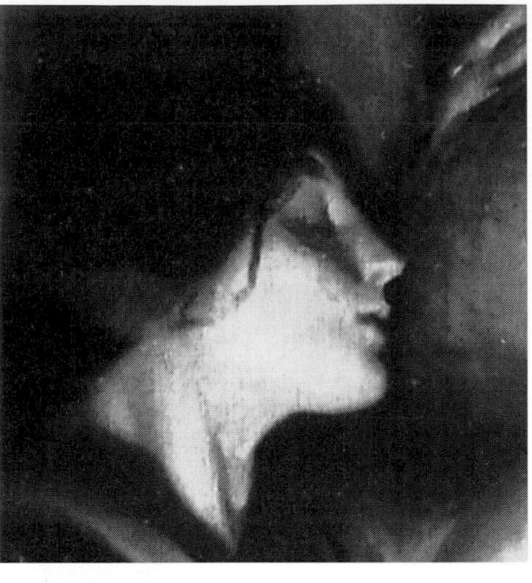

7.8.

John White Alexander. *Isabella, or the Pot of Basil,* 1897. Boston, Museum of Fine Art.

7.9.

Detail of Isabella's face.

remote, its white profile turned inward from the picture plane and lit from below, approaches the smooth cheek of the vase. We do not see the basil plant at all—which, along with much else, makes this picture very little like Holman Hunt's masterpiece. One thinks, instead, of some of Amy Lowell's poems and, of course, of Whistler—*The White Girl.* Alexander stylishly concentrates the girl's head, arm, flowers, and pot at the very top of his tall scene. And he devotes the whole of the rest of the picture to the slow uninterrupted fall of gown to floor, the left-hand fall curving leftward and the right-hand fall to the right, following the girl's slightly bent knee.

So far the picture is pure glamour without much hint of decadence. But there is a grotesqueness, and what would be a grisly decadence in Nordau's eyes, to the picture's basic *concetto*. We recall that Isabella, a character from Boccaccio by way of Keats, has planted her lover's head inside this pot. So Alexander is portraying Isabella as she makes love to a severed head. She has deposited white blossoms near the base of the vase, perhaps as an offering. The girl's figure, which is haunted by the forms of thick blossoms and nodding stems, transforms her into a sort of graceful plant. This gives rise to mental crosscurrents about the severed head and its invisible crown of basil. Note that, ever so gently, she is kissing the round surface of the pot—drinking in the kiss of the buried bloody head. So here one almost has to think about Lombroso and his theories about blood-drinking maenads.

These artists, then, and many others, are for Max Nordau biologically degenerate. And biological degeneration is pandemic, he says, among those who view these images and pattern themselves after them. One sees this particularly among fashionable women, in their dress, hairdos, and ornaments, so often imitated from Whistler, Boldini, and the rest. Art and life reinforce each other. Real women "reproduce" the painted and sculptured reproductive goals they worship. Here again ornament is a particular evil. It is wrong for women to decorate themselves with the spoil of lesser species' selective armaments, for example, feathers, furs, and flower forms. It is even more wrong when they do so in some past style. Coiffures are a case in point. "Among the women, one wears her hair combed smoothly back and down like Raphael's Maddalena Doni in the Uffizi at Florence," says Nordau; "another wears it drawn up high over the temples like Julia, the daughter of Titus, or Plotina, wife of Trajan, in the busts in the Louvre; a third has hers cut short in front on the brow and long in the nape, waved and slightly puffed, after the fashion of the fifteenth century, as may be seen in the pages and young knights of Gentile Bellini, Botticelli, and Mantegna."[34]

Such misoneism, as Lombroso called hatred of the new, is particularly bad when different parts of a costume, coiffure, or both are chosen from different times and cultures. Then we have not only primary atavism, or using ornament, and secondary atavism, copying past styles, but now a third kind—the *eclectic* copying of the past, borrowing from two or more different periods. "Thus," says Nordau, "we get heads set on shoulders not belonging to them, costumes the elements of which are as disconnected as though they belonged to a dream, colours that seem to have been matched in the dark." It is the costume equivalent of bodily dysplasia. Nordau likens the general effect of a fashionable Paris gathering to "a mythical mortuary [with] fragments of bodies, heads, trunks, limbs . . . clothed in the garments . . . of all epochs and countries" (*Degeneration*, 8ff.).

Here Nordau touches on one of the earlier themes of this book: the evolution of attractors is concerned with borrowing them from ever-widening contexts—different periods, different sexes, different species. This cult of bygone body parts, says Nordau, intensifies the diseased sexual feelings from which these people already suffer. Nordau the physician recognizes in these symptoms "the confluence of two well-defined conditions of disease . . . viz. degeneration (degeneracy) and hysteria, of which the minor stages are designated as neurasthenia" (16).

What is to be done to, for, or against these artists with their optical diseases, erotomanias, and brain decay? What is to be done about the purveyors of misoneism in dress? Can the authorities not take proper measures? Here Nordau presents the most ominous part of his thesis: "Those degenerates whose mental derangement is too deep-seated must be abandoned to their inexorable fate. They are past cure or amelioration. They will rave for a season, and then perish" (551). What this turns out to mean is that biologically unfit cultural figures must not be allowed to survive. These are artists "who dirty their canvases like children, who stammer instead of speak," who "compose music like that of the yellow natives of East Asia," who "confound all the arts, and lead them back to the primitive forms they had before evolution differentiated them" (555); they, like

mystics . . . especially ego-maniacs and filthy pseudo-realists, are direct enemies of society. Society must unconditionally defend itself against them. Whoever believes with me that society is the natural organic form of humanity, in which alone it can exist, prosper, and continue to develop itself to higher destinies; whoever looks upon civilization as a good, having value and deserving to be defended, must mercilessly crush under his thumb the anti-social vermin. (557)

Let there be criminal trials. Let modern professional psychiatry identify these sick individuals (559). Let the malefactors then be sent to psychiatric hospitals or, if necessary, to permanent camps where they will receive intensive supervision and where, as with Galton's subnormal classes and Lombroso's atavists, they will eventually die off without reproducing. Rodin, Whistler, Verlaine—to the camps!

It is hard to know what to make of Max Nordau's artistico-biological prophecies and suggested remedies. If we resolutely expunge the symptoms of our culture's weakness, Nordau implies, we may be able to root out the disease itself. But like Galton and Lombroso he does not consider the practical implications of this course of treatment. What laws would be written in order to achieve these totalitarian ends? Who would run the criminal trials? What about individual human rights, such as free speech, not to mention the freedom to dress and do one's hair as one likes? What about a possible legal right not to be put in a concentration camp for painting like Whistler or modeling like Rodin? Or for portraying, as attractive, people considered by the law to be criminally thin?

Nordau preaches his fatalism with a certain joyfulness. Were his proposals for totalitarian remedies simply a way of saying that the situation was already impossible? Was he himself, in a way, dancing just before the deluge? I will let him finish our chapter with a Spenglerian coda: "And such is the spectacle presented by the doings of men in the reddened light of the Dusk of the Nations. Massed in the sky the clouds are aflame in the weirdly beautiful glow which was observed for the space of years after the eruption of Krakatoa. Over the earth the shadows creep with deepening gloom, wrapping all objects in a mysterious dimness, in which all certainty is destroyed and any guess seems plausible" (*Degeneration*, 6).

8 Into Nazism

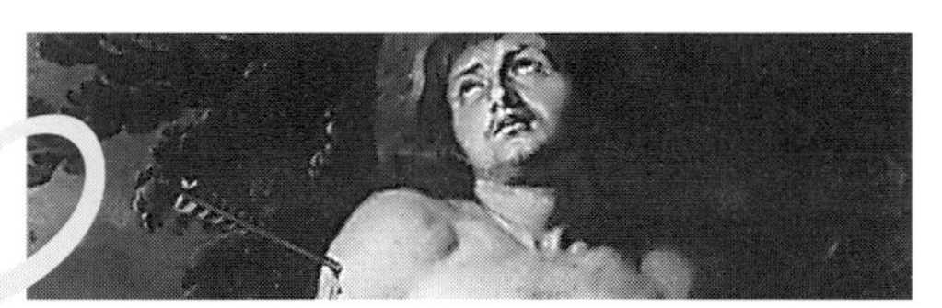

Paul Schultze-Naumburg: Rubens and Rembrandt

As everyone knows, it was the Nazis more than anyone else whose totalitarianism made practical the notions that in Lombroso, Galton, and Nordau had remained merely propaganda. The Holocaust may be understood, in part at least, as a piece of applied eugenics, though it was based mostly on racial categories rather than on the individual physical characteristics that were the focus of these three precursors' primary analysis. And well before the Nazis came to power organizations such as the Reichsverband für Geburtenregelung und Sexualhygiene (National Association for Birth Control and Sexual Hygiene)—and there were many others—served the cause of a eugenics that was already at least partly racial, though it certainly also condemned Nordics or Aryans who were diseased, retarded, or criminal. Books on eugenics for a specifically German audience were written by a host of authors like Roderich von Engelhardt, Paul Kranhals, and Edgar Jung. By 1934, Wilfried van der Will reports, in Prussia alone 31,000 compulsory sterilizations were performed on such *Minderwertigen* (undesirables), and there were 50,000 in 1935. Heinrich Himmler calculated that by following these procedures, in concert with a strict policy of state-supervised breeding for the "sexually healthy," the German people would be completely Nordic within 120 years.[1] All this was a development of the Great Fear. Following Nordau's lead (though without mentioning him, since he was Jewish), the movement summoned the assistance of reproductively healthy art and condemned its opposite.

The most arresting figure who brings us from late-nineteenth-century proto-Nazi thought about the body directly into Nazi practice is Paul Schultze-Naumburg. Schultze-Naumburg was an architect, painter, art-school administrator, and prolific writer.[2] In *Kunst und Rasse* (1928), his most relevant book for us, he claimed that art—specifically that of Rubens and Rembrandt—ought to constitute a major source of positive and negative reproductive goals, respectively, for all Germanic peoples.

Schultze-Naumburg writes that Rubens was an artist of superabundantly strong, full-blooded humanity. Physiologically the man himself was pink and white in complexion and possessed round limbs with small hands and feet. We see that body type everywhere in his art—and quintessentially in his famous self-portrait of 1609–1610 with Isabella Brant in Munich (8.1). Isabella clearly belongs to Rubens's "race." It is true that her globelike skull gives a rotundity to her

8.1.
Rubens. Portrait of the artist with Isabella Brant, 1609–1610. Munich, Alte Pinakothek.

8.2.
Rubens. Self-portrait, 1639. Vienna, Kunsthistorisches Museum.

features that is absent from her husband's more vertical face. And the axis of her eyes, unlike his, follows a downward arc. But these two people still have much in common—hands with long, supple fingers developing out of carpal/metacarpal areas that are relatively small, for example. And the couple's eyes (liquid, clearly edged, and with a strong, direct gaze) their mouths (sculptured, red, and fleshy), and noses (long, straight, rather sharp) are almost perfect matches. Only Isabella's nostrils appear on the rounded undersurface of her nose, and hence are not deep-cut flared openings like her husband's.

Rubens retained this phenotype into old age. If we look at a 1639 self-portrait made at the age of sixty-two (8.2—he was thirty-two in the double portrait) in the Kunsthistorisches Museum, Vienna, we see, along with the expected aging, this same countenance and physique. But now the artist is portly rather than simply rounded, and his cheeks are worked with long muscular ridges, while his nose has blossomed, as happens to some older people, and his hair and beard are somewhat thinner though not gray.

Do we see Rubens's "self-portrait," in a Schultze-Naumburg sense, also in his representations of other people—of humanity in general? Let us look at two nude images: the *St. Sebastian* and the *Andromeda*, both in Berlin (8.3, 8.4).[3] No one could say that either is really a self-portrait; but in the spirit of Leighton, Morelli, and now Schultze-Naumburg, we look at the round skull, heavy red lips, strong axial nose, and soft hair as certainly of the same physi-

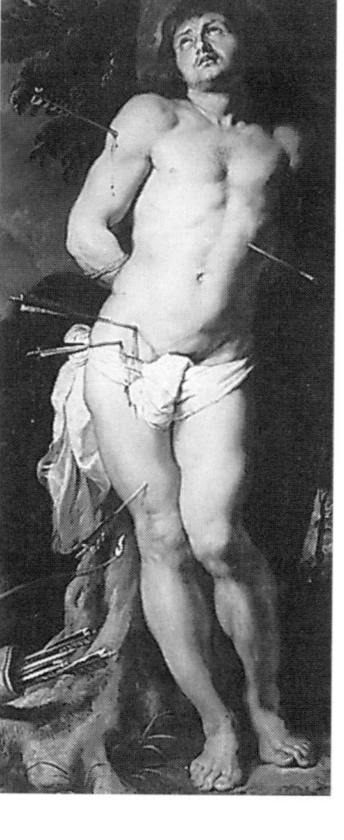

8.3.

Rubens. *St. Sebastian,* c1618.

Berlin, Gemäldegalerie.

8.4.

Rubens. *Andromeda*, c1638.

Berlin, Gemäldegalerie.

cal type as in Rubens's true self-portraits. Other "somatotypical indexes," as Sheldon would call them, also apply: short tibiae and fibulae, pronounced calves, a soft, columnar torso, all with muscle fiber rounded into cupped masses. But the saint's feet are large, Michelangelesque ones, unlike Rubens's dainty feet. These go back to the tradition of the heroic Italian nude. In turn, Andromeda's phenotype in all these same ways is close to Isabella Brant's (and also to those of Hélène Fourment, the painter's second wife). And so we can now look at an equally famous picture, the nude portrait of Hélène with a fur coat in the Kunsthistorisches Museum, Vienna (8.5). Indeed one suspects that Andromeda in a way *is* Hélène. (And why not? Ἀνδρί μειδιᾷ is a trope for "she smiles on her husband.") Here, too, Hélène has a straighter, more "classical" nose, but otherwise she possesses those same bee-stung dewy lips, clear eyes, round face and head, and soft, well-padded, even pebbly (but muscularly articulated) body that belongs to what Schultze-Naumburg would call Fourment's and Rubens's "race." Note, particularly, that Andromeda's legs are quite muscular, with developed gastrocnemii interiores and laterales, marked muscle-clusters around the kneecaps, and even vestiges of the thigh muscles—the sartorius and the two vasti—so relished in male figures at this period. It may well be that Schultze-Naumburg, following and greatly developing Lombroso/Morelli, is right—that part of what we recognize as Rubens's "hand" in a picture like this is not just his hand but his whole body.

Other artists in Rubens's circle are subject to quite different readings. Schultze-Naumburg compares heads, legs, and hands from Van Dyck, Jacob Jordaens (Brussels: *Allegory of Fertility*, c1625; 8.6) and others. From these comparisons we discover more about Rubens's ideally selectable physique. We see that, more than his contemporaries, he possesses, and in his art celebrates, legs with wide, pronounced patellae or kneecaps, with the short bones in the lower leg having a slight outward bow, and with stout calves. The toes, except for the big toe, are long, articulate, and sharply curled. The ankles are flexible, constantly arching outward and inward. The thighbones are long, and the muscle called the biceps femoris, around the lower thighbone as it joins the knee, is protuberant, as is the iliotibial tract next to it. All these features are well bedded in, but not hidden by, delicate garnishes of fat. In contrast to these highly articulated Rubensian legs, the woman's legs in Jordaens's Brussels allegory, seen from the back, are as smooth and solid as the legs of a modern professional model. But, discussing this picture, Schultze-Naumburg allows this body type as a healthy variant in the Germanic "race."

8.5.
Rubens. *Hélène Fourment in Fur*, 1630s. Vienna, Kunsthistorisches Museum.

8.6.
Jacob Jordaens. *Allegory of Fertility*, c1625. Detail. Brussels, Musées royaux d'art et d'histoire.

For Schultze-Naumburg the main delineator of reproductive countertypes—that is, of deselectables—is, astonishingly, Rembrandt.[4] Like all artists Rembrandt draws and paints his own body; and he himself, rather than possessing Rubens's healthy physique, is short, thickset, and scruffy, with a craggy face whose deep eyes and full glance betoken a troubled brain. And his art is a world of undesirable genetic clones.

Schultze-Naumburg cites the *Adam and Eve* in Rembrandt's famous 1638 etching (8.7). Adam and Eve indeed! To the author of *Kunst und Rasse* these pathetic wretches are anything but the begetters of our noble race; they are more like the aboriginal parents of the famous Jukes family.[5] Adam stands uncertainly, leaning against a rock, his pigeon-toed right foot drawn slightly up as he speaks to Eve, at the same time reaching out for the apple she holds. A contrast with Rubens's *St. Sebastian* suggests the immense anatomical distance between this pitiful creature and a true Nordic hero.

Psychologically, moreover—and I continue to paraphrase Schultze-Naumburg—Rembrandt's first human male is a study in fraudulent indecision. His head is

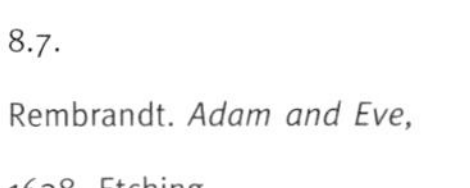

8.7.

Rembrandt. *Adam and Eve,*

1638. Etching.

set down into his chunky body and, with his sharp widow's peak, twisted nose, and scraggly beard, he is almost a satyr—the very quintessence of unregulated, irresponsible sexual selection. He has an animal face, large-lipped and beetle-browed—almost a snout. Eve is solider and rounder than Adam, less wiry and hairy, more symmetrical but still bestial, her head framed by a long, ratty ponytail. Lombroso would have emphasized the couple's megacephaly, asymmetry, and physiognomical atavism. Nordau would probably have discoursed on their pathological hirsuteness. By all these criteria Adam and Eve are as *minderwertig* as they come. But Rembrandt, says Schultze-Naumburg, would have seen nothing wrong with his two heroes. He himself, according to the theories of the age, would have looked just like them. He loved such faces and bodies. Rembrandt's whole art, his world of Christian heroes and saints, of gods and goddesses, of peasants and bourgeois, is a vast, insidious *Gegenauslese*—insidious because, of course, Rembrandt remains through it all (and Schultze-Naumburg emphasizes this) one of the greatest artists who ever lived: great but fatally degenerate.

From Rembrandt, furthermore, as a mark of that very greatness in all its perversity, there flows a stream of Northern European painting that perpetuates and develops this population. The polluted swarm, according to Schultze-Naumburg, runs onward and broadens, eventually to produce the expressionists of Schultze-Naumburg's own period. That race of Jukes-like anthropoids now dominates art completely, while the Rubensian Nordic type has all but disappeared from the galleries.

In figure scenes exotic features reign. Among these types, furthermore, there is a strong tendency not to portray the nobler examples but rather a tendency that runs from primitive humans to grinning grotesques of bestial cavemen showing off their very disfigurements. Over it all we see the preference for the signs of decadence, an army of the fallen, the sick, and the bodily deformed. . . . If one wants the art most symbolic of our own time it is that of the idiot, the prostitute, and the woman with pendulous breasts. One must call things by their right name. It is truly a hell of subhumans that here spreads before us, and one breathes a sigh of relief when one moves from this atmosphere to the pure air of other cultures, especially the antique and the early Renaissance.[6]

These purveyors of the deselectable are especially evil when they paint women: "Almost never has woman been so dishonorably and unappetizingly displayed

8.8.
Otto Dix. *Café Couple*, 1921. Watercolor and pencil. New York, Museum of Modern Art.

as in German exhibitions during the last twelve years," says Schultze-Naumburg, writing in 1928, "to the point that disgust and loathing overcome us again and again. Here there is not the slightest hint of the health of the human body and the splendor of the divinely naked form, but rather voracious lust of the kind felt only by outcasts of the lowest stamp."[7] The approach Nordau had taken to Whistler and Rodin, Schultze-Naumberg now applies to Rouault, Chagall, and Kokoschka. Otto Dix's work (8.8) is also an example.

And, Schultze-Naumburg adds in quiet horror, and again echoing Nordau, all these monstrosities were created *on purpose*. The artists themselves, inwardly and outwardly pathological in every Lombrosan sense, seek out pathological models. They visit leper colonies, homes for the retarded, and psychiatric clinics to find sitters. This, I would note, is a tradition that goes back to the German sculptor Messerschmidt and to Courbet, as well as to Rodin. For that matter Leonardo sometimes sought out people with deformed faces and drew them.[8] What Schultze-Naumburg deplores is that, now, these creatures are being presented as sexually selectable—or at least as not being particularly deselectable.

Jacob Epstein and Racial Treachery

Schultze-Naumburg, then, reintroduces the concept of race into our discussions, a concept revived or continued from Gobineau, Curtius, and the Aryan controversies of Victorian Britain. The change during the 1930s from a eugenics based on individuals, or individual types, to one based on race was not confined to

Germany. We return briefly to Britain, where the case of Schultze-Naumburg's contemporary, Jacob Epstein, is instructive. That he was an American Jew who made it on the British art scene is always remarked on—and not always favorably.[9] Many luminaries in the art establishment weighed in with opinions about Epstein's work that were race-based and intended to point out, in that work, its bio-moral degeneracy. Even those who defended Epstein did so on racial grounds. Thus Walter Crane explained that the artist's much-criticized nude statues for the facade of the British Medical Association (1907–1908) were not indecent: they portrayed Mediterranean body types, and there nudity has always been acceptable. To have portrayed characteristically British physiques, to supply Crane's suppressed corollary, *would* have been indecent. In a different vein the Slade Professor of Art at Cambridge, Martin Conway, held that this Mediterranean racial stock was so superior to the native British or "Arctic" strain that it deserved to be displayed in the nude as a kind of punitive admonition to the ill-shaped British.

But most British critical opinion was not about to accept propositions such as these. Some even argued that a "Mediterranean," that is, Polykleitan, physique was a sign of biological inferiority. Narrow shoulders and spindleshanks betokened their possessors' high intellectual level. But once again the major fear was that such images would beget real-life imitation, that British women would prefer, as mates, men built like Apollo rather than like G. B. Shaw.

And a final irony: these unworthy reproductive goals were being proposed by the British *Medical* Association, which at the time was of course full of eugenicists. The guardians of health were now the propagators of decay and disease. Father Bernard Vaughn of the National Vigilance Society feared that the portrayal of these handsome but clearly inferior sun-people would help bring about a lowering of British culture to primitive levels. He complained in particular that Epstein, himself already lamentably exotic, was trying to "convert London into a Fiji island." Even Epstein's clothed figures caused a racial stir. His *Risen Christ* reminded Fr. Vaughn of "some degraded Chaldean or African . . . Asiatic-American or Hun-Jew . . . emaciated Hindu or badly-grown Egyptian." Other cultural leaders found that Epstein perversely specialized in Mongolian morons, Asiatic monstrosities, and "dark blood, itself not pure but drawn from African, the Aztec and many other races"; this latter, meant in praise, came from Anthony Blunt, at the time the art critic of *The Spectator*.[10]

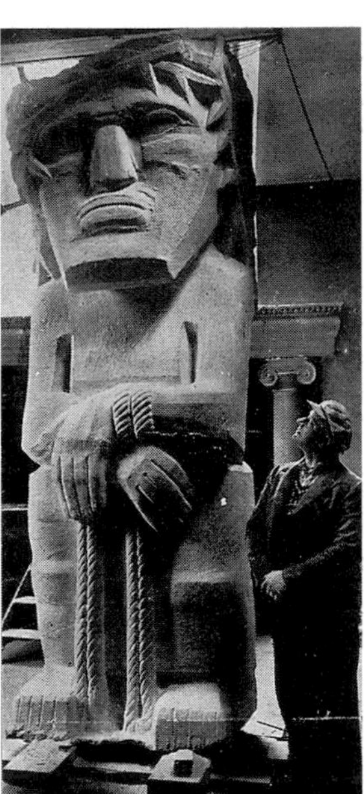

8.9.

Georges Rouault. *Head of Christ*, 1905. Norfolk, Va., Chrysler Museum of Art. Gift of Walter P. Chrysler, Jr.

8.10.

Jacob Epstein's *Behold the Man*, 1934–1935, with the artist. From the *New York Times*, 17 March 1935. The statue is now at Coventry Cathedral.

Thus what Schultze-Naumburg saw when he looked, say, at Rouault (8.9) was probably not too different from what Fr. Vaughn saw when he looked either at one of Epstein's statues or at Epstein himself (8.10). And, if we look at both images from the Schultze-Naumburg/Fr. Vaughn viewpoint, Rembrandt's fatal genes (8.7) surely might be said to show up in Rouault's painting of Christ. Here is an ur-catalogue of anthropometric decadence: a huge prognathous jaw with predator's mandible and recessed maxilla; a large, thick asymmetrical mouth that Lombroso would call African and atavistic; a nose whose seemingly broken bone is attached to an overlong, crooked septum; goose ears; close-set, deep eyes like those of Michelangelo's Minos (see fig. 6.12) but even more asymmetrical; and in the cranium an exceedingly low frontal bone. From what we can see, the rest of the body has narrow shoulders and a very wide neck. Almost all of this can be said about the Epstein Christ, and to it we can add preternaturally narrow shoulders, asymmetrical eyes, and Kretschmer's "shield-shaped" face (which the Nazis would paradoxically take up as a positive diagnostic). From the viewpoint of anthropometry, the Christ is just 3 heads high, so macrocephaly is monstrously present. The lack of bodily articulation in chest, arms, and legs also marks the figure as atavistic. From the viewpoint of the 1930s right wing, it would be hard to conjure up a more deselectable vision of a human being. That the image represented the savior of humankind and the central Christian doctrine of the incarnation only made it all worse.

The 120-Year Reich

In 1933 the satirical magazine *Kladderadatsch* (Mischief) published a cartoon (8.11) in which Hitler visits the studio of a probably Jewish sculptor. The Führer is examining the artist's wet clay *modello* of a scene of naked bodies writhing in struggle. With one blow he brings his fist down on the work. Then he models from the mashed-up clay a single figure of a hypermuscular nude male with the proper Nazi long legs, superwide shoulders, and tall face. With one violent act Hitler has eliminated a struggling mass of inferior human clay and kneaded their flesh into a single perfect man. The cartoon well sums up Nazi attitudes to sexual selection, human breeding, and eugenics.[11]

But it is not often pointed out that, in real life, the new Nazi race remained very much in the future. We have seen that Himmler said it would take 120 years to breed it. Indeed, even those who most ardently stigmatized degenerate humans could themselves be atavistic. Look at Himmler himself (8.12).

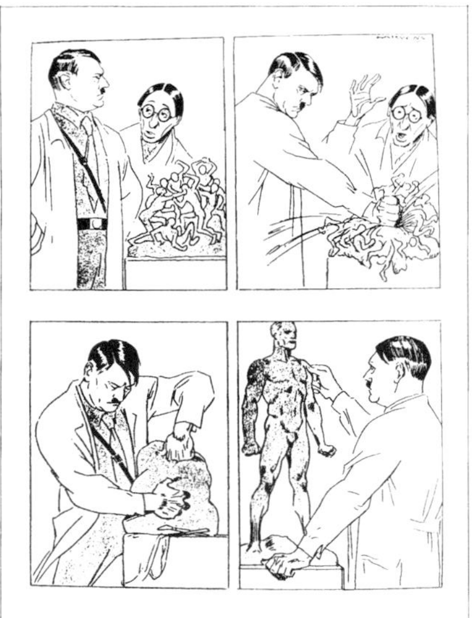

8.11.
Hitler creates a new man. From the Nazi magazine *Kladderadatsch* (1933).

8.12.
Heinrich Himmler. From Bettina Arnold, "The Past as Propaganda," *Archaeology* 45 (July/August 1992).

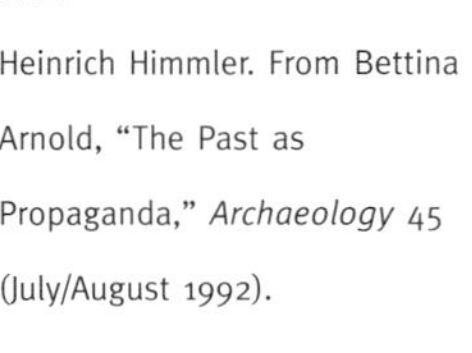

8.13.
Thersites. Redrawn detail from a Hellenic vase. From Günther, *Rassengeschichte.*

8.14.
After Kresilas. Head of Pericles. Roman copy. Antikensammlungen, Staatliche Museen zu Berlin, Preussischer Kulturbesitz. From Günther, *Rassengeschichte.*

According to Nazi physiognomists like Hans Günther, a receding lower lip and weak chin flowing diagonally into the neck, ears at a 45-degree angle, and the rictus or dimple next to the mouth are all signs of inferiority, of Near Eastern racial origins. Lombroso had agreed that these features were degenerate (though not because they were Near Eastern), as was weak eyesight (note the pince-nez). And Günther illustrates his point with Thersites (8.13), famous in the *Iliad* for ugliness and loquacity—no bad characterization of Himmler himself, by the way.[12] Thersites has exactly Himmler's nose, chin, sagging throat, pinched lips, and rictus. (I must make it clear that Günther himself makes no mention of Himmler at this point.)

Moreover, the contrast between Himmler's face and the faces of the "Hellenic" and "Nordic" heroes that Günther points to as breeding models—for example, Pericles (8.14)—could not be greater. Pericles' profile lines up along a perfect vertical. His chin (as far as one can tell with the beard) is as deep, square, and

notably prominent as Himmler's is shallow, round, and hypoplasic. Pericles' (restored) nose is as delicate and nuanced as Himmler's is thick and short. (Günther, however, does not allude to the legend that the unusual shape of Pericles' helmet hid a malformation of his skull—an aberration, as noted in chapter 4, that ought to have ruled him out as a valid Aryan.)

These are things that one divines by looking at images. But the Nazis themselves frankly acknowledged that they and their generation suffered from phenotypal shortcomings. Alfred Rosenberg argued (I paraphrase) that modern history no longer produces the sterling specimens of Aryan warriorship that characterized earlier epochs, especially the Renaissance. He lists a number of representative figures on the German political scene and contrasts their faces and physiques with the Polykleitan ideal. Rosenberg, convinced that Parsifal, Roland, Charlemagne, and Henry II *did* have the proper sort of bodies and faces, cites the distinction between the ancient heroes and the modern leaders as the reason why the vanished faces and physiques must be vigorously selected for.[13] Of course, like all racial theorists who appealed to figures from the past, he was relying completely on works of art for his anthropometric data.

Rosenberg recommends the "lean, strong, aristocratic" physiques in Greek vase painting. He mentions especially the Euphronios painter. "Collective Europe's hero-ideal," he adds, "is synonymous with a tall, lean figure with shining eyes, high forehead, muscular but not muscle-bound." Other useful reproductive models are Donatello's *St. George* in Florence and Gattamelata statue in Padua, and Verrocchio's Colleoni monument in Venice. But the new emerging type is no mere repetition from the past. "Today," Rosenberg writes, "a more internalized dynamic predominates: will and brain, drawing upon a centre, direct millions [of people]. . . . Forehead, nose, eyes, mouth and chin become bearers of a will, of a particular direction of thought. . . . It is at this point that Nordic-Western art is differentiated from the Greek Ideal."

A 1941 book by K. R. Ganzer on the faces of German heroes contains a photograph of Arno Breker's bust of Hitler, whose face, at least in Breker's hands, does indeed project Rosenberg's idea of a newly muscularized physiognomy, redolent of heavy thought, powerful decisions, and a wary fierceness (8.15). It is, as Rosenberg says, a face marked by the responsibility of directing the destinies of millions.[14] The muscles are strongly exerted. The frontalis, along the brow, is clenched into a powerful X-shape. The heavy overfold of the eye (which

8.15.
Arno Breker. Bust of Adolf Hitler, 1941. From Johannes Sommer, *Arno Breker.*

8.16.
Arno Breker. *Bereitschaft* (*Readiness*), 1939. *Modello* for sculpture at the zeppelin field of the Reichsparteiaggeländ, Nuremberg. Location unknown.

8.17.
Benvenuto Cellini. *Modello* for the *Perseus,* commissioned 1545. Florence, Museo Nazionale del Bargello.

the Germans considered to be particularly Aryan, though Lombroso and Hooton called it degenerate), forms the center of a nest of muscular creases and corrugations, especially in the orbiculares oculi. Meanwhile the muscles that raise the upper lip, and which rise diagonally across the cheeks when flexed, produce an expression of lordly and unconscious disdain.

Arno Breker, who was the most gifted of the Nazi sculptors, specialized in a type of male physique that actually went beyond Renaissance norms and the Polykleitan tradition as we have studied it.[15] A typical work is a six-foot statue called *Readiness*, a *modello* for a colossal figure that remained unexecuted (8.16). If we compare it to one of the Rosenberg-recommended prototypes, Cellini's *Perseus* (8.17), we see immediately that Breker is up to something new. The *Perseus* is exactly 7 heads high, with the breaks coming properly at nipples, navel, groin, and so on. The other measurements are equally orthodox. *Readiness*, however, is fully 8 heads high—the kind of extremism we see in Michelangelo. But Breker's real departure is in the breadth of the shoulders, which are almost $1/3$ of the total body height: huge beyond all precedents discussed in this book. Other notable Nazisms are the massive flat articulations of the abdominals and, elsewhere, the Rubensian mounded islands of muscle. Note also the tall, shield-shaped facial mask and long neck.

The ideal Nazi woman was also frequently portrayed. Hitler was particularly fond of nudity,[16] and decorated his various living quarters, for example in the Führerhaus in Munich, with allegorical nudes by artists such as Adolf Ziegler.[17] Ziegler and his fellow Nazi painters belonged to an artistic tradition reaching back to the European academic nude through Böcklin and Feuerbach, and perhaps through Cabanel, Gérôme, and even Leighton. But the French midcentury bodies are more marmoreal than those created by the Victorians and the Germans. Above all the French faces are often Near Eastern, Slavic, and the like, and the French bodies lack the long bones, flat stomachs, shallow breasts, and sharp distinctions of one part from another that the Aryanists demanded. I illustrate with figures by Julius Engelhard and Ivo Saliger (8.18, 8.19). What is also specifically Aryan about the two women is their very fair skins, whose whiteness is emphasized by projected highlights and reflected shadows. In all these things the women are Leighton-like, as they are also in their languorous expectancy. Schultze-Naumburg, in his book *Nordische Schönheit* (1937), added that such bodies are beautiful because they express logic and truthfulness of mind.[18] But note that in Saliger's figure (8.19), the woman's shield-shaped face is so tall, and her head so dolichocephalic, that her total body measures only about 6 heads. This is probably just a mistake. One notes, too, her extremely narrow shoulders, little more than $1/5$ of her total body height. The artist has ruined the Polykleitan formula in his zeal for the Nazi cephalic trademark.

8.18.
Julius Engelhard. *Bath in a Mountain Lake*, c1930–1945. Detail. Location unknown. From Hinz, *Die Malerei im deutschen Faschismus*.

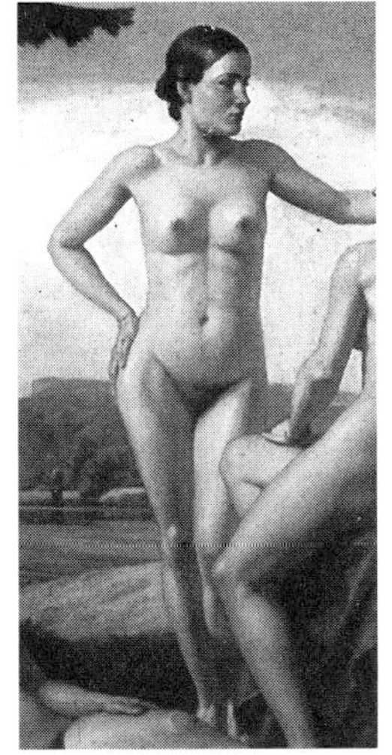

8.19.
Ivo Saliger. *Diana's Rest*, c1930–1945. Detail. Location unknown. From Hinz, *Die Malerei im deutschen Faschismus*.

While Breker's males, and those of other Nazi artists, owe quite a bit to Rubens's musculatures, they are not otherwise Rubensian or even baroque. German neoclassicism seems the more relevant source. And the same is true of both Engelhard's and Saliger's female figures. Or, if one seeks sources in the art recommended by Schultze-Naumburg, Jordaens rather than Rembrandt fills the bill (see fig. 8.6). Such smooth solid masses of flesh, clear arching silhouettes, crystalline backlighting, and satiny skin surfaces are extraordinarily like a great deal of Nazi nude painting.

As to breeding more such types, most people today think of the SS purely as a military organization. But it was also a genetic pool. "All SS members who sought to marry were required to submit their families' genealogical backgrounds," writes the *New York Times* of the documents in the SS archives, "and those of their prospective wives, dating to 1800, or 1750 if they were officers." This assured that they had no undesirable blood. In short the SS files became the German equivalent of Galton's *Golden Book of Thriving Families.* Specialists also analyzed applicants' facial structure in terms of twenty-one categories with an intricate grading scale. All men with large noses or ears, asymmetrical eyes, and swarthy complexions were eliminated.[19] Successful candidates, meanwhile, went to *Lebensborn* or procreation centers where they mated with appropriate women.[20] Thus while the death camps were eliminating unhealthy blood, the SS was regenerating it—the same double process we saw in the cartoon in figure 8.11.

In this chapter we have demonstrated, I trust with new insights, something often said about Nazism—that it added no really new ideas to the ideologies it appropriated. Nazism's only true novelty was the totalitarianism that put these older notions horrifically into effect.[21] Both race-based and individual visions of biological decay had been current throughout the latter part of the nineteenth century. Galton, Lombroso, and Nordau concentrated on the diagnosis of individuals. Schultze-Naumburg, building on their ideas, proposed a new Nordic race with Rubens providing the reproductive goals and Rembrandt the types to be selected against—all this long before Hitler came to power. What might be called artistic racism is also readable in British criticism of Jacob Epstein. He was accused of impugning superior British types by portraying, and implicitly praising, lesser breeds—African, Oceanic, Near Eastern—in his sculpture.

Within the Nazi world, Schultze-Naumburg, Himmler, and Alfred Rosenberg became spokesmen for the planned new Nordic race. Its physiological nature was illustrated with Italian Renaissance sculpture, and by the work of such artists as Arno Breker, Paul Engelhard, and Ivo Saliger. The women were to be tall, long-legged, dolichocephalic, fair, exceedingly white-skinned and with shield-shaped facial masks. The men are represented by Breker's heroes: most of these same characteristics plus Rubensian musculatures and extraordinarily wide shoulders. While the women could be as little as 6 heads high, the men were apt to be 8, showing a degree of sexual dimorphism, I would suppose, that is not often found in real-life human populations.

9 Hyperdevelopment Today

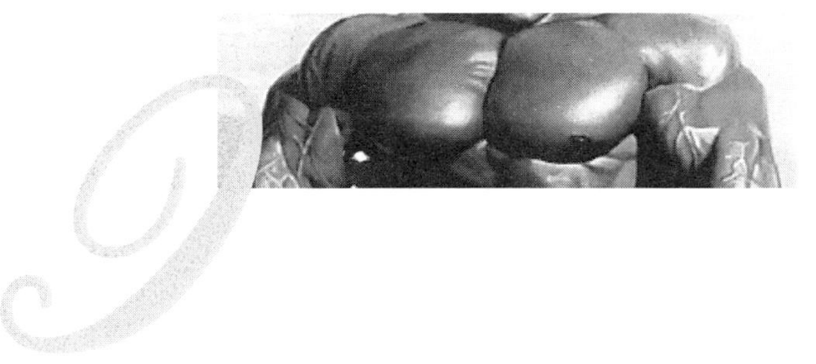

Augmentation: Hercules and Batman

The thesis that body type and personality are linked together, and that by manipulating this relationship the state could establish a program in eugenics, led to the Nazi atrocities we are all familiar with. In the aftermath of World War II, and even still today, these ideas persist, but they have taken second place to the development of a purely bodily extremism. In this last chapter I want to talk about three forms of sexual hyperdevelopment—augmentation, exchange, and dimorphism (i.e., the male's being much larger than the female).

We saw in chapter 5 that mesomorphs, male and female, are considered more selectable than ectomorphs and endomorphs.[1] And not only are mesomorphs more selectable, they seem to be getting more mesomorphic. Two of Sheldon's followers, Barbara Heath and J. E. Lindsay Carter, working in the 1970s and 1980s, have found degrees of mesomorphy that exceed Sheldon's top value of 7.[2] Such physiques have occurred naturally among both males and females in the Pacific Islands and in many other populations that Sheldon did not study. But even these glorious bodies are meager by the standards of today's professional bodybuilders, who, with the aid of specialized exercise, diet, and often steroids, are able to push their muscles and eliminate body fat to a degree well beyond anything seen earlier in human history. Today, the muscles of the legs and upper body can be mounded into huge, intricate sculptural masses interwoven with hoselike arteries. When pumped, a modern set of male biceps can measure twenty inches around or more.[3] This exceeds the muscularity even of antiquity's mightiest mesomorphs, at least as we can know them from works of art. Only Arno Breker's work (fig. 8.16), discussed in the last chapter, anticipates today's hypermesomorph. It is true, of course, that not everyone admires these hyperphysiques. But they seem to work their magic on much of the relevant population.[4]

These new degrees of bulk and of plastic detail give the viewer a great deal of new information. Each muscle hyperbolizes its identity and shape, redefining its place within the body with its own life, properties, and personality. This arises partly from the newfound ability preternaturally to isolate and expand individual muscles, to "peak" them, as the bodybuilders say; and we also gain from the very terminology of the muscles themselves. Thus the Latin word *musculus,* from which we get "muscle," means "little mouse." Many of the most prominent muscles—the biceps and the triceps, for example, which respectively mean "two-headed" and "three-headed"—also have names suggesting independent creatures. We can therefore think of ourselves as covered with two- and three-headed mice, and with sets of smaller and larger creatures that, at least if we are bodybuilders, dart around under our skins, popping up, sliding behind each other, ever on the go, creating an outer carapace of clinging creatures—a sort of kinetic subcutaneous clothing. It is not at all uncommon, among bodybuilders and their fans, to see them showing off by popping specific muscles that, in the bodybuilders' psyches, function something like pets.

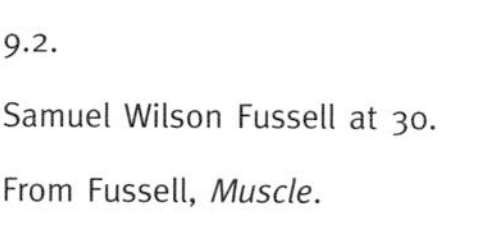

9.1.

Samuel Wilson Fussell at 22.

From Fussell, *Muscle*.

9.2.

Samuel Wilson Fussell at 30.

From Fussell, *Muscle*.

This idea of muscles as an outer garment made of small animals is not as strange as at first it might seem. Real clothes, after all, are frequently made from animal parts or even from whole animals. Think of the dozens of little creatures that make up a mink or chinchilla coat. And someone in a mouse jacket would literally be clad in *musculi.* The same applies to other animals used for these purposes—fox, beaver, and some seals. All are small, curvaceous, furry things—strongly reminiscent, by the way, of genital hair.

Like coats of fur, coats of muscle can be put on or taken off, though at much greater expense of time and effort. Samuel Wilson Fussell's 1991 book, *Muscle: Confessions of an Unlikely Bodybuilder*, illustrates the author's multiyear rise from ectomorphic twenty-two-year-old (9.1) to full-rigged hypermesomorphy (9.2).[5] The book shows that a determined person can change from ectomorph to mesomorph, a possibility that Sheldon himself denied. But I doubt that even he would classify the 1992 version of Fussell as anything but a mesomorph—and possibly as one who had developed himself somewhat beyond Sheldon's maximum of 172. Indeed Fussell is more muscular than even the Farnese Hercules (9.3), who has for centuries exemplified the Polykleitan muscular

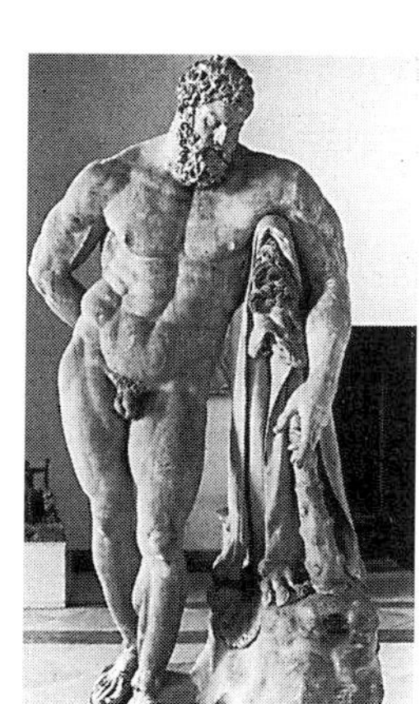

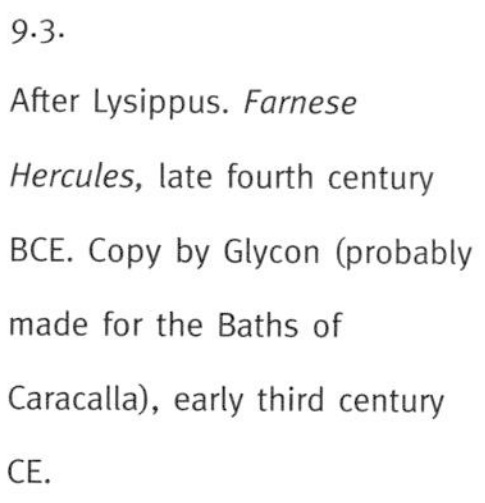

9.3.

After Lysippus. *Farnese Hercules,* late fourth century BCE. Copy by Glycon (probably made for the Baths of Caracalla), early third century CE.

extreme, even though its legs are not original (and are too small).[6] It is only when the hypermesomorphs begin to appear in our own day that Hercules' legs begin to look knock-kneed and his shoulders narrow. No wonder he looks weary; he has been surpassed. Thus, comparing Hercules with Fussell at his mesomorphic peak (and by his own account Fussell is far from the most perfectly developed of his colleagues), we see that Hercules' muscles lack the bulge, the definition, the edged "cutting" that modern bodybuilders achieve by reducing their body fat to insignificant (and dangerous) levels. The result, in living human beings, is the outward appearance of an *écorché* figure—a skinned, all-muscle male. Why would anyone wish to achieve this look? One answer, I suppose, is that it comes from a common object in life-drawing studios and anatomy: the *écorché* thus exerts selective pressure on art students.

Further on Fussell versus Hercules: Fussell is just under 7 heads high; his shoulders, even hunched as in the picture, are just under $1/3$ of his total body height and his arms are a desirably short $1/4$ of that height. So, in proportion, he approaches the Arno Breker ideal. Hercules, meanwhile, is also 7 heads high, his chest is more canonically $1/4$ of his body height, and his forearm-and-hand actually is somewhat less than the prescribed $1/4$ of that measurement. So the hero-god is slightly shorter-armed (and shorter-legged) than the ideal. Fussell is *more* Polykleitan, in fact, except that he is wider-shouldered than the canon. It is worth noting that this comparison between Fussell and Hercules is real, not academic. Bodybuilders often strike the pose of this statue and that of Michelangelo's *David*, or even that of the *Dying Gaul*, as part of their competition routines.[7]

Such increases and shifts in bodily proportions reintroduce the subject of body canons. Bodybuilders spend a great deal of time measuring themselves and each other. They live in a world of numbers. Articles about the movement's heroes and heroines are as rich in this way as are Lomazzo's descriptions of solar and lunar physiques, or Sheldon's account of his "Northeasterners" and "Southerners." On arriving in America, we learn, Arnold Schwarzenegger, now the retired king of the bodybuilders, weighed 235 pounds, was 6′1″, had an 18″ neck, a 55″ chest, a 31″ waist, and biceps that were 20″ around when pumped. We also learn that his 1992 exercise routine consisted of 430 full squats, 410 bench presses, 285 curls, 390 clean jerks, and more of the same. These numbers exist as challenges to be surpassed. As Fussell writes: "I couldn't stop.

Seventeen-inch arms were not enough, I wanted 20. And when I got to 20, I was sure I'd want 22. My retreat to the weight room was a retreat into the simple world of numbers. Numerical gradations were the only thing left in my life that made sense."[8]

Most of these people, furthermore, enter bodybuilding competitions in which still more numbers are assigned, a process that culminates in the prize money (e.g., $40,000 for a first-place showing in the Junior USA Middleweight Championship for Women—with up to ten times that amount in endorsements). The careful recording of all these numbers maps out the progress of the successive winners. Each year, too, in proportion they seem to get better—longer-legged, wider-shouldered, narrower-waisted, and always more massively muscled. No evolutionary biologist or somatotyper could measure his or her subjects more vigilantly than these men and women measure themselves. There will be a regression factor to limit their infinite increase. But even so, a sort of cultural microevolution occurs through each given bodybuilder's progressive surpassing of his or her predecessors. We do not get a new species but we do get new, ever more exaggerated reproductive goals. And that, of course, might some day lead to true genetic evolution, as from *Homo erectus* to *Homo sapiens*—if, as Sheldon predicts, the mesomorphs come to outbreed their competitors.

One great pool of reproductive goals in modern life has been comic-book art. We have already noted that Sheldon called attention to Superman, Smilin' Jack, and Li'l Abner as heroic mesomorphs. But, like Fussell, these characters in their current versions have transformed themselves into hypermesomorphs.

In 1970 Batman was hardly more than a 172 (see fig. 5.7). He presents himself with only a few negligently indicated blobs of fiber at the shoulders, on his chest, and on his upper legs. Just 7 heads high, his shoulders were considerably less than $1/4$ of his total height, his waist a bit more than half his shoulder width. In considerable contrast, the Batman of our own day (9.4) is much wider, much more articulated, and much more mesomorphic than his earlier self. His shoulders are just less than *half* his total body height. His many muscles have excellent symmetry and edge definition, and most of them are anatomically real (as opposed to 1970 Batman's nameless protuberances). Batman 1992's arms are huge and long, almost equaling his legs (a relationship that is supposedly regressive, of course) and his head is equally outsize, giving him a total body 4 $1/2$ heads high.

9.4.
Batman in 1992. From *Batman*, DC Comics, February 1992. Cover by Jim Aparo.

9.5.
Michelangelo. *Last Judgment*, 1535–1541. Detail of Christ. Vatican, Sistine Chapel.

Batman 1992 also has the especially wide waist of the Christ in Michelangelo's Sistine *Last Judgment* (9.5). But then Michelangelo's Christ, strangely for its own or any time, has shoulders and waist of almost equal width. Perhaps it is the familiarity of Michelangelo's figure that has permitted Batman's (and his many colleagues') growth in the same direction to seem natural or permissible. But these changes can also be chalked up to our having habituated ourselves to new levels of attractor augmentation. Such augmentations are particularly appropriate to saviors who fly through the cosmos and summon souls from frightened, fateful cities of the dead.

Exchange: Arnold, Diana of Ephesus, Kristy Ramsey, and Hannah Höch

Among the most prominent muscles in today's hypermesomorphs are the pectorales majores, which cover the breast area in a three-part trapezoidal formation. These can be developed so massively into outward compound domes that they resemble female breasts (9.6). Arnold Schwarzenegger's magnificent shoulders and upper arms are such that his whole upper body frames his pectorals with particular decision. Thus may muscles mimic the enlargements that plastic implants achieve on women (see fig. 9.11). Of course there is still a contrast of hardness with softness, of engorged fiber for the males versus pneumatic viscosity for the females, and the women's breasts are larger and more balloonlike than Arnold's. But the surface curve is often remarkably the same, and

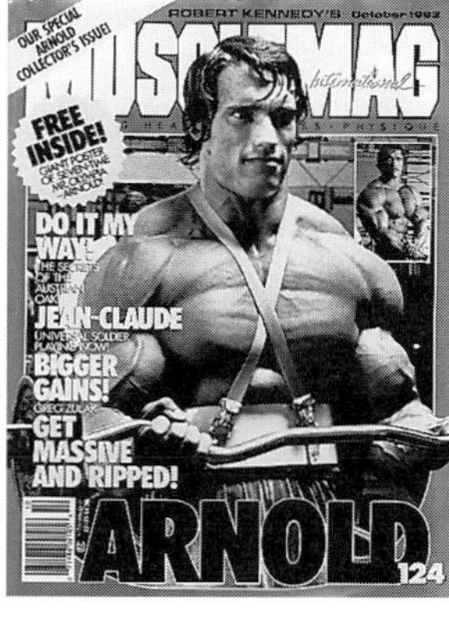

9.6.

Arnold Schwarzenegger. From *Musclemag International*, October 1992. Cover.

9.7.

Artemis, Ephesian type. Roman copy after an original of c500 BCE. Detail. Naples, Museo Nazionale.

the degree of departure from the norm for the sex is the same. And in both sexes we observe extreme augmentation of attractors, with the males at the same time borrowing from the females. Many of the hypermesomorphic male's other muscles have this same breastlike quality, which means augmented frequency as well as size.[9]

The most heavily breasted figure from antiquity is the Artemisia Hypermammia (9.7). It has been conjectured in some quarters that in fact her multiple mammaries are not breasts at all but the scrota of sacrificed bulls (they are without nipples), which would make the goddess a good instance of attractor exchange.[10] Even simply as breasts, however, these organs manage to anticipate the mammary mountain ranges with which Arnold Schwarzenegger and other male bodybuilders have clothed their bodies.

We have been looking at augmentations that border on exchange—men with breasts. Another sort of exchange-cum-augmentation involves women developing their muscles to a male degree and simultaneously *reducing* their breasts. In Kristy Ramsey (9.8) every muscle has been enlarged, engorged, and chemically goaded into sculptural life. Her upper arms are huge and hard, along with her deltoids, biceps, and triceps, and even the flexor carpi radialis and palmaris longus (long, thin muscles in each inner lower arm) are solidly eminent. Her breasts are now mere caps on the massive pectorals flowing into her armpits and rising vertically in the center of her chest to die into the base of the mastoids where the neck begins. Her washboard stomach vies, in its corrugations, with that of the Farnese Hercules (9.2). Her upper body is in fact almost fully male so that here the attractor exchange is virtually complete. Her pelvis and thighs, though, have lost nothing of their female outlines, albeit even they seem hard as marble. And her hands, head, and hair are all completely feminine, as is her bathing suit. There is attractor exchange, then, but it is exchange that does nothing to disguise the fact that the body in question is female. Quite the contrary: by reframing the genital area in male muscles, she makes her upper body into an unexpected, hence forceful, genital vector.

What does this have to do with art? Kristy Ramsey and her sisters are predicted by some of the 1930s collages of the dada artist Hannah Höch. I cannot introduce these works as instances of art being consciously used to propose reproductive goals, as has been the case earlier. Rather, now, it is at the unconscious, possibly even fortuitous level, that one makes the comparison. An example is *Dompteuse* (*Dominatrix*, 9.9). Like Kristy, Höch's woman mixes strongly male and strongly female attractors. A sleek, sloe-eyed, marmoreal mannequin's face stares down at what appear to be her own hard hairy male arms basking in hot crosslighting, the arms being far more fleshly and human than the face and neck. Her blouse, however, is exceedingly female—sleeveless, with a shaped neck, and decorated with huge paisley teardrops rimmed like toothed vulvas. She has no apparent breasts but her hip, like her face and neck, is completely female. In this sense the dominatrix is exactly what Kristy is: female head, male torso and arms, female thighs, but wearing woman's gear on her torso and lower body. A sea lion (as the future source of a fur?) looks out from the lower right. The animal's heavy-lidded, slitlike eyes echo those of the mannequin head. Note that both the young woman and the animal have just exploded through a set of riveted wall plates. The overtones of sadomasochism are clear.

9.8.
Kristy Ramsey. From *Women's Physique World*, September 1992.

9.9.
Hannah Höch. *Dompteuse*, c1930. Kunsthaus, Zurich. Copyright © 1993 ARS NY/Bild-Kunst, Bonn.

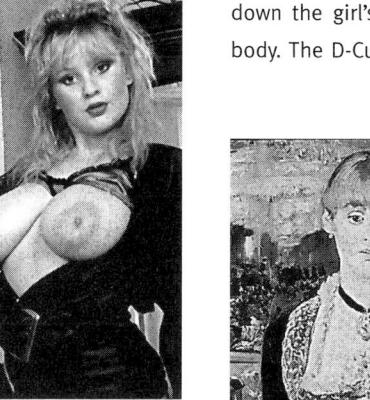

Just as men and women have augmented their muscles, so women (and perhaps a few men who have undergone sex changes), have augmented their breasts. Sometimes their desire has been to achieve really huge appendages like those in the earliest fertility idols (9.10).[11] There is a modern subculture devoted to these augmentations (9.11), with magazines like *D-Cup Superstars*, videos, films, and even telephone sex services that cater to the interest.

Yet women's clothes, much more innocently (or "innocently"), have long achieved similar effects. In Manet's *Bar at the Folies Bergères* (1882; 9.12) the girl's breasts are framed and presented by bordering margins of lace, including a see-through panel over the dark dress with a ruched trapezoidal edging, offsetting a parallel panel, that veils but thus also points out and enlarges the breasts themselves. The visual effect is to double the breasts' apparent size. (And we note, in this connection, the strong flavor of sexual display in the Folies Bergères performances themselves.)[12] In a way, the D-Cup superstar's image simply translates into flesh, or flesh and silicone, an ageless tradition. Note that in the Lemba figure the two upper lateral protuberances, while they may be arms, can also be read as wide-swung breasts. In the Manet the girl's jacket, furthermore, reflects the Lemba figure's bunched, shortened shape, both having chevronlike genital vectors and widened hips. There is similar emphasis on the throat in the girl's black choker and pendant and in the idol's lengthened, thickened neck. Note too the similar groin vectoring in the row of buttons leading down the girl's abdomen and the vertical fissure down the front of the idol's body. The D-Cup superstar has also lengthened her neck, both by means of her

9.10.
Goddess from Lemba, Cyprus. Limestone, Chalcolithic, c2500 BCE. Nicosia, Cyprus Museum.

9.11.
Julie. From *D-Cup Superstars*, February 1992.

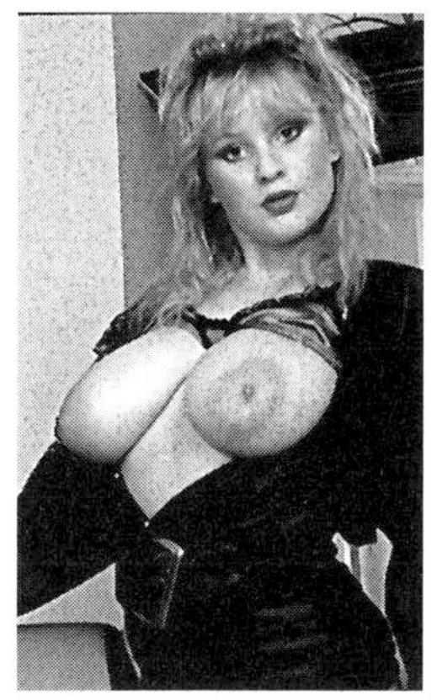

9.12.
Edouard Manet. *The Bar at the Folies Bergères*, 1882. Detail. London, Courtauld Institute Galleries.

hunched-shoulder pose and by the way the two sides of her blouse form a vase-like frame: they flow down her neck and sweep out into a pair of wide mirror-symmetrical loops to present her breasts. The visual results—quite unconsciously—are equally close to the Lemba figure and to the Manet.

Dimorphism: The Incredible Hulk, His Friends, and the Sage Grouse

Another result of the interplay between exchange and augmentation can be dimorphism—the exaggeration of differences rather than the similarities between the sexes. Four-hundred-pound male mountain gorillas and their relatively diminutive female companions are the classic example. But there is human dimorphism, too. On the one hand, Arnold and Kristy, after strenuous body-developing measures, end up looking superficially *like* each other, isomorphic. So do "America's Fittest Couple" (9.13). The translated attractors gain in appeal by being shared and also by appearing in the unexpected setting of the female body. With dimorphism, on the other hand, one sex gains in augmentation by exaggerating its contrast with the other.

The Incredible Hulk (9.14), for example, has been scaled up and muscularized far beyond anything we have seen so far. He weighs over 400 pounds, probably twice as much as 1970 Batman. Even allowing for the foreshortening in the illustration, the Hulk's massive arm is much thicker than his head—indeed the latter becomes almost a vestigial polyp on the hero's bright green landscape of

9.13.
"America's Fittest Couple": Laura Creavalle and Chris Aceto. From *Muscular Development*, October 1992.

9.14.
The Incredible Hulk emerges from undersea captivity. From Marvel Comics, *The Incredible Hulk*, vol. 1, no. 408 (August 1993). The Incredible Hulk Copyright © & TM 1996 Marvel Entertainment Group, Inc. Used with permission.

muscle. The Hulk's microevolution, then, has been toward shorter arms, longer legs, and a thinner head. Note that, as in a good bodybuilder with minimal surface fat, the infraspinatus muscle across the Hulk's shoulder is subdivided into serried layers. (However, this somatotype comes over the Hulk only when he is angered at some piece of evil, which, with his new body, he can proceed to correct. Otherwise he is Dr. Bruce Banner, a scientist, who is of normal proportions and musculature, with normally pigmented skin.)

One of the Hulk's allies is Killpower, who resembles his friend in physique and who has more of a sex life. He dates a foul-mouthed, long-legged girl named Motormouth (9.15). In Killpower one is invited to admire, particularly, the tumescent fantasies of thigh and calf (*all* his limbs are thicker than his head). And Killpower is not merely more muscled but more "evolved" than his 172+ predecessors. He takes Batman's extreme width and stretches it into hyperbolic height. His upper arms are the same length as his thighs, whereas 1970 Batman's ratio in this respect is only 3:2 in favor of the thighs; 1992 Batman's arm/thigh ratio is somewhere in between.

The Hulk and Killpower, then, compared to Motormouth, exemplify dimorphic augmentation in the sense of increased size of the whole body and increased musculature. But Killpower, in contrast to the unarmed Hulk, in his gear also exemplifies augmentation-by-multiplication. Images of male sex organs colonize his whole body. His upper chest is ablaze with groin vectors. Note that his jockstrap or mitra is the same size and shape as his head and even has a similar expression. Indeed this device of a smirking face is repeated four times around his belt, which naturally intensifies the sense of groin/head interchange. And across his shoulder Killpower has slung a set of grenades that constitute a supplementary squad of dummy penises. His pelvic vectors are immense—a massive

9.15.
Killpower and Motormouth. From Marvel Comics, *The Incredible Hulk*. The Incredible Hulk, Killpower and Motormouth Copyright © & TM 1996 Marvel Entertainment Group, Inc. Used with permission.

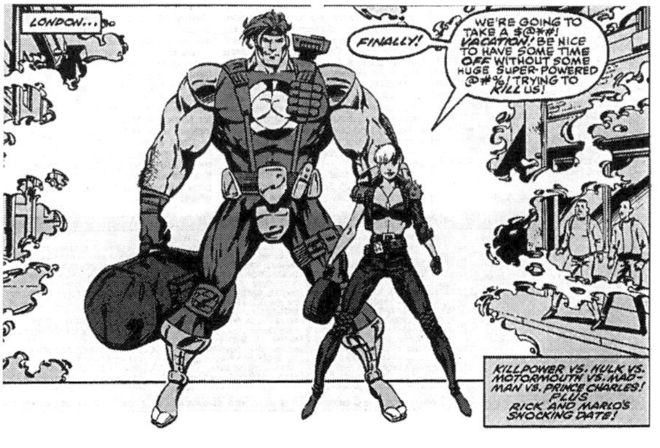

constructed framework flowing down from his shoulders, across his chest and stomach, and on to his groin with its dual prosopographic codpiece.

But all this is only true of Killpower himself. Motormouth is completely orthodox at 7 heads and has a litheness that approaches the anorexic. Thus she too works on widening the dimorphic gap between herself and her boyfriend. As to her apparel, she wears a simplified version of Killpower's clothes, omitting the phallic and testicular symbols. A small pendant vector—a cross or a key—hangs around her neck and delicately points between her breasts downward to her prominently belted groin.

Sexual dimorphism, even to the degree exhibited by Killpower and Motormouth, is extremely common in nature. I have already referred to mountain gorillas. A good example among birds is that between the male and female sage grouse (9.16). And, interestingly, the male of this species indulges in some of the most exuberant sexual displays to be found anywhere—worthy of Killpower or the Hulk. A group of males will gather on a lek or seduction arena and dance, strut, gurgle, and puff out their breasts in mutual competition as a jury of females watches from the sidelines. The females will bestow the palm on the winner and will try to mate with him alone, more or less excluding the runners-up from that season's reproductive enterprise.

This winner-take-all mode of sexual selection is undoubtedly what has bred the male sage grouse into the sexual signboard he now is. As to his particular charms, note the inflatable sac covered with contrastingly colored feathers that is formed around his throat, and the stiff, spiny Elizabethan ruff behind his head. In addition to these displays, he has a specialized esophagus that, during the seduction routine, emits a fetching chortle. The whole complex of head,

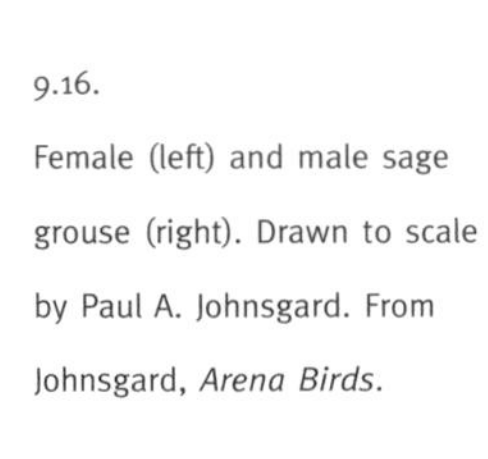

9.16.
Female (left) and male sage grouse (right). Drawn to scale by Paul A. Johnsgard. From Johnsgard, *Arena Birds*.

breast, and ruff, together with the sound these visual elements frame, is a good example of Eberhard's "genital extravagance" translated to the upper body. Indeed the male's entire extra body mass, in contrast to that of his female, almost *solely* comprises attractors. Note, meanwhile, that the male's head and bill are actually smaller than those of his consort.

Art and nature seem to be progressively testing each other's power to exaggerate. Killpower's attractors may be huge, his gear may be extraordinary in its augmentation, and his dimorphism vis-à-vis Motormouth may greatly enhance his scale. But even greater artistic exaggerations can be found. A case in point is Paul Rienzo's portrait of the bodybuilder Lee Haney (9.17). As seen through the portraitist's eyes, Lee is a bit short, 6 3/4 heads high, and with a particularly short torso (1 3/4, 2 1/2, 3 1/2 for nipples, umbilicus, and groin instead of Killpower's neat 2, 3, 4). But in their prodigious width Lee's shoulders equal the entire height of that torso. And his thighs could almost be inscribed on a square whose sides equal the length of the femur. Once again the head becomes a mere incident, a bud in the craggy muscular landscape. He has no neck whatever.

To find other art that approximates this vision one is driven back to the very early figures with which this book began—prehistoric Venus images. The Venus of Lespugue (9.18) possesses equally expanded domical protuberances that

9.17.
Paul Rienzo. Portrait of Lee Haney. From *Muscular Development*, October 1992.

9.18.
The "Venus of Lespugue," Gravettian Period, c7000 BCE? From H. Delporte, *L'Image de la femme dans l'art préhistorique* (Paris, 1979).

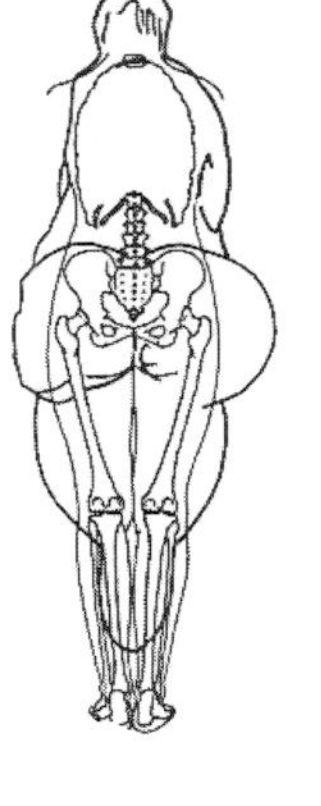

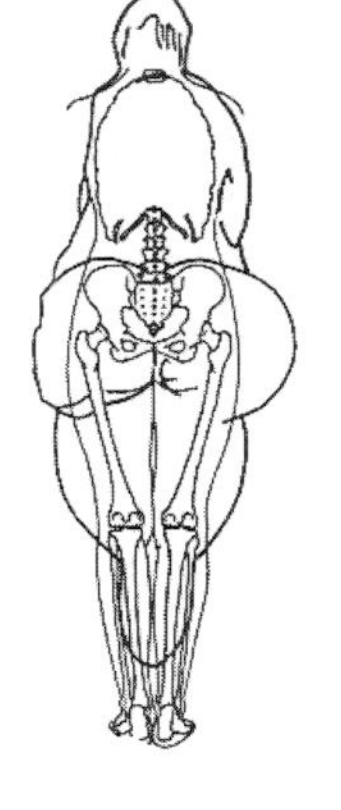

9.19.
Diagram of the Venus of Lespugue superimposed on the skeleton and exterior body of a normal female. After Pales, from Delporte, *L'Image de la femme dans l'art préhistorique.*

9.20.
Photograph of Lee Haney. From *Muscular Development*, October 1992.

add to her enormous width—not muscles this time but areas of mounded fat, that is, the buttocks and thighs. Unlike Lee Haney, however, these exaggerations are not distributed equally all over her body: her upper torso is normal. And indeed, as shown in the diagram in figure 9.19, her seemingly extravagant physique can be normalized when a modern female skeleton and body outline are inscribed on it. But then the same thing would happen with the Lee Haney illustration. Indeed, we can look at a photo of Lee Haney (9.20). His real-life body is hypermesomorphic, certainly, but perfectly Polykleitan. His likeness to the Venus of Lespugue is in the realm of art, not life.

This last chapter has looked at what I call the hyperdevelopment of male and female attractors, and the new ways in which they are being augmented, borrowed, and translated. First we noticed historically unprecedented increases in simple augmentation—muscle size and breast size. However, these new colossal musculatures stem from the Polykleitan tradition even as they transcend it, a fact underlined by the bodybuilders' penchant for mimicking the poses of classical statues. But at the same time, paradoxically, hyperdeveloped males like Arnold often develop musculatures that look like massed female breasts.

Similarly, women can develop their muscles in ways that, while borrowing male musculatures, highlight the women's femininity via contrast. Huge biceps are flourished over carefully sculptured female pelvises. And here again there is multimammary extravagance, for the large pectoral muscles of these women form a second set of breastlike forms. When similar extravagances show up in a dimorphic setting, as with Motormouth and Killpower, the difference in scale between the male and the female increases the net effect of augmentation.

Finally, some bodybuilding art seems to lead beyond even the greatest achievements of real-life bodybuilders, aiming at superhuman width, mass, and volume. Such hyperbolic phenotypes go directly back to the pre-Polykleitan period in art, and to the parahuman varieties of physique we see in prehistoric sculptures and graphic renderings. Nothing could more clearly mark the end of the "canonic" period in figure design that we have been investigating throughout this book. Bodybuilding and cosmetic surgery have made new links between art and sexual selection, links involving the *bizarrerie* of the stranger sorts of ancient art, of comic books, of dada, while also making novel parallels with nonhuman nature. All of which only underlines the complex continuing dialogue between sexual selection and the visual arts—concepts the are, of course, themselves in constant evolution.

Notes

Introduction: Aphrodite's Daughters

1
For a full account see Francis Haskell and Nicholas Penny, *Taste and the Antique: The Lure of Classical Sculpture, 1500–1900* (New Haven, 1981), s.v. See also Martin Robertson, *A History of Greek Art* (Cambridge, 1975), 1:392; Theodor Kraus, *Die Aphrodite von Knidos* (Bremen, 1957); and Christine Havelock, *The Aphrodite of Knidos and Her Successors* (Ann Arbor, Mich., 1995).

2
C. S. Blinkenberg, *Knidia: Beiträge zur Kenntnis der Praxitelischen Aphrodite* (Copenhagen, 1933).

3
Jacqueline Karageorghis, *La grande Déesse de Chypre et son culte* (Lyons, 1977), esp. 33ff.

4
Caroline Walker Bynum, "The Female Body and Religious Practice in the Later Middle Ages," *Zone: Fragments for a History of the Body* 1 (1989), 161ff. See also idem, *The Resurrection of the Body in Western Christianity, 200–1336* (New York, 1995).

5
Bynum, "The Female Body," 161ff., as quoted by Katharine Park, "The Criminal and Saintly Body: Autopsy and Dissection in Renaissance Italy," *Renaissance Quarterly* 47 (1994), 21.

1 Sexual Selection

1
For the early history of sexual selection, see Carl Jay Bajema, *Evolution by Sexual Selection: Theory Prior to 1900* (New York, 1984); the best general review and bibliography is offered by Malte Andersson, *Sexual Selection* (Princeton, 1994). See also Randy Thornhill and Steven Gangestad, "Human Facial Beauty: Averageness, Symmetry, and Parasite Resistance," *Human Nature* 4.3 (1993), 237ff.

2
Charles Darwin, *The Descent of Man and Selection in Relation to Sex* (1871), in *The Works of Charles Darwin,* ed. Paul H. Barrett and R. B. Freeman (London, 1989), 22:611. This edition will be cited throughout.

3
Joseph Arthur de Gobineau, *Essai sur l'inégalité des races humaines* (1853; Paris, 1967), 124.

4
Yet the equation is borne out in the literature of experimental psychology. See Linda A. Jackson, *Physical Appearance and Gender: Sociobiological and Sociocultural Perspective* (Albany, 1992), and S. W. Gangestad, R. Thornhill, and R. A. Yeo, "Facial Attractiveness, Developmental Stability, and Fluctuating Asymmetry," *Ethology and Sociobiology* (in press). Jackson points out that if Sheldon's correlations between temperament and body type fail to prove out observationally, they succeed in the realm of stereotypes *about* those correlations (156ff.).

5
Darwin, *Descent of Man, Part 2*, 408.

6
William G. Eberhard, *Sexual Selection and Animal Genitalia* (Cambridge, Mass., 1985), 15ff.; James L. Gould and Carol Grant Gould, *Sexual Selection* (New York, 1989), 71ff.

7
M. Andersson, "Female Choice Selects for Extreme Tail Length in a Widowbird," *Nature* 299 (1982), 818ff.

8
W. Wickler, "Ursprung und biologische Deutung des Genitalpraesentierens männlicher Primaten," *Zeitschrift für Tierpsychologie* 23 (1966), 422ff.; idem, "Socio-Sexual Signals and Their Intraspecific Imitation among Primates," in *Primate Ethology*, ed. Desmond Morris (Chicago, 1969), 89ff.

9
Ernst Mayr, "Sexual Selection and Natural Selection," in Bernard G. Campbell, ed., *Sexual Selection and the Descent of Man 1871–1971* (London, 1971), 88.

10
Eberhard, *Sexual Selection*, 12, 65ff. See also R. V.

Short, "Sexual Selection and Its Component Parts, Somatic and Genital Selection, as Illustrated by Man and the Great Apes," *Advances in the Study of Behavior* 9 (1979), 131ff., and Paul A. Johnsgard, *Arena Birds: Sexual Selection and Behavior* (Washington, D.C., 1994). For the diagram see also R. Martin and R. May, "Outward Signs of Breeding," in *Nature* 293 (1981), 7ff.

11
Eberhard, *Sexual Selection*, 72ff.

12
J. M. Diamond, "Borrowed Sexual Ornaments," *Nature* 349 (1991), 105ff. A. F. Dixson, "Observations on the Evolution of the Genitalia and Copulatory Behaviour in Male Primates," *Journal of Zoology* 213 (1978), 423ff., shows that penises in social systems where females have more than one partner are longer and more complex, and the baculum (penis bone) is longer when intromission lasts beyond the moment of ejaculation. See also A. H. Harcourt, P. H. Harvey, S. G. Larson, and R. V. Short, "Testis Weight, Body Weight, and Breeding Systems in Primates," *Nature* 293 (1981), 55ff.; M. Kirkpatrick, "Is Bigger Always Better?," *Nature* 337 (1989), 116ff.

13
Short, "Sexual Selection," 131ff.

14
Wickler, "Socio-Sexual Signals," 69ff.

15
J. H. Crook, "Sexual Selection, Dimorphism, and Social Organization in the Primates," in Campbell, *Sexual Selection and the Descent of Man, 1871–1971*, 231ff. Randy Thornhill, a leading expert on sexual selection and sperm competition, points out to me that these features in colobi may simply constitute handicaps (displays whose riskiness expresses greater ultimate fitness) for both sexes.

16
For Michael Ghiselin's interpretation of the law of battle as the "copulatory imperative of male combat" (a form of capitalism), see his *Economy of Nature and the Evolution of Sex* (Berkeley, 1974), 138ff.

17
Richard Dawkins, *The Selfish Gene* (Oxford, 1976). For sperm competition see Robert L. Smith, ed., *Sperm Competition and the Evolution of Animal Mating Systems* (Orlando, 1984), and T. R. Birkhead, *Sperm Competition in Birds: Evolutionary Causes and Consequences* (London, 1992), both with earlier bibliography. For the dawn chorus, see Birkhead, 172ff.

18
Randy Thornhill, "The Allure of Symmetry," *Natural History*, September 1993, 30ff.

19
Dixson, "Observations."

20
Darwin, *Descent of Man*, 521.

21
Darwin, *Descent of Man*, 586.

22
Judith K. Brown, "A Note on the Division of Labor by Sex," in Sharon W. Tiffany, ed., *Women and Society: An Anthropological Reader* (Montreal, 1979), 36ff.; Peggy Reeves Sanday, *Female Power and Male Dominance: On the Origins of Sexual Inequality* (New York, 1981), 76ff.

23
N. Burley, "Sex Ratio Manipulation and Selection for Attractiveness," *Science* 211 (1981), 721ff.

24
A. P. Møller, "Female Choice Selects for Male Sexual Tail Ornaments in the Monogamous Swallow," *Nature* 332 (1988), 640ff.

25
J. Höglund, M. Eriksson, and L. E. Lindell, "Females of the Lek-Breeding Great Snipe, *Gallinago media*, Prefer Males with White Tails," *Animal Behaviour* 40 (1990), 23ff.

26
Anne Hollander, *Seeing through Clothes* (New York, 1978), especially the brilliant chapter 1, "Drapery."

27
For codpieces: K. G. Heider, "Attributes and Categories in the Study of Material Culture: New Guinea Dani Attire," *Man* 4 (1969), 379ff.; and Wickler, "Ursprung" and "Socio-Sexual Signals."

28
Charles McCorquedale, *Bronzino* (New York, 1981), 139ff. For details about Ludovico's romance and marriage see L. Becherucci, "Per un ritratto di Bronzino," *Studi in onore di Matteo Marangoni* (Florence, 1957), 203ff., with earlier bibliography; also F. Angiolini, *Dizionario biografico degli italiani* (Rome, 1976), s.v.

29
Joseph Braun, S.J., *Die liturgische Gewandung im Occident und Orient . . .* (Freiburg im Breisgau, 1907), 424ff.

30
Francis Galton, *Inquiries into Human Faculty and Its Development* (New York, 1883), 180.

31
Darwin, *Descent of Man*, 588, 621.

32
For the genesis of the modern man's suit see Anne Hollander, *Sex and Suits* (New York, 1994), esp. 63ff.

33
Darwin, *Selection*, 642. In a similar vein, and having looked at much more recent data, C. Owen Lovejoy concludes: "Evidence provided by the fossil record, primate behavior, and demographic analysis shows that . . . the unique sexual and reproductive behavior of man may be the sine qua non of human origin." "The Origin of Man," *Science* 211 (1981), 341 (summary).

2

Incarnate Christs and Selectable Saints

1
Françoise Bardon, "Le thème de la Madeleine pénitente au XVIIème siècle en France," *Journal of the Warburg and Courtauld Institutes* 31 (1968), 274ff.; see n. 29 below. Bardon quotes many similar examples devoted to Magdalens by Le Brun, Vouet, and others.

2
Leo Steinberg, *The Sexuality of Christ in Renaissance Art and in Modern Oblivion* (New York, 1983).

3
Stefano De Fiores and Salvatore Meo, eds., *Nuovo dizionario di mariologia* (Milan, 1986), 687.

4
Cited in Bernard Aikema, "Titian's Mary Magdalen in Palazzo Pitti: An Ambiguous Painting and Its Critics," *Journal of the Warburg and Courtauld Institutes* 57 (1994), 48ff., esp. 54.

5
See also Steinberg, *Sexuality of Christ*, 89.

6
H. Herter, *De Priapo,* Religionsgeschichtliche Versuche und Vorarbeiten, 23 (Giessen, 1932); H. D. Rankin, "Petronius, Priapus, and the Priapeum LXVIII," *Classica et Mediaevalia* 27 (1966), 125ff.

7
Hippolytus, *Refutatio omnium haeresium*, ed. P. Wedland (Leipzig, 1916), 5.26, 32.

8
Roberto Bellarmino, *Opera omnia* (1617ff.; rpt. Naples, 1856–1862), 6:228.

9
Timothy G. Verdon, introduction, in Verdon, ed., *Monasticism and the Arts* (Syracuse, 1984), 2.

10
De Fiores and Meo, *Nuovo dizionario*, 958.

11
De Fiores and Meo, *Nuovo dizionario*, 961, quoting Max Scheler. For Scheler on Christian reproductive goals, see M. Scheler, "Vorbilder und Führer," in *Schriften aus dem Nachlass* (Bern, 1979), 1:255ff.

12
Alan of Lille, *The Art of Preaching (Ars Praedicandi)* (Kalamazoo, Mich., 1981).

13
Wolfgang Beinert and Heinrich Petri, eds., *Handbuch der Marienkunde* (Regensburg, 1984). See also De Fiores and Meo, *Nuovo dizionario*, s.v. "Immacolata"; also René Laurentin, *Court traité sur la Vierge Marie*, trans. Charles Neumann as *A Short Treatise on the Virgin Mary* (Washington, N.J., 1991), esp. 68ff., 106ff., 184ff.; Suzanne L. Stratton, *The Immaculate Conception in Spanish Art* (Cambridge, 1994); Kathleen Ashley and Pamela Sheincorn, eds., *Interpreting Cultural Symbols: Saint Anne in Late Medieval Society* (Athens, Ga., 1990); and Michael P. Carroll, *The Cult of the Virgin Mary: Psychological Origins* (Princeton, 1986).

14
For a biologist's thought on the subject, see A. Mitterer, *Dogma und Biologie der heiligen Familie* (Vienna, 1952). He holds that Christ was born in the normal way but without the sexual act. There was a flurry of controversy at this. In 1960 the Holy Office prohibited Catholics from writing on the subject; see De Fiores and Meo, *Nuovo dizionario*, 1419, and bibliography, 1469ff.

15
Eadmer, *Tractatus de conceptione sanctae Mariae* (c1134); *Patrologia Latina* 159:305. Cf. also Franz von Retz (d. 1425), *Defensorium inviolatae virginitatis Mariae* (facsimile, Weimar, 1910). This author argues that Danaë (whom he calls Diana!) was made pregnant by a rain of gold, so why not Mary by something similar? Eagles, vines, and other organisms, he adds, are said to reproduce by virgin birth. The point was reinforced by the age-old belief that bees were capable of parthenogenesis. The *Physiologus*, a late Greek treatise on animals, cites cases in which a female's eggs have been fertilized by the male's breath. If so, says Franz, why not the Virgin by the very breath with which Gabriel utters his speech?

16
Clearly this belief in the fetus's sinfulness might have reinforced the belief that it is somehow less human than would be a baptized newborn. Thus do these matters rather unexpectedly tie into the abortion controversy.

17
De Fiores and Meo, *Nuovo dizionario*, 687.

18
J.-C. Brousolle, *Etudes sur la sainte Vierge*, vol. 1, *De la conception immaculée à l'annonciation angélique* (Paris, 1908); Dom Gaston Dimaret, *Marie de qui est né Jésus* (Paris, 1937–1939).

19
Léon Maxe-Werly, *Iconographie de l'immaculée conception* (Paris, 1903).

20
Louis Réau, *Iconographie de l'art chrétien* (Paris, 1957), 2.2:75ff.

21
The Authorized Version shamelessly bowdlerizes here and elsewhere. In Song 1.3 it is not her breasts but her love that is better than wine. And in 5.4 the *foramen* is "the hole of the door" of their room, not the woman's vagina.

22
Anna Jameson, *Legends of the Madonna as Represented in the Fine Arts* (London, 1852), xix.

23
Jameson, *Legends of the Madonna*, xxff.

24
Gianfranco Ravasi, ". . . Kî Tôb: 'Dio vide che era bello!'" in T. Verdon, ed., *L'Arte e la Bibbia: Immagine come esegesi biblica*, Atti del Convegno internazionale di studi l'Arte e la Bibbia, Venice, 14–16 October 1988 (Bergamo, 1992), 48.

25
W. Ludwig, *Das Rechts-Links Problem im Tierreich und beim Menschen* (Berlin, 1932); Randy Thornhill, Stephen W. Gangestad, and Randall Comer, "Human Female Orgasm and Mate Fluctuating Asymmetry," *Animal Behaviour* (in press).

26
Randy Thornhill, "The Allure of Symmetry," *Natural History*, September 1993, 30ff.

27
Randy Thornhill, personal communication. I should add that in Thornhill's articles cheekbone symmetry is also measured, and also sometimes the distance between the pupils of the eyes. See Karl Grammer and Randy Thornhill, "Human (Homo sapiens) Facial Attractiveness and Sexual Selection: The Role of Symmetry and Averageness," *Journal of Comparative Psychology* 108 (1994), 233ff.; Randy Thornhill and Steven W. Gangestad, "Human Fluctuating Asymmetry and Sexual Behavior," *Biological Abstracts* 97.8 (1994), 21ff.; A. R. Palmer and C. Strobeck, "Fluctuating Asymmetry: Measurement, Analysis, and Patterns," *Annual Review of Ecology and Systematics* 17 (1986), 391ff.; P. J. Watson and R. Thornhill, "Fluctuating Asymmetry and Sexual Selection," *Trends in Ecology and Evolution* 9 (1994), 21ff.

28
Anna Jameson, *Sacred and Legendary Art* (London, 1870), 349 n.

29
The sonnet is quoted in Bardon, "La Madeleine Pénitente," 282; she quotes many similar examples devoted to Magdalens by Le Brun, Vouet, and others.

30
Cesare Baronius, *Annales ecclesiastici* (Antwerp, 1727), vol. 1, ann. 35, ch. 5. Réau, *Iconographie*, part 3, 2:942; Carolus Stengelius, *Sanctae Mariae Magdalenae vitae historia* (Ingolstadt, 1622), 219, 315ff.; Claude Cortez, O.P., *Vie de sainte Marie-Madeleine*, 3rd ed. (Aix, 1643), 85ff.; Adrien Baillet, *Les Vies des saints* (Paris, 1701), sub fasto; and Susan Haskins, *Mary Magdalen: Myth and Metaphor* (London, 1994).

31
Marjorie M. Malvern, *Venus in Sackcloth: The*

Magdalen's Origins and Metamorphoses (Carbondale, Ill., 1975), 57ff., 89ff. For the Renaissance, see Monika Ingenhoff-Danhäuser, *Maria Magdalena: Heilige und Sünderin in der italienischen Renaissance* (Tübingen, 1984), esp. 44ff. More significant for the points raised here is Aikema, "Titian's Mary Magdalen."

32
The picture was painted for the Donne Convertite della Maddalena, former prostitutes; see Luigi Salerno, *I dipinti del Guercino* (Rome, 1988), no. 88.

33
William James, *The Varieties of Religious Experience* (1902; rpt. New York, 1987), 316.

34
Giorgio Vasari, *Le vite dei più eccellenti pittori, scultori, ed architettori*, ed. Rosanna Bettarini and Paola Barocchi (Florence, 1966–), 3:574.

35
Jameson, *Legends of the Madonna*, xxxiii.

36
For discussions, see J. J. Pollitt, *The Ancient View of Greek Art* (Cambridge, 1974), 173ff.

37
Vasari, *Le vite*, 2:312.

38
Vasari, *Le vite*, 2:303.

39
Vasari, *Le vite*, 5:28.

40
Vasari, *Le vite*, 5:33.

41
Richard E. Spear, *Domenichino* (New Haven, 1982), text vol., 23.

3

Body Canons

1
Herbert Oppel, "ΚΑΝΩΝ: Zur Bedeutungs-geschichte des Wortes und zeiner Lateinischen Entsprechungen (*regula-norma*)," *Philologus*, suppl. 30.4 (1937), 14ff. For the κανῶν or *regula* in architecture, see 78ff.

2
For the figure canons in Egyptian art, which conditioned those of Greek, see Whitney Davis, *The Canonical Tradition in Ancient Egyptian Art* (Cambridge, 1989). See also Gay Robins, *Proportion and Style in Ancient Egyptian Art* (Austin, Tex., 1994); Heinrich Schäfer, *Principles of Egyptian Art*, 4th ed., ed. Emma Brunner-Traut (Oxford, 1974), 277ff.; and Erwin Panofsky, "The History of the Theory of Human Proportions as a Reflection of the History of Styles," *Meaning in the Visual Arts* (New York, 1955), 55ff.

3
See J. J. Pollitt, *The Ancient View of Greek Art* (Cambridge, 1974), 14ff. See also J. E. Raven, "Polyclitus and Pythagoreanism," *Classical Quarterly* 45 (1951), 147ff.; H. von Steuben, *Der Kanon des Polyklet: Doryphoros und Amazon* (Tübingen, 1973); Andrew Stewart, "The Canon of Polykleitos: A Question of Evidence," *Journal of Hellenic Studies* 98 (1978), 122ff., with a full bibliography. For the most recent ideas, see the 1990 exhibition catalog *Polyklet: Der Bildhauer der griechischen Klassik* Liebieghaus Museum alter Plastik, Frankfurt-am-Main (Mainz-am-Rhein, 1990): see especially the articles by Norbert Kaiser, "Schriftquellen zu Polyklet," 48ff.; Hanna Philipp, "Zu Polyklets Schrift 'Kanon,'" 135ff.; Ernst Berger, "Zum Kanon des Polyklet," 156ff., which gives detailed analyses of the proportional system of the Doryphoros; Hans von Steuben, "Der Doryphoros," 185ff., and cat. 41–58; and Renate Bol, "Die Amazone des Polyklet," 213ff., and cat. 82–102.

4
Von Steuben, *Der Kanon*, 31ff. For the Naples statue, see also Andrew Stewart, *Greek Sculpture* (New Haven, 1990), 1:68ff., where the canons of Vitruvius and Leonardo are also discussed; and for the quesion in general, see Joseph Rykwert, *The Dancing Column: On the Orders of Architecture* (Cambridge, Mass., 1996).

5
Martin Robertson, *A History of Greek Art* (Cambridge, 1975), 1:328ff.

6
See George L. Hersey and Richard Freedman, *Possible Palladian Villas (Plus Some Instructively Impossible Ones)* (Cambridge, Mass., 1992), chapter 1.

7
Galen, *Ars medica* (*De usu partium corporis humani* 2.441), quoted by Robertson, *Greek Art*, 1:328ff.; idem, *De placitis Hippocratis et Platonis* 5.

8
Quintilian 12.10, 7–9; R. Bianchi Bandinelli, *Policleto* (Florence, 1938), nos. 21, 23.

9
Plutarch, *Moralia* 45*C–D* on Polykleitos's canon. See also Aristotle, *Physics* Γ 4, 203–210 (DK 58 B 28).

10
Robertson, *Greek Art*, 1:329ff.; Bianchi Bandinelli, *Policleto*, passim.

11
Stewart, *Greek Sculpture*, 1:162ff., 262, 264ff.

12
Robertson, *Greek Art*, 1:391. For kouroi and korai, see G. M. A. Richter, *Kouroi*, 3rd ed. (London, 1970), and idem, *Korai* (London, 1968).

13
Robertson, *Greek Art*, 1:391; Antonio Corso, *Prassitele: Fonti epigrafiche e letterarie, vita e opere* (Rome, 1988–1990); Stewart, *Greek Sculpture*, 1:176ff.

14
For Polykleitos and Vitruvius, see Frank Zöllner, *Vitruvs Proportionsfigur* (Worms, 1987), with earlier bibliography.

15
Stewart, "The Canon of Polykleitos," 130.

16
Raven, "Polyclitus and Pythagoreanism."

17
L. B. Alberti, *"On Painting and on Sculpture": The Latin Texts of "De pictura" and "De statua,"* ed. and trans. Cecil Grayson (London, 1972); *De statua*, 133ff.

18
Jane Andrews Aiken, "Leon Battista Alberti's System of Proportions," *Journal of the Warburg and Courtauld Institutes* 42 (1980), 68ff., and Gustina Scaglia, "Instruments Perfected for Measurements of Man and Statues Illustrated in Leon Battista Alberti's *De statua*," *Nuncia: Annali di storia della scienza* 8 (1993), 555ff.

19
Scaglia, "Instruments," figs. 5, 6; Cosimo Bartoli, *Opuscoli morali* (1568).

20
In his text Alberti has only two measurements in common with those given by Vitruvius, the Doryphoros, and Leonardo: foot length and throat-to-crown, both as 1/6 of the total height.

21
Vitruvius's other measurement—of the face into horizontal thirds marked by chin, nose base, eyes, and top of forehead—is observed in all four physiques, so there is no point in including them in the tables.

22
I repeat that this statue type was almost certainly unknown to Alberti, at least as representing the famous Polykleitan work; and this makes me think that Alberti may have been privy to antique formulas other than Vitruvius's.

23
The claim is made by Erwin Panofsky, *The Life and Art of Albrecht Dürer* (Princeton, 1955), 261ff.

24
Panofsky, *Dürer*, 263. For more on Dürer's theories, see Ludwig Justi, *Konstruierte Figuren und Köpfe unter den Werken Albrecht Dürers* (Leipzig, 1902); Panofsky, "Theory of Human Proportions"; and J. Giesen, *Dürers Proportionstudien im Rahmen der allgemeinen Proportionsentwicklung* (Bonn, 1930).

25
See Jean Julia Chai, *Gian Paolo Lomazzo and the Art of Expression* (Ann Arbor, Mich., 1990), with earlier bibliography. Lomazzo's *Trattato dell'arte de la pittura* was first published in Milan in 1584.

26
Another aspect of Renaissance body measurement lies first in the revival, and then the overthrow, of the classical anatomical tradition. The human body that had been described by Hippocrates and Galen was transformed and modernized in the sixteenth and seventeenth centuries—sometimes in the face of considerable ideological opposition. Both Leonardo and Michelangelo, meanwhile, contemplated creating their own anatomical treatises, and Leonardo made a large number of drawings for such a work. See Bernard Schultz, *Art and Anatomy in Renaissance Italy* (Ann Arbor, Mich., 1985), 25.

27
David R. Hay, *The Natural Principles of Beauty in the Human Figure* (London and Edinburgh, 1852).

28
William Wetmore Story, *The Proportions of the Human Figure, According to a New Canon, for Practical Use; with a Critical Notice of the Canon of Polycletus, and of the Principal Ancient and Modern Systems* (London, 1864).

29
Story, *Proportions*, preface.

30
Mary Cowling, *The Artist as Anthropologist: The Representation of Type and Character in Victorian Art* (Cambridge, 1989), lists and analyzes the main authorities on this subject who were known in the nineteenth century. See also Gottfried Schadow, *Polyclet oder von den Maassen des Menschen, nach dem Geschlechte und Alter mit Angabe der wirklichen Naturgrösse* (Berlin, 1834), published in English as *The Sculptor and Student's Guide to the Proportions of the Human Form*, trans. James J. Wright (London, 1883), which discusses Polykleitos's, Leonardo's, Dürer's, and Gérard de Lairesse's proportional teachings in relation to "national physiognomies"; also David R. Hay, *On the Science of those Proportions by which the Human Head and Countenance as represented in Works of Ancient Greek Art are Distinguished from those of Ordinary Nature* (London and Edinburgh, 1849). See also Petrus Camper, *Vorlesungen . . . über die bewunderswürdige Ähnlichkeit im Bau des Menschen, der vierfüssigen Thiere . . .* (Berlin, 1793). In his text Camper derives much of his anthropometric data from works of art.

31
William Wetmore Story, *Conversations in a Studio* (Boston and New York, 1890), 2:481, 483. The squaring of the circle consists of constructing a square with the same area as that of a given circle, using straightedge and compass only. It is apparently impossible.

4

Aryans and Semites

1
See Doris Mendlewitsch, *Volk und Heil: Vordenker des Nationalsozialismus im 19. Jahrhundert* (Bielefeld, 1988), 18ff. For Aryanism generally see Martin Bernal, *Black Athena: The Afroasiatic Roots of Classical Civilization*, vol. 1, *The Fabrication of Ancient Greece, 1785–1985* (New Brunswick, N.J., 1987), 239ff.; also Thomas W. Thompson, *James Anthony Froude on Nation and Empire* (New York and London, 1987), 15ff.; Léon Poliakov, *The Aryan Myth: A History of Racist and Nationalist Ideas in Europe* (New York, 1971). For Houston Stewart Chamberlain see, especially, his *Arische Weltanschauung* (Berlin, 1905), and Fritz Stern, *The Politics of Cultural Despair: A Study in the Rise of Germanic Ideology* (1961; rpt. New York, 1965).

2
Madhar M. Deshpande and Peter Edwin Hooke, eds., *Aryan and Non-Aryan in India* (Ann Arbor, Mich., 1979); see especially A. L. Basham, "Aryan and Non-Aryan in Southeast Asia," 1ff. See also Ramesh Chandra Majundar, *Expansion of Aryan Culture in Eastern India* (Imphal, 1968).

3
Sir John Muir, *Original Sanskrit Texts on the Origin and History of the People of India: the Vedas . . .*, 2nd ed. (London, 1871), 1:174ff., 2:213ff., 267ff.; idem, *The Hymns of the Rig Veda* (London, 1873).

4
Joseph Arthur de Gobineau, *Essai sur l'inégalité des races humaines* (1853; rpt. Paris, 1967), 328ff., 481.

5
Ernst Curtius (1814–1896), not to be confused with the later historian, Ernst Robert Curtius (1886–1956), author of *European Literature in the Latin Middle Ages*. For the continuum between Ernst Curtius's generation and the Nazis, see Peter Weingart, Jürgen Kroll, and Kurt Bayertz, *Rasse, Blut und Gene: Geschichte der Eugenik und Rassenhygiene in Deutschland* (Frankfurt am Main, 1988), 98ff.

6
Quoted as in Bernal, *Black Athena*, 1:334–335.

7
Curtius, *Griechische Geschichte* (Berlin, 1857–1867), 1:24ff. Much of this is very close to Johann Joachim Winckelmann, *Gedanken über der griechischen Werke in der Malerei und Bildhauerkunst* (1755). See the text and translation, *Reflections on the Imitation of Greek Works in Painting and Sculpture*, by Elfriede Heyer and Roger C. Norton (La Salle, Ill., 1987).

8
His upper skull was greatly elongated and squill-shaped (Plutarch, *Pericles* 3). Cf. Robert Garland, *The Eye of the Beholder: Deformity and Disability in the Graeco-Roman World* (Ithaca, N.Y., 1995), 111.

9
Curtius, *Geschichte*, 1:25. For recent views on eugenics in ancient Greece, see Andros Loizon and Henry Lesser, eds., *Polis and Politics: Essays in Greek Moral and Political Philosophy* (Aldershot, 1990), especially Ruth Chadwick, "Feminism and Eugenics: The Politics of Reproduction in Plato's Republic," 101ff.

10
Gotthold Ephraim Lessing, *Laocoön*, trans. Ellen Frothingame (New York, 1957), 10ff.

11
Frederic Leighton, *Addresses Delivered to the Students of the Royal Academy by the Late Lord Leighton*, 2nd ed. (London, 1897). This work will hereafter be cited parenthetically in the text.

12
Gobineau, *Essai*, 326.

13
Gobineau, *Essai*, 158, 159n, 160.

14
See Nirad C. Chaudhuri, *Scholar Extraordinary: The Life of Professor the Rt. Hon. Friedrich Max Müller P.C.* (London, 1974), 313ff.

15
See Thomas Thompson, *James Anthony Froude on Nation and Empire: A Study in Victorian Racialism* (New York, 1987), 15ff.

16
These Sanskrit texts were part of a larger series edited by Müller, published under the general title *The Sacred Books of the East*.

17
Georg Bühler, *Sacred Laws of the Aryas*, part 1 (1879; rpt. Oxford, 1969), 11.

18
Bühler, *Aryas*, part 1, 102.

19
Matthew Arnold, *Culture and Anarchy* (1869; rpt. New York, 1908), 111ff.

20
This and subsequent quotations from Arnold, *Culture and Anarchy*, 124.

21
Emile Bournouf, *La Science des religions* (Paris, 1872).

22
Quoted by Frederic E. Faverty, *Matthew Arnold the Ethnologist* (Evanston, Ill., 1951), 171, from Arnold's essay "Literature and Dogma"; this is Arnold's translation of Bournouf.

23
See also Annemarie De Waal Malefijt, *Images of Man: A History of Anthropological Thought* (New York, 1974), with bibliography.

24
Friedrich Engels, *The Origin of the Family, Private Property, and the State in the Light of the Researches of Lewis H. Morgan,* ed. Eleanor Burke Clark (1884; rpt. New York, 1972), 91, 166.

25
In Thomas Henry Huxley, *Evidence as to Man's Place in Nature* (London, 1863); there were many later editions.

26
Huxley, *Man's Place*, 160.

27
For continuities from this period onward, see Paul Weindling, *Health, Race, and German Politics between National Unification and Nazism, 1870–1945* (Cambridge, 1989).

28
Huxley, *Man's Place*, 162.

29
Charles Wentworth Dilke, *Greater Britain* (Philadelphia, 1869), 346ff.

30
Leonée and Richard Ormond, *Lord Leighton* (London, 1975), with earlier bibliography. Dilke was a member of Leighton's circle, especially through his wife, the former Emilia Pattison (see 72ff.).

31
Gaston Phoebus is a portrait of Leighton, though the name belongs to a fifteenth-century Gascon knight. Leighton also appears as Lord Mellifont in Henry James's story "The Private Life."

32
Benjamin Disraeli, *Lothair*, ed. Vernon Bogdanor (1870; rpt. London, 1975).

33
Disraeli, *Lothair*, 105.

34
Ronald Pearsall, *Tell Me, Pretty Maiden: The Victorian and Edwardian Nude* (Exeter, 1981); Christopher Wood, *Olympian Dreamers: Victorian Classical Painters, 1860–1914* (London, 1983).

35
Disraeli, *Lothair*, 105.

36
Ormond and Ormond, *Leighton*, cat. 350 (Tate Gallery, London, on loan to Leighton House). The Ormonds note the derivation from the Aphrodite Callipygos.

37
Francis Haskell and Nicholas Penny, *Taste and the Antique: The Lure of Classical Sculpture, 1500–1900* (New Haven, 1981), 317. Athenaeus, *Deipnosophistae* 12.554; Martin Robertson, *A History of Greek Art* (Cambridge, 1975), 1:553; Theodor Kraus, *Die Aphrodite von Knidos* (Bremen, 1957); Gösta Säfflund, *Aphrodite Kallipygos* (Stockholm, 1963).

38
Haskell and Penny, *Taste and the Antique*, 317; Athenaeus, *Deipnosophistae*, 12.554.

39
This thought, I will add, comes amiss from an artist whose reputation was made with a picture entitled *Cimabue's Madonna Is Carried in Procession through the Streets of Florence* (1853–1855; Royal Collection). The painting Leighton portrays was made in 1285 for Santa Maria Novella and is now in the Uffizi. Vasari is the source of this story but the picture, known as the Rucellai Madonna, is in fact not by Cimabue but by Duccio of Siena. See Giovanna Ragionieri, *Duccio: Catalogo dei dipinti* (Florence, 1989), no. 3.

40
Ormond and Ormond, *Leighton*, cat. 388.

41
W. H. Roscher, *Ausführliches Lexikon der Griechischen und Römischen Mythologie* (Leipzig, 1902–1909), 3.2, col. 1155ff.

42
Roscher, *Lexikon*, 2.2, col. 1924.

43
Something else in the Leda image that has been corrected is Michelangelo's (or his copyist's) faulty foreshortening of Leda's right lower leg.

44
Disraeli, *Lothair*, 103.

45
Henry James, *William Wetmore Story and His Friends* (1903; rpt. New York, 1957), 1:33, 2:75ff.

46
William Wetmore Story, *Poems* (Boston, 1886), 133.

47
James, *Story*, 2:72. For the Cleopatra and the Sibyl, see also Mary E. Phillips, *Reminiscences of William Wetmore Story* (Chicago and New York, 1897), 130ff.

48
James, *Story*, 2:78ff.

49
Quoted by Haskell and Penny, *Taste and the Antique*, 134.

50
Disraeli, *Lothair*, 105.

51
Another version was on the art market in Christie's London sale of 4 November 1982.

52
Nathaniel Hawthorne, *The Marble Faun* (1859; rpt. New York, 1961), chap. 14, 97.

53
I describe the Metropolitan version, 1861 (1979.266). Another version is now in the National Gallery, Washington, D.C.

54
James, *Story*, 2:70ff.

55
Quoted by James, *Story*, 2:71.

56
The crossed legs, according to Story's friend Harriet Beecher Stowe, are a sign of secrecy and of the power to bind. See Harriet Beecher Stowe, "Sojourner Truth, the Libyan Sibyl," *Atlantic Monthly* 11 (1863), esp. 480ff., which claims that Story's statue was inspired by Stowe's account of the famous African-American preacher.

5

More Body Prescribers

1
Michel Feher, Ramona Naddaff, and Nadia Tazi, eds., *Fragments for a History of the Human Body*, 3 vols. (New York, 1989), gives an idea of the extent of the literature. Stephen Kern, *Anatomy and Destiny: A Cultural History of the Human Body* (Indianapolis, 1975), deals mainly

with the nineteenth century. J. G. Schadow, *Polyclet oder von den Maassen des Menschen, nach dem Geschlechte und Alter mit Angabe der wirklichen Naturgrösse* (Berlin, 1834); Johann Ludwig L. Choulant, *Geschichte und Bibliographie der anatomischen Abbildungen* (Leipzig, 1852), trans. Mortimer Frank as *History and Bibliography and the Relation to Anatomic Science and the Graphic Arts*, with essays by others (New York, 1945); Adolf Quetelet, *Anthropométrie ou mésure des différentes facultés de l'homme* (Brussels, 1871); C. A. Roberts, *A Manual of Anthropometry* (London, 1878); and P. Topinard, *Eléments d'anthropologie générale* (Paris, 1885), are essential *points d'appui* in an enormous literature. Quetelet is particularly important (a) because he studies proportions, not absolute dimensions, and (b) because he has numerous tables comparing contemporary physiques with those depicted in art.

2
For Le Brun see J. Baltrusaitis, *Aberrations: Essai sur la légende des Formes* (Paris, 1983). For J. C. Lavater, see his *Fragmente—Physiognomische Fragmente, zur Beförderung der Menschenkenntniss und Menchenliebe*, 4 vols. (Leipzig, 1775–1778; facsimile Zurich, 1968); idem, *Essai sur la Physiognomie destinée à faire connoître l'homme et à le faire aimer*, 4 vols. (The Hague, 1781–1801); and Joan K. Stemmler, "The Physiognomical Portraits of Johann Caspar Lavater," *Art Bulletin* 75 (1993), 151ff., with earlier bibliography. See also Barbara Maria Stafford, *Body Criticism: Imaging the Unseen in Enlightenment Art and Medicine* (Cambridge, Mass., 1991), whose chapter on internal anatomy (47ff.) forms a brilliant counterpart to the subjects I here more leadenly discuss. For discussion and recent bibliography on phrenology, see Philippe Sorel, "La Phrénologie et l'art," in Jean Clair, ed., *L'Ame au corps: arts et sciences 1793–1993* (Paris, 1994), 266ff.

3
As quoted by Stemmler, "Physiognomical Portraits," 159.

4
Karl Pearson, *The Life, Letters, and Labours of Francis Galton* (Cambridge, 1914–1930), 3a; 279ff.

5
As quoted by Stemmler, "Physiognomical Portraits," 157.

6
Francis Darwin, ed., *Charles Darwin's Autobiography* (New York, 1950), 36.

7
Paul Weindling, *Health, Race, and German Politics between National Unification and Nazism, 1870–1945* (Cambridge, 1989), 49. For Rudolf Virchow, see his *Collected Essays on Public Health and Epidemiology*, ed. L. J. Rather (Canton, Mass., 1985); idem, *Disease, Life, and Man* (Stanford, Calif., 1958); L. J. Rather, *A Commentary on the Medical Writings of Rudolf Virchow* (San Francisco, 1990).

8
Charles Goring, *The English Convict: A Statistical Study* (London, 1913).

9
Weindling, *Health*, 99.

10
Tönnies, "Ammons Gesellschaftstheorie," *Archiv für Sozialwissenschaft und Sozialpolitik*, 19 [n.s., 1] (1904), 53, 54, 110.

11
Weindling, *Health*, 100. See also Otto Ammon, *Die Gesellschaftsordnung und ihre natürlichen Grundlagen*, 2nd ed. (Jena, 1896), 59ff.; F. Tönnies, "Ammons Gesellchaftstheorie," 88ff.

12
Ernst Kretschmer, *Geniale Menschen*, 2nd ed. (Berlin, 1931); *Die Personlichkeit der athletiker* (Leipzig, 1936); *Körperbau und Charakter*, new ed. (Berlin, 1944). An earlier edition of *Körperbau und Charakter* was translated by E. Miller as *Physique and Character*, 2nd rev. ed. (London, 1936); Miller himself wrote *Types of Mind and Body* (London, 1927) and *Psychology of Men of Genius* (New York, 1931). This edition of *Physique and Character* has a useful appendix, by Miller, on work in anthropometry and constitutional psychology from 1925 to 1936.

13
Kretschmer, *Physique and Character*, 80.

14
Kretschmer, *Geniale Menschen*.

15
N. Pende, *Constitutional Inadequacies* (Philadelphia, 1928).

16
G. Viola, "L'habitus phthisicus et l'habitus apoplecticus comme conséquence d'une loi qui déforme normalement le type moyen de la race en ces deux types antithétiques," *Comptes rendus de l'association des*

anatomistes (Turin, 1925); idem, *La costituzione individuale* (Bologna, 1933); idem, "Il mio metodo di valutazione della costituzione individuale," *Riforma medicale* 51 (1935), 1635ff.; A. Di Giovanni, *Clinical Commentaries Deduced from the Morphology of the Human Body* (London and New York, 1919). Cf. S. Naccarati, "The Morphologic Aspect of Intelligence," *Archives of Psychology*, no. 45 (August 1921).

17
This work is discussed, with bibliography, in W. H. Sheldon, with S. S. Stevens and B. B. Tucker, *Varieties of Human Physique: An Introduction to Constitutional Psychology* (New York, 1940), 10ff. For Sheldon's career, see J. E. Lindsay Carter and Barbara Honeyman Heath, *Somatotyping—Development and Applications* (Cambridge, 1990), 3ff.

18
Sheldon, *Human Physique*, 15. See Naccarati, "Morphologic Aspect," 25, where the morphologic index is defined as the degree to which the subject's physique partakes of three bodily types: microsplachnic, macrosplachnic, and normosplachnic—measures of small, large, and normal trunks. The index number is produced by dividing the total length of arm plus leg by the volume of the trunk.

19
Mark H. Haller, *Eugenics: Hereditarian Attitudes in American Thought* (New Brunswick, N.J., 1963), 142. Robert C. Bannister, *Social Darwinism: Science and Myth in Anglo-American Social Thought* (Philadelphia, 1979); Richard Hofstadter, *Social Darwinism and American Thought* (Philadelphia, 1944). For Hooton, see Jonathan Marks, *Human Biodiversity: Genes, Race, and History* (New York, 1995), 99ff.; also Annemarie De Waal Malefijt, *Images of Man: A History of Anthropological Thought* (New York, 1974), 215ff., 261ff.

20
Haller, *Eugenics*, 73.

21
In the years just before World War II, Hooton began addressing a wider audience. Taking his cue from his early book *Up from the Ape* (1931), he produced a series of witty popular works: *Apes, Men, and Morons* (1937), *The Twilight of Man* (1939), and *Why Men Behave Like Apes and Vice Versa* (1940).

22
Earnest A. Hooton, *The American Criminal*, vol. 1, *The Native White Criminal of Native Parentage* (Cambridge, 1939), 301. No further volumes were published.

23
Hooton, *American Criminal*, 1:197ff.

24
Hooton, *American Criminal*, 1:199.

25
Earnest A. Hooton, *Why Men Behave Like Apes and Vice Versa: or, Body and Behavior* (Princeton, 1940), 197.

26
The first person to start doing this, thus rescuing physical anthropology from its earlier oversimplifications, was George Draper in *The Human Constitution* (1924): cf. Hooton, *Why Men Behave Like Apes*, 200.

27
Hooton, *Why Men Behave Like Apes*, 202.

28
See the discussion after Sheldon's paper "The Somatotype, the Morphophenotype, and the Morphogenotype," in *Cold Spring Harbor Symposium on Quantitative Biology* 15 (1950), 378. For more on Sheldon and his followers see Ron Rosenbaum, "The Great Ivy League Nude Posture Photo Scandal," *New York Times Magazine*, 15 January 1995, 26ff.

29
H. Sheldon, with Emil M. Hartl and Eugene McDermott, *Varieties of Delinquent Youth: An Introduction to Constitutional Psychiatry* (New York, 1949), 20.

30
H. Sheldon, *Psychology and the Promethean Will: A Constructive Study of the Acute Common Problem of Education, Medicine, and Religion* (New York, 1936).

31
Sheldon, *Promethean Will*, 81ff., 95ff.

32
Sheldon, *Human Physique*, 7.

33
Sheldon, *Human Physique*, 34ff.

34
Sheldon, *Human Physique*, 40.

35
Sheldon, *Delinquent Youth*, 16.

36
Sheldon, *Delinquent Youth*, 18.

37
Sheldon, *Human Physique*, 47.

38
Sheldon, *Human Physique*, 7, 68ff.

39
Sheldon, *Human Physique*, 71.

40
Sheldon, *Human Physique*, 8.

41
H. Sheldon, *Varieties of Temperament: A Psychology of Constitutional Differences* (New York, 1942), 29off.

42
Sheldon, *Delinquent Youth*, 79off.

43
Sheldon, *Human Physique*, 19off.

44
Sheldon, *Temperament*, 58.

45
Sheldon, *Temperament*, 298.

46
H. Sheldon, *An Atlas of Men* (New York, 1954), 126.

47
Sheldon, *Temperament*, 53.

48
Sheldon, *Temperament*, 56ff.

49
Sheldon, *Delinquent Youth*, 17f.

50
Sheldon's "Neoplatonism" could stem from his admiration for Jung, who wrote on alchemy and whom Sheldon frequently cites. For Sheldon's later influence, see Emil M. Hartl, Edward P. Monnelly, and Roland D. Elderkin, *Physique and Delinquent Behavior: A Thirty-Year Follow-Up of William H. Sheldon's "Varieties of Delinquent Youth"* (New York, 1982); also Carter and Heath, *Somatotyping*, 3ff. and passim, for their developments of the spherical triangle. For current preferences for mesomorphs, see Marc E. Mishkind, Judith Rodin, Lisa R. Silberstein, and Ruth H. Striegel-Moore, "The Embodiment of Masculinity: Cultural, Psychological, and Behavioral Dimensions," *American Behavioral Scientist*, 29 (1986), 545ff.; also Joseph Lyons, *Ecology of the Body: Styles of Behavior in Human Life* (Durham, N.C., 1987). There is much more bibliography on latter-day Sheldonism in C. Peter Herman, "The Shape of Man," *Contemporary Psychology* 37 (1992), 525ff. I thank Ellery Lanier, who is writing a doctoral dissertation on Sheldon, for this latter reference.

6

Galton and Lombroso

1
The classic view, though it comes late in the game, is of course Oswald Spengler, *The Decline of the West* (1918; rpt. New York, 1957), 1:104ff. See also Manfred P. Fleischer, ed., *The Decline of the West?* (New York, 1970), for a useful overview with contributions by Spengler himself, H. R. Trevor-Roper, P. A. Sorokin, Arnold Toynbee, and others. Stephen Jay Gould, *The Mismeasure of Man* (New York, 1981), tells the story well, as does Daniel Pick, *The Faces of Degeneration: A European Disorder, c1848–c1918* (Cambridge, 1989).

2
Cited by Thomas S. Savage, M.D., "Notice of the External Characters and Habits of Troglodytes Gorilla, a New Species of Orang from the Gaboon River," *Boston Journal of Natural History* 5 (December 1847), 417ff. (Today the term *orangutan* is applied only to the ape known as *Pongo pygmaeus* of Borneo and Sumatra.)

3
Bernard Schultz, *Art and Anatomy in Renaissance Italy* (Ann Arbor, Mich., 1985), 25. For Vesalius's moves toward the acceptance of a less ideal, more varied concept of the normal human body see Nancy G. Siraisi, "Vesalius and Human Diversity in *De humani corporis fabrica*," *Journal of the Warburg and Courtauld Institutes* 57 (1994), 60ff., with earlier bibliography.

4
Savage, "New Orang," 420n.

5
Helena Cronin, *The Ant and the Peacock: Altruism and Sexual Selection from Darwin to Today* (Cambridge, 1991), 45; Peter J. Bowler, *The Eclipse of Darwinism: Anti-Darwinian Evolution Theories in the Decades around 1900* (Baltimore, 1983), 141ff.

6
Friedrich Engels, *The Origin of the Family, Private Property, and the State in the Light of the Researches of Lewis H. Morgan*, ed. Eleanor Burke Clarke (1884; rpt. New York, 1972), 252.

7
Quoted in the *New York Times*, 23 May 1994.

8
Peter Rivière, introduction, *Primitive Marriage: An Inquiry into the Origin of the Form of Capture in Marriage Ceremonies*, by John F. McLennan (1865; rpt. Chicago, 1970).

9
Westermarck's observations, made at a public meeting, are cited by Karl Pearson, *The Life, Letters and Labours of Francis Galton* (Cambridge, 1914–1930), 3a:268.

10
Pearson, *Galton*, 2:341. The prettiest girls were in London, the ugliest in Aberdeen.

11
Pearson, *Galton*, 2:283ff.

12
Francis Galton, *Inquiries into Human Faculty and Its Development* (New York, 1883), 6.

13
Galton, *Inquiries*, 8.

14
Some of these things may have occurred naturally in Galton's photographic process. But it seems clear to me that someone has touched up the highlights on the nose, chin, and upper lip of the officer type, thus artificially enhancing both his selectability and his exact similarity to other desirable types.

15
Galton, *Inquiries*, 18.

16
Milo Keynes, ed., *Sir Francis Galton, FRS: The Legacy of His Ideas*, Proceedings of the 27th Annual Symposium of the Galton Institute, London, 1991 (Houndmills, England, 1993). The volume contains updated discussions of many Galton subjects—heredity, statistics, race, genetics, evolution—that are of interest here.

17
Pearson, *Galton*, 2:323ff.

18
Pearson, *Galton*, 3a:279ff.

19
Pearson, *Galton*, 2:323.

20
Pearson, *Galton*, 3a:422.

21
Stephen Pepper, *Guido Reni, l'opera completa* (Novara, 1988), cat. 40, with bibliography.

22
Of all classical authors, so far as I know, only the obscure Quintus Smyrnaeus (*Fall of Troy* 1.50, 2.593) connects the Hours with both Apollo and Aurora, and makes them her companions.

23
See Pindar, frag. 1.394 (Bergk); Callimachus, *Hymn to Apollo*, 80.

24
It is a paradox that Galton made contributions to statistics, one of the bases of modern population genetics, and yet disdained the work of Gregor Mendel, who discovered the existence and action of genes. See Ruth Schwartz Cowan, *Sir Francis Galton and the Study of Heredity in the Nineteenth Century* (New York, 1985).

25
Quoted in Pearson, *Galton*, 3a:260 and n.

26
Charles Darwin, *The Descent of Man and Selection in Relation to Sex* (1871), in *The Works of Charles Darwin*, ed. Paul H. Barrett and R. B. Freeman (London, 1989), 22:643ff. See also Eveleen Richards, "Darwin and the Descent of Woman," in David Oldroyd and Ian Langham, eds., *The Wider Domain of Evolutionary Thought* (Boston, 1983), 58.

27
Pearson, *Galton*, 3a:121.

28
Pearson, *Galton*, 3a:229.

29
Galton, *Inquiries*, 305.

30
Galton, *Inquiries*, 321.

31
Pearson, *Galton*, 3a:375.

32
Pearson, *Galton*, 3a:231. Pearson prints the text of a proposed diploma (292ff.).

33
Richard A. Soloway, *Demography and Degeneration: Eugenics and the Declining Birthrate in Twentieth-Century Britain* (Chapel Hill, N.C., 1990), 66.

34
Francis Galton, *Hereditary Genius* (New York, 1870), xx.

35
Quoted in Pearson, *Galton*, 3a:231.

36
Pearson, *Galton,* 3a:217.

37
R. A. Fisher, "The Evolution of Sexual Preference," *Eugenics Review* 7 (1915), 184ff. More definitively these views reappeared in his *Genetical Theory of Natural Selection* (Oxford, 1930).

38
For Lombroso, see Stephen Jay Gould, *The Mismeasure of Man* (New York, 1981), 113ff., and Pick, *Faces of Degeneration*, 109ff. The standard biography is Luigi Bulferetti, *Cesare Lombroso* (Turin, 1975). See also Delfina Dolza Carrara, *Essere figlie di Lombroso* (Milan, 1990), and Peter Strasser, "Cesare Lombroso: l'homme délinquent ou la bête sauvage au naturel," in *L'Ame au corps: arts et sciences 1793–1993* (Paris, 1994), 352ff. Lombroso is a bibliographer's nightmare. His books were almost all translated into French, German, English, and other languages. Frequently Lombroso, or Lombroso plus a new coauthor, expanded and rewrote the translations.

39
Richard Dawkins, *The Extended Phenotype: The Gene as the Unit of Selection* (Oxford, 1982). Dawkins's basic conception of the person's culture being biologically determined like his or her phenotype (i.e., physique) is remarkably similar to Otto Ammon's notion that craft and art products are biologically comparable to their makers. See F. Tönnies, "Ammons Gesellschaftstheorie," *Archiv für Sozialwissenschaft und Sozialpolitik* 19 [n.s., 1] (1904), 90. It is also similar to the ideas of Kretschmer (see above, chapter 5).

40
Quoted by Gould, *Mismeasure*, 124.

41
Lombroso, *L'Homme criminel* (Paris, 1895), 1:224.

42
Gould, *Mismeasure*, 122ff.

43
Lombroso, *L'Homme criminel*, 1:226.

44
Lombroso, *L'Homme criminel*, 1:xii.

45
Lombroso, *L'Homme criminel*, 1:120.

46
Lombroso, *L'Homme criminel*, 1:26.

47
Lombroso, *Genio e Follia* (Turin, 1882), 6.

48
Lombroso and G. Ferrero, *La donna delinquente* (Turin, 1894), 14. This work will hereafter be cited parenthetically in the text.

49
Erwin Panofsky, *Tomb Sculpture: Four Lectures on Its Changing Aspects from Ancient Egypt to Bernini* (New York), 1964, 80.

50
Lombroso and Ferrero, *La donna delinquente*, 346, with illustration. In calling Messalina a prostitute Lombroso is probably thinking of the notorious incident when the empress, challenged by the number of tricks per twenty-four-hour period a famous prostitute could turn, outdid her rival by fucking twenty-five different partners in the same span of time (Pliny, *Epistulae* 10.192).

51
Lombroso, *L'Homme criminel*, 1:223.

52
Lombroso, *Genio e follia*, 331ff.

53
Lombroso, *Genio e follia*, 126ff.

54
Lombroso, *L'Homme criminel*, 1:317.

55
See Anthea Callen, "Anatomie et physiognomie: 'la Petite Danseuse de quatorze ans,' de Degas," in *L'Ame au corps: arts et sciences 1793–1993* (Paris, 1994), 352ff. Also idem, *The Spectacular Body: Science, Method, and Meaning in the Work of Degas* (New Haven, 1995).

56
For Morelli, see Richard Wollheim, "Giovanni Morelli and the Origins of Scientific Connoisseurship," *On Art and*

the Mind: Essays and Lectures (London, 1974), 177ff.; Henri Zerner, "Morelli et la science de l'art," *Revue de l'art* 40–41 (1978), 209ff.; Donata Levi, "Fortuna di Morelli: appunti sui rapporti fra storiografia artistica tedesca ed inglese," and M. Panzeri and G. O. Bravi, "La figura e l'opera di Giovanni Morelli: Materiali e ricerca," both in *La figura di Giovanni Morelli: studi e ricerche* (Bergamo, 1987), 19ff. and 349ff.; and Jaynie Anderson, "Dietro lo pseudonimo," in *Giovanni Morelli: Della pittura italiana: Studii storico-critici* (Milan, 1991), 491ff. See also two essays in *Giovanni Morelli e la coltura dei conoscitori. Atti del convegno nazionale*, vol. 2 (Bergamo, 1993): Richard Pau, "Le origini scientifiche del metodo morelliano," 301ff., and David Alan Brown, "Giovanni Morelli and Bernard Berenson," 389ff.

57
Ivan Lermolieff [Giovanni Morelli], *Kunstkritische Studien über italienische Malerei* (Leipzig, 1890), 1:ixff.

58
For Morelli and Cuvier, see Anderson, "Dietro lo pseudonimo," 500ff. The reference is to Georges Baron Cuvier, *Le Règne animal distribué d'après son organisation* (Paris, 1817).

59
And so archaeologists claimed, from a couple of ribs or a door shaft, to be able to reconstruct a demolished medieval cathedral.

7

Max Nordau

1
Daniel Pick, *Faces of Degeneration: A European Disorder, c1848–c1918* (Cambridge, 1989).

2
Francis Galton and August Weismann had already studied degeneration under various names—Galton as "cessation of selection" and Weismann as "Panmixia," i.e., irresponsible mate choice. See Karl Pearson, *The Life, Letters, and Labours of Sir Francis Galton* (Cambridge, 1914–1930), 3a:340.

3
Stephen Jay Gould, *Ontogeny and Phylogeny* (Cambridge, Mass., 1977).

4
See Adolf Opel, ed., *Adolf Loos: Kontroversen* (Vienna, 1984), especially Arthur Rundt, "Ornament und Verbrechen," 122ff., and Karin Michaelis, "Der Überwinder des Ornaments," 152ff.

5
See also G. Schmidt, *Die literarische Rezeption des Darwinismus* (Berlin, 1974), 132ff.

6
Jules Chaix-Roy, *The Superman from Nietzsche to Teilhard de Chardin* (Notre Dame, Ind., 1968).

7
Wagner, *Oper und Drama* (Leipzig, 1852); Robert Donington, *Wagner's "Ring" and Its Symbols* (London, 1963), 180, 189.

8
Richard Gilman, *Decadence: The Strange Life of an Epithet* (New York, 1979), 73ff.

9
Max Nordau is a pen name: he was born Max Südfeld, "south field," which he turned into Nordau, "north meadow."

10
See Anna and Maxa Nordau, *Max Nordau, centinela de la civilisación* (Buenos Aires, 1943).

11
Max Nordau, *Degeneration* (1892; rpt. New York, 1968), 17.

12
We recall that Sheldon was to call endomorphs underevolved, ectomorphs overevolved, and mesomorphs properly evolved.

13
Nordau, *Degeneration*, 556.

14
A. Morel, *Traité des dégénérescences physiques, intellectuelles, et morales* (Paris, 1857).

15
Quoted by Nordau, *Degeneration*, 16.

16
Lombroso and G. Ferrero, *La donna delinquente* (Turin, 1894), 346.

17
Nordau, *Degeneration*, 119ff. He bases his physical description of Verlaine in part on Jules Huret, *Enquête*

sur l'évolution littéraire (Paris, 1891), 65 (rpt. Vanves, 1982, 80).

18
The best discussion of Nordau and Rodin is in J. A. Schmoll gen. Eisenwerth, *Rodin-Studien* (Munich, 1983), 344, 353. In the Vienna *Neuen Freien Presse* of 2 July 1908, Nordau published another attack on Rodin. See also Nordau, "Sur Auguste Rodin," *Revue des revues* (Paris, 1905).

19
Max Nordau, *On Art and Artists* (London, 1907), 279ff. See Georges Didi-Huberman, *Invention de l'hystérie: Charcot et l'iconographie photographique de la Salpêtrière* (Paris, 1982). Curiously enough, the sufferers from mental disease depicted here are all quite good-looking—no Lombrosan atavists or Nordauian degenerates, but rather healthy solid bodies and well-shaped faces.

20
Nordau, *Art and Artists*, 279.

21
Albert E. Elsen, *Rodin's Thinker and the Problems of Modern Public Sculpture* (New Haven, 1985), with bibliography. See also Frederic V. Grunfeld, *Rodin: A Biography* (New York, 1987), 501.

22
Nordau, *Art and Artists*, 291.

23
Nordau, *Art and Artists*, 279.

24
Nordau, *Degeneration*, 28.

25
Roy McMullen, *Victorian Outsider: A Biography of J. A. M. Whistler* (New York, 1973), 28, 58ff., 98ff., 103. For the painting, see *From Realism to Symbolism: Whistler and His World*, catalogue of exhibition organized by the Department of Art History and Archaeology of Columbia University in cooperation with the Philadelphia Museum of Art (New York, 1971), no. 12.

26
Nordau, *Art and Artists*, 153ff.

27
McMullen, *Whistler*, 210ff.

28
Mrs. Julian Hawthorne, quoted by G. H. Fleming, *James Abbott McNeill Whistler, a Life* (New York, 1991).

29
Giorgio Ruggeri, *Saette e carezze di un ironico libertino: Giovanni Boldini (1842–1931)* (Bologna, 1980).

30
Nordau, *Degeneration*, 7ff.

31
Ruggeri, *Saette*, 15, 17, and passim.

32
An oil sketch for the picture was on auction at Sotheby's, London, 22 June 1988. There is a pencil sketch for the composition in a private collection in Bologna. See Carlo L. Ragghianti, *L'opera completa di Boldini* (Milan, 1970).

33
John White Alexander (1856–1915), by Mary Anne Goley, Exhibition Catalogue, National Collection of Fine Arts, Smithsonian Institution (Washington, D.C., 1976).

34
Nordau, *Degeneration*, 7ff. This work will hereafter be cited parenthetically in the text

8

Into Nazism

1
Brandon Taylor and Wilfried van der Will, eds., *The Nazification of Art: Art, Music, Architecture, and Film in the Third Reich* (Winchester, England, 1990), 43. See also Robert Wistrich, *Weekend in Munich: Art, Propaganda, and Terror in the Third Reich* (London, 1995).

2
Norbert Borrmann, *Paul Schultze-Naumburg, 1869–1949, Maler, Publizist, Architekt* (Essen, 1989). On *Kunst und Rasse* (Munich, 1928), see 215ff. Schultze-Naumburg's other books are equally germane: *Nordische Schönheit: ihr Wunschbild im Leben und in der Kunst* (Munich and Berlin, 1937); *Kunst als Blut und Boden* (Leipzig, 1934), and the article also entitled "Kunst und Rasse" that appeared in *Die Sonne* 6.2 (1929), 49ff. Borrmann (245ff.) gives a full bibliography.

3
Jan Kelch, *Peter Paul Rubens,* Kritischer Katalog der Gemälde im Besitz der Gemäldegalerie, Berlin (Berlin, 1978), nos. 798-4, 776C.

4
Astonishingly because one of the important proto-Nazi

books was Julius Langbehn's *Rembrandt als Erzieher* (Rembrandt as a Teacher), published in 1890. For this book and its Nazi career, see Fritz Stern, *The Politics of Cultural Despair: A Study of the Rise of the Germanic Ideology* (1961; New York, 1965), 131ff. Langbehn says nothing in his very strange book that is apropos the present discussion. The idea that Rembrandt produces antiselectable types is explored, in its eighteenth-century setting, by Barbara Maria Stafford, *Body Criticism: Imaging the Unseen in Enlightenment Art and Medicine* (Cambridge, Mass., 1991), 327ff.

5
Schultze-Naumburg, *Kunst und Rasse*, fig. 89, and adjacent discussion. The Jukes family had been studied (1875) by the sociologist Richard L. Dugdale, who found genetic feeblemindedness and criminality across several generations. Cf. Dugdale, *The Jukes: A Study in Crime, Pauperism, Disease, and Heredity*, 4th ed. (New York, 1910).

6
Schultze-Naumburg, *Kunst und Rasse*, 87.

7
Schultze-Naumburg, *Kunst und Rasse*, 42.

8
Kenneth Clark, *The Drawings of Leonardo da Vinci in the Collection of Her Majesty the Queen at Windsor Castle*, 2nd ed. (London, 1969), nos. 12447–12495.

9
Malcolm Bull, "Caught in the Crossfire: Epstein, the Avant-Garde, and the Public," *TLS*, 25 September 1992, 20ff. For Epstein, see Richard Buckle, *Jacob Epstein, Sculptor* (Cleveland, 1963); Evelyn Silber, *The Sculpture of Epstein* (Oxford, 1986), esp. *Behold the Man,* no. 246. See also Terry Friedman, *Epstein's Rima, "The Hyde Park Atrocity," Creation, and Controversy* (Leeds, 1988), 35ff.

10
Vaughn and Blunt are quoted in Bull, "Caught in the Crossfire," 20ff.

11
See Peter Weingart, Jürgen Kroll, and Kurt Bayertz, *Rasse, Blut und Gene: Geschichte der Eugenik und Rassenhygiene in Deutschland* (Frankfurt-am-Main, 1988), 367ff.; Paul Weindling, *Health, Race, and German Politics between National Unification and Nazism, 1870–1945* (Cambridge, 1989), 489ff.; Aly Götz, Peter Chroust, and Christian Pross, *Cleansing the Fatherland: Nazi Medicine and Racial Hygiene*, trans. Belinda Cooper (Baltimore, 1994).

12
Hans F. K. Günther, *Rassengeschichte des hellenischen und des römischen Volkes* (Munich, 1929), 21. For Himmler's personality, see Peter Padfield, *Himmler: Reichsführer-SS* (London, 1990), e.g., 10, 135ff.

13
Alfred Rosenberg, *Des Mythos des 20. Jahrhunderts: eine Wertung der seelisch-geistigen Gestaltenkämpfe unserer Zeit* (Munich, 1930); idem, *Revolution in der bildenden Kunst?* (Munich, 1934); see also the translation of *Mythos der 20. Jahrhunderts, The Myth of the Twentieth Century: An Evaluation of the Spiritual-Intellectual Confrontations of Our Age* (Torrance, Calif., 1982), 169ff. Like Schultze-Naumburg, Rosenberg contrasts the healthy Rubens to the unhealthy Rembrandt. But Rembrandt is nonetheless Nordic—even his so-called Jewish Bride!

14
R. Ganzer, *Das deutscher Führergeschicht: 204 Bildnisse deutscher Kämpfer und Wegsucher aus zwei Jahrtausenden* (Munich, 1941).

15
Johannes Sommer, *Arno Breker* (Bonn, 1943); B. John Zavrel, *Arno Breker, His Art and Life* (Amherst, N.Y., 1985.)

16
Wilfried van der Will, "The Body and the Body Politic as Symptom and Metaphor in the Transition of German Culture into National Socialism," in Taylor and van der Will, *The Nazification of Art*, 14ff. The essay discusses the nudist movement in Germany, which the Nazis took up as part of their program for showcasing proper reproductive goals.

17
Berthold Hinz, *Die Malerei im deutschen Faschismus: Kunst und Konterrevolution* (Munich, 1974), 111.

18
Schultze-Naumburg, *Nordische Schönheit.*

19
Stephen Kinzer in the *New York Times*, 1 April 1994. See also Richard M. Lerner, *Final Solutions: Biology, Prejudice, and Genocide* (University Park, Penn., 1992), 21ff.

20
The Nazification of Art, 43.

21
Stern, *Politics of Cultural Despair*, brings out the point well.

9

Hyperdevelopment Today

1
For additional bibliography, see Marc E. Mishkind, Judith Rodin, Lisa R. Silberstein, and Ruth H. Striegel-Moore, "The Embodiment of Masculinity: Cultural, Psychological, and Behavioral Dimensions," *American Behavioral Scientist* 29 (1986), 545ff.; Joseph Lyons, *Ecology of the Body: Styles of Behavior in Human Life* (Durham, N.C., 1987); also A. E. Fallon and P. Rozin, "Sex Differences in Perception of Desirable Body Shape," *Journal of Abnormal Psychology* 94 (1985), 102ff.; Kenneth R. Dutton, *The Perfectible Body: The Western Ideal of Male Physical Development* (New York, 1995).

2
E. Lindsay Carter and Barbara Honeyman Heath, *Somatotyping—Development and Applications* (Cambridge, 1990), 1ff. The authors discuss bodybuilders on 210ff.

3
Charles Gaines, *Pumping Iron: The Art and Sport of Bodybuilding* (New York, 1974); Alan M. Klein, *Little Big Men: Bodybuilding Subculture and Gender Construction* (Albany, 1993), especially the chapter entitled "Comic Book Masculinity and Cultural Fiction," 234ff.

4
See the interviews in Gaines, *Pumping Iron*. Also, for artificially created musculature and maleness, see John M. Hoberman and Charles E. Yesalis, "The History of Synthetic Testosterone," *Scientific American* 272 (February 1995), 76ff.

5
Samuel Wilson Fussell, *Muscle: Confessions of an Unlikely Bodybuilder* (New York, 1991).

6
Francis Haskell and Nicholas Penny, *Taste and the Antique: The Lure of Classical Sculpture, 1500–1900* (New Haven, 1981), 230.

7
Fussell, *Muscle*, 133, 191. See also V. Bok, "A Comparison of Selected Illustrations of Creative Works from the Point of View of Constitutional Typology," *Acta universitatis carolinae (gymnica)* 10 (1974), 79ff.; idem, "Comparison of Somatotypes of Certain Works of Art with the View to the Beauty of the Living Human Body," in R. Line, ed., *International Conference on Physical Education* (Prague, 1976), 191ff.; idem, "The Comparison of Adam's and Eve's Depiction in Selected Style Periods from the Point of View of the Somatotype," *Acta universitatis carolinae (gymnica)* 19 (1983), 73ff.

8
Fussell, *Muscle*, 122.

9
Here is an old joke: someone asked Groucho Marx if he wanted to see a Tarzan movie starring Johnny Weissmuller and Linda Darnell. "No," said Groucho, "I don't go to no movie where the boy has bigger boobs than the girl." My thanks to Professor Jonathan Marks for this.

10
Andrew Stewart, *Greek Sculpture* (New Haven, 1990), 1:126.

11
In some cases this may have been done in order to cure breast asymmetry, which is particularly apparent in large-breasted women; A. P. Møller, M. Soler, and R. Thornhill, "Breast Asymmetry, Sexual Selection, and Human Reproductive Success" (with earlier bibliography, submitted to *Ethology and Sociobiology*). See also R. E. Frisch, "Fatness and Fertility," *Scientific American* 258 (March 1988), 70ff.; R. W. Smuts, "Fat, Sex, Class, Adaptive Flexibility, and Cultural Change," *Ethology and Sociobiology* 13 (1992), 523ff.; and B. S. Low, R. D. Alexander, and K. M. Noonan, "Human Hips, Breasts, and Buttocks: Is Fat Deceptive?" *Ethology and Sociobiology* 8 (1987), 249ff.

12
Robert L. Herbert, *Impressionism: Art, Leisure, and Parisian Society* (New Haven, 1988), 79ff.

Selected Bibliography

Aikema, Bernard. "Titian's Mary Magdalen in the Palazzo Pitti: An Ambiguous Painting and Its Critics." *Journal of the Warburg and Courtauld Institutes* 57 (1994), 48ff.

Aiken, Jane Andrews. "Leon Battista Alberti's System of Proportions." *Journal of the Warburg and Courtauld Institutes* 42 (1980), 68ff.

Alberti, Leone Battista. *"On Painting and on Sculpture": The Latin Texts of "De Pictura" and "De Statua."* Ed. and trans. Cecil Grayson. London, 1972

Ammon, Otto. *Die Gesellschaftsordnung und ihre natürlichen Grundlagen.* 2nd ed. Jena, 1896.

Anderson, Jaynie. "Dietro lo pseudonimo." In *Giovanni Morelli: Della pittura italiana: Studii storico-critici.* Milan, 1991. 491ff.

Arnold, Matthew. *Culture and Anarchy* (1869). New York, 1908.

Baltrusaitis, Jurgis. *Aberrations: Essai sur la légende des Formes.* Paris, 1983.

Bannister, Robert C. *Social Darwinism: Science and Myth in Anglo-American Social Thought.* Philadelphia, 1979.

Bardon, Françoise. "Le thème de la Madeleine pénitente au XVIIème siècle en France." *Journal of the Warburg and Courtauld Institutes* 31 (1968), 274ff.

Beinert, Wolfgang, and Heinrich Petri, eds. *Handbuch der Marienkunde.* Regensburg, 1984.

Bernal, Martin. *Black Athena: The Afroasiatic Roots of Classical Civilization.* Vol. 1, *The Fabrication of Ancient Greece, 1785–1985.* New Brunswick, N.J., 1987.

Bianchi Bandinelli, Ranuccio. *Policleto.* Florence, 1938.

Blinkenberg, C. S. *Knidia: Beiträge zur Kenntnis der Praxitelischen Aphrodite.* Copenhagen, 1933.

Bok, V. "The Comparison of Adam's and Eve's Depiction in Selected Style Periods from the Point of View of the Somatotype." *Acta universitatis carolinae (gymnica)* 19 (1983), 73ff.

Bok, V. "A Comparison of Selected Illustrations of Creative Works from the Point of View of Constitutional Typology." *Acta universitatis carolinae (gymnica)* 10 (1974), 79ff.

Bok, V. "Comparison of Somatotypes of Certain Works of Art with the View to the Beauty of the Living Human Body." In *International Conference on Physical Education,* ed. R. Line. Prague, 1976. 191ff.

Borrmann, Norbert. *Paul Schultze-Naumburg, 1869–1949: Maler, Publizist, Architekt.* Essen, 1989.

Bournouf, Emile. *La Science des religions.* Paris, 1872.

Bowler, Peter J. *The Eclipse of Darwinism: Anti-Darwinian Evolution Theories in the Decades around 1900.* Baltimore, 1983.

Buckle, Richard. *Jacob Epstein, Sculptor.* Cleveland, 1963.

Bulferetti, Luigi. *Cesare Lombroso.* Turin, 1975.

Bull, Malcolm. "Caught in the Crossfire: Epstein, the Avant-Garde, and the Public." *TLS,* 25 September 1992, 20ff.

Bynum, Caroline Walker. "The Female Body and Religious Practice in the Later Middle Ages." *Zone: Fragments for a History of the Body* 1 (1989), 161ff.

Bynum, Caroline Walker. *The Resurrection of the Body in Western Christianity, 200–1336.* New York, 1995.

Callen, Anthea. "Anatomie et physiognomie: 'la Petite Danseuse de quatorze ans,' de Degas." In *L'Ame au corps: arts et sciences, 1793–1993.* Paris, 1994.

Callen, Anthea. *The Spectacular Body: Science, Method, and Meaning in the Work of Degas.* New Haven, 1995.

Camper, Petrus. *Vorlesungen . . . über die bewunderswürdige Ähnlichkeit im Bau des Menschen, der vierfüssigen Thiere . . .* Berlin, 1793.

Carroll, Michael P. *The Cult of the Virgin Mary: Psychological Origins.* Princeton, 1986.

Chai, Jean Julia. *Gian Paolo Lomazzo and the Art of Expression.* Ann Arbor, Mich., 1990.

Chamberlain, Houston Stewart. *Arische Weltanschauung.* Berlin, 1905.

Chaudhuri, Nirad C. *Scholar Extraordinary: The Life of Professor the Rt. Hon. Friedrich Max Müller, P.C.* London, 1974.

Choulant, J. L. *Geschichte und Bibliographie der anatomischen Abbildungen* (1852). Trans. Mortimer Frank as *The History and Bibliography of Anatomic Illustration in Its Relation to Anatomic Science and the Graphic Arts.* Chicago, 1920.

Clark, Kenneth. *The Drawings of Leonardo da Vinci in the Collection of Her Majesty the Queen at Windsor Castle.* 2nd ed. London, 1969.

Corso, Antonio. *Prassitele: Fonti epigrafiche e letterarie, vita e opere.* Rome, 1988–1990.

Cowan, Ruth Schwartz. *Sir Francis Galton and the Study of Heredity in the Nineteenth Century.* New York, 1985.

Cowling, Mary. *The Artist as Anthropologist: The Representation of Type and Character in Victorian Art.* Cambridge, 1989.

Cronin, Helena. *The Ant and the Peacock: Altruism and Sexual Selection from Darwin to Today.* Cambridge, 1991.

Curtius, Ernst. *Griechische Geschichte.* 3 vols. Berlin, 1857–1867.

Darwin, Francis, ed. *Charles Darwin's Autobiography.* New York, 1950.

Davis, Whitney. *The Canonical Tradition in Ancient Egyptian Art.* Cambridge, 1989.

Dawkins, Richard. *The Extended Phenotype: The Gene as the Unit of Selection.* Oxford, 1982.

Dawkins, Richard. *The Selfish Gene.* Oxford, 1976.

De Fiores, Stefano, and Salvatore Meo, eds. *Nuovo dizionario di mariologia.* Milan, 1986.

Deshpande, Madhar M., and Peter Edwin Hooke, eds. *Aryan and Non-Aryan in India.* Ann Arbor, Mich., 1979.

De Waal Malefijt, Annemarie. *Images of Man: A History of Anthropological Thought.* New York, 1974.

Di Giovanni, A. *Clinical Commentaries Deduced from the Morphology of the Human Body.* London and New York, 1919.

Dilke, Charles Wentworth. *Greater Britain.* Philadelphia, 1869.

Disraeli, Benjamin. *Lothair* (1870), ed. Vernon Bogdanor. London, 1975.

Dolza Carrara, Delfina. *Essere figlie di Lombroso.* Milan, 1990.

Dugdale, Richard L. *The Jukes: A Study in Crime, Pauperism, Disease, and Heredity.* 4th ed. New York, 1910.

Dutton, Kenneth R. *The Perfectible Body: The Western Ideal of Male Physical Development.* New York, 1995.

Elsen, Albert E. *Rodin's Thinker and the Problems of Modern Public Sculpture.* New Haven, 1985.

Engels, Friedrich. *The Origin of the Family, Private Property, and the State in the Light of the Researches of Lewis H. Morgan* (1884). Ed. Eleanor Burke Clark. New York, 1972.

Fallon, A. E., and P. Rozin. "Sex Differences in Perception of Desirable Body Shape." *Journal of Abnormal Psychology* 94 (1985), 102ff.

Faverty, Frederic E. *Matthew Arnold the Ethnologist.* Evanston, Ill., 1951.

Fisher, R. A. "The Evolution of Sexual Preference." *Eugenics Review* 7 (1915), 184ff.

Fisher, R. A. *The Genetical Theory of Natural Selection.* Oxford, 1930.

Fleischer, Manfred P., ed. *The Decline of the West?* New York, 1970.

Fleming, G. H. *James Abbott McNeill Whistler, a Life.* New York, 1991.

Friedman, Terry. *Epstein's Rima, "The Hyde Park Atrocity," Creation, and Controversy.* Leeds, 1988.

Frisch, R. E. "Fatness and Fertility." *Scientific American* 258 (March 1988), 70ff.

From Realism to Symbolism: Whistler and His World. Exhibition catalogue, Department of Art History and Archaeology of Columbia University in cooperation with the Philadelphia Museum of Art. New York, 1971.

Fussell, Samuel Wilson. *Muscle: Confessions of an Unlikely Bodybuilder.* New York, 1991.

Gaines, Charles. *Pumping Iron: The Art and Sport of Bodybuilding.* New York, 1974.

Galton, Francis. *Hereditary Genius.* New York, 1870.

Galton, Francis. *Inquiries into Human Faculty and Its Development.* New York, 1883.

Galton, Francis. *See also* Pearson, Karl.

Ganzer, K. R. *Das deutscher Führergeschicht: 204 Bildnisse deutscher Kämpfer und Wegsucher aus zwei Jahrtausenden.* Munich, 1941.

Garland, Robert. *The Eye of the Beholder: Deformity and Disability in the Graeco-Roman World.* Ithaca, N.Y., 1995.

Gaunt, William. *Victorian Olympus.* London, 1952.

Giesen, J. *Dürers Proportionstudien im Rahmen der allgemeinen Proportionsentwicklung.* Bonn, 1930.

Gilman, Richard. *Decadence—the Strange Life of an Epithet.* New York, 1979.

Giovanni Morelli e la coltura dei conoscitori: Atti del convegno nazionale. Vol. 2. Bergamo, 1993.

Gobineau, Joseph Arthur de. *Essai sur l'inégalité des races humaines* (1853). Paris, 1967.

Goley, Mary Anne. *John White Alexander (1856–1915).* Exhibition catalogue, National Collection of Fine Arts, Smithsonian Institution, Washington, D.C., 1976.

Götz, Aly, Peter Chroust, and Christian Pross. *Cleansing the Fatherland: Nazi Medicine and Racial Hygiene.* Trans. Belinda Cooper. Baltimore, 1994.

Gould, Stephen Jay. *The Mismeasure of Man.* New York, 1981.

Gould, Stephen Jay. *Ontogeny and Phylogeny.* Cambridge, Mass., 1977.

Grammer, Karl, and Randy Thornhill. "Human (Homo sapiens) Facial Attractiveness and

Sexual Selection: The Role of Symmetry and Averageness." *Journal of Comparative Psychology* 108 (1994), 233ff.

Grunfeld, Frederic V. *Rodin: A Biography*. New York, 1987.

Günther, Hans F. K. *Rassengeschichte des hellenischen und des römischen Volkes*. Munich, 1929.

Haller, Mark H. *Eugenics: Hereditarian Attitudes in American Thought*. New Brunswick, N.J., 1963.

Hartl, Emil M., Edward P. Monnelly, and Roland D. Elderkin. *Physique and Delinquent Behavior: A Thirty-Year Follow-Up of William H. Sheldon's "Varieties of Delinquent Youth."* New York, 1982.

Haskell, Francis, and Nicholas Penny. *Taste and the Antique: The Lure of Classical Sculpture, 1500–1900*. New Haven, 1981.

Haskins, Susan. *Mary Magdalen: Myth and Metaphor*. London, 1994.

Havelock, Christine. *The Aphrodite of Knidos and Her Successors*. Ann Arbor, Mich., 1995.

Hay, David R. *The Natural Principles of Beauty in the Human Figure*. London and Edinburgh, 1852.

Hay, David R. *On the Science of Those Proportions by which the Human Head and Countenance as Represented in Works of Ancient Greek Art Are Distinguished from Those of Ordinary Nature*. London and Edinburgh, 1849.

Herbert, Robert L. *Impressionism: Art, Leisure, and Parisian Society*. New Haven, 1988.

Herman, C. Peter. "The Shape of Man." *Contemporary Psychology* 37 (1992), 525ff.

Herter, H. *De Priapo*. Religionsgeschichtliche Versuche und Vorarbeiten, 23. Giessen, 1932.

Hinz, Berthold. *Die Malerei im deutschen Faschismus: Kunst und Konterrevolution*. Munich, 1974. Trans. Robert and Rita Kimber as *Art in the Third Reich*. New York, 1979.

Hoberman, John M., and Charles E. Yesalis. "The History of Synthetic Testosterone." *Scientific American* 272 (February 1995), 76ff.

Hofstadter, Richard. *Social Darwinism and American Thought*. Philadelphia, 1944.

Hooton, Earnest A. *The American Criminal*. Vol. 1, *The Native White Criminal of Native Parentage*. Cambridge, Mass., 1939.

Hooton, Earnest A. *Apes, Men, and Morons*. New York, 1937.

Hooton, Earnest A. *The Twilight of Man*. New York, 1939.

Hooton, Earnest A. *Why Men Behave Like Apes and Vice Versa*. Princeton, 1940.

Huxley, Thomas Henry. *Evidence as to Man's Place in Nature*. London, 1863.

Ingenhoff-Danhäuser, Monika. *Maria Magdalena: Heilige und Sünderin in der italienischen Renaissance*. Tübingen, 1984.

James, Henry. *William Wetmore Story and His Friends* (1903). 2 vols. New York, 1957.

James, William. *The Varieties of Religious Experience* (1902). New York, 1987.

Jameson, Anna. *Legends of the Madonna as Represented in the Fine Arts*. London, 1852.

Jameson, Anna. *Sacred and Legendary Art*. London, 1870.

Johnsgard, Paul A. *Arena Birds: Sexual Selection and Behavior.* Washington, D.C., 1994.

Justi, Ludwig. *Konstruierte Figuren und Köpfe unter den Werken Albrecht Dürers*. Leipzig, 1902.

Karageorghis, Jacqueline. *La grande Déesse de Chypre et son culte*. Lyons, 1977.

Kelch, Jan. *Peter Paul Rubens. Kritischer Katalog der Gemälde im Besitz der Gemäldegalerie, Berlin*. Berlin, 1978.

Kern, Stephen. *Anatomy and Destiny: A Cultural History of the Human Body*. Indianapolis, 1975.

Keynes, Milo, ed. *Sir Francis Galton, FRS: The Legacy of His Ideas*. Proceedings of the 27th Annual Symposium of the Galton Institute, London, 1991. Houndmills, England, 1993.

Klein, Alan M. *Little Big Men: Bodybuilding Subculture and Gender Construction*. Albany, 1993.

Kraus, Theodor, *Die Aphrodite von Knidos*. Bremen, 1987.

Kretschmer, Ernst. *Geniale Menschen*. 2nd ed. Berlin, 1931.

Kretschmer, Ernst. *Körperbau und Charakter*. New ed. Berlin, 1944

Kretschmer, Ernst. *Die Persönlichkeit der Athletiker.* 1936.

Kretschmer, Ernst. *Physique and Character.* Trans. E. Miller. 2nd rev. ed. London, 1936.

Langbehn, Julius. *Rembrandt als Erzieher.* Leipzig, 1890.

Lavater, J. C. *Fragmente—Physiognomische Fragmente, zur Beförderung der Menschenkenntniss und Menschenliebe*. Leipzig, 1775–1778; facsimile Zurich, 1968.

Leighton, Frederic. *Addresses Delivered to the Students of the Royal Academy by the Late Lord Leighton*. 2nd ed. London, 1897.

Lermolieff, Ivan. *See* Morelli, Giovanni.

Lerner, Richard M. *Final Solutions: Biology, Prejudice, and Genocide*. University Park, Penn., 1992.

Lessing, Gotthold Ephraim. *Laocoön*. Trans. Ellen Frothingame. New York, 1957.

Levi, Donata. "Fortuna di Morelli: appunti sui rapporti fra storiografia artistica tedesca ed inglese." In *La Figura di Giovanni Morelli: studi e ricerche*. Bergamo, 1987. l9ff.

Lindsay Carter, J. E., and Barbara Honeyman Heath. *Somatotyping—Development and Applications*. Cambridge, 1992.

Lombroso, Cesare. *Genio e follia*. Turin, 1882.

Lombroso, Cesare. *L'Homme criminel*. 2 vols. Paris, 1895.

Lombroso, Cesare. *La donna delinquente*. Turin, 1894.

Low, B. S., R. D. Alexander, and K. M. Noonan. "Human Hips, Breasts, and Buttocks: Is Fat Deceptive?" *Ethology and Sociobiology* 8 (1987), 249ff.

Lyons, Joseph. *Ecology of the Body: Styles of Behavior in Human Life*. Durham, N.C., 1987.

Majundar, Ramesh Chandra. *Expansion of Aryan Culture in Eastern India*. Imphal, 1968.

Malvern, Marjorie M. *Venus in Sackcloth: The Magdalen's Origins and Metamorphoses*. Carbondale, Ill., 1975.

Marks, Jonathan. *Human Biodiversity: Genes, Race, and History*. New York, 1995.

McMullen, Roy. *Victorian Outsider: A Biography of J. A. M. Whistler*. New York, 1973.

Mendlewitsch, Doris. *Volk und Heil: Vordenker des Nationalsozialismus im 19. Jahrhundert*. Bielefeld, 1988.

Miller, E. *Types of Mind and Body*. London, 1927.

Mishkind, Marc E., Judith Rodin, Lisa R. Silberstein, and Ruth H. Striegel-Moore. "The Embodiment of Masculinity: Cultural, Psychological, and Behavioral Dimensions." *American Behavioral Scientist* 29 (1986), 545ff.

Mitterer, A. *Dogma und Biologie der heiligen Familie*. Vienna, 1952.

Møller, A. P., M. Soler, and R. Thornhill. "Breast Asymmetry, Sexual Selection, and Human Reproductive Success." *Ethology and Sociobiology*, in press.

Morel, B. A. *Traité des dégénérescences physiques, intellectuelles, et morales*. Paris, 1857.

Morelli, Giovanni [Ivan Lermolieff]. *Kunstkritische Studien über italienische Malerei*. 2 vols. Leipzig, 1890.

Muir, John. *The Hymns of the Rig Veda*. London, 1873.

Muir, John. *Original Sanskrit Texts on the Origin and History of the People of India: The Vedas* . . . 2nd ed. 5 vols. London, 1871.

Naccarati, S. "The Morphologic Aspect of Intelligence." *Archives of Psychology*, no. 45 (August 1921).

Nordau, Anna, and Maxa Nordau. *Max Nordau, centinela de la civilisación.* Buenos Aires, 1943.

Nordau, Max. *Degeneration* (1892). New York, 1968.

Nordau, Max. *On Art and Artists.* London, 1907.

Opel, Adolf, ed. *Adolf Loos: Kontroversen.* Vienna, 1984.

Oppel, Herbert. "KANΩN: Zur Bedeutungs-geschichte des Wortes lateinischen Entsprechungen *(regula-norma).*" *Philologus* suppl. 30.4 (1937), 14ff.

Ormond, Leonée, and Richard Ormond. *Lord Leighton.* London, 1975.

Padfield, Peter. *Himmler: Reichsführer-SS.* London, 1990.

Palmer, A. R., and C. Strobeck. "Fluctuating Asymmetry: Measurement, Analysis, and Patterns." *Annual Review of Ecology and Systemics* 17 (1986), 391ff.

Panofsky, Erwin. "The History of the Theory of Human Proportions as a Reflection of the History of Styles." In *Meaning in the Visual Arts.* New York, 1955. 55ff.

Panofsky, Erwin. *The Life and Art of Albrecht Dürer.* Princeton, 1955.

Panofsky, Erwin. *Tomb Sculpture: Four Lectures on Its Changing Aspects from Ancient Egypt to Bernini.* New York, 1964.

Panzeri, M., and G. O. Bravi. *La figura e l'opera di Giovanni Morelli: Materiali e ricerca.* Bergamo, 1987.

Park, Katherine. "The Criminal and Saintly Body: Autopsy and Dissection in Renaissance Italy." *Renaissance Quarterly* 47 (1994), 21ff.

Pearsall, Ronald. *Tell Me, Pretty Maiden: The Victorian and Edwardian Nude.* 3 vols. Exeter, 1981.

Pearson, Karl. *The Life, Letters, and Labours of Francis Galton.* Cambridge, 1914–1930.

Pende, N. *Constitutional Inadequacies.* Philadelphia, 1928.

Pepper, Stephen. *Guido Reni, l'opera completa.* Novara, 1988.

Phillips, Mary E. *Reminiscences of William Wetmore Story.* Chicago and New York, 1897.

Pick, Daniel. *The Faces of Degeneration: A European Disorder, c1848–c1918.* Cambridge, 1989.

Poliakov, Léon. *The Aryan Myth: A History of Racist and Nationalist Ideas in Europe.* New York, 1971.

Polyklet: Der Bildhauer der griechischen Klassik. Exhibition catalogue, Liebieghaus Museum alter Plastik, Frankfurt am Main. Mainz am Rhein, 1990.

Pollitt, J. J. *The Ancient View of Greek Art.* Cambridge, 1974.

Quetelet, Adolphe. *Anthropométrie ou mésure des différentes facultés de l'homme.* Brussels, 1871.

Ravasi, Gianfranco. ". . . Kî Tôb: 'Dio vide che era bello!'" In T. Verdon, ed., *L'arte e la Bibbia: Immagine come esegesi biblica.* Atti del Convegno internazionale di studi l'Arte e la Bibbia, Venice, 14–16 October 1988. Bergamo, 1992.

Raven, J. E. "Polyclitus and Pythagoreanism." *Classical Quarterly* 45 (1951), 147ff.

Réau, Louis. *Iconographie de l'art chrétien.* Paris, 1957.

Richards, Eveleen. "Darwin and the Descent of Woman." In David Oldroyd and Ian Langham, eds., *The Wider Domain of Evolutionary Thought.* Boston, 1983.

Richter, G. M. A. *Korai.* London, 1968.

Richter, G. M. A. *Kouroi.* 3rd ed. London, 1970.

Roberts, C. A. *A Manual of Anthropometry.* London, 1878.

Robertson, Martin. *A History of Greek Art.* 2 vols. Cambridge, 1975.

Robins, Gay. *Proportion and Style in Ancient Egyptian Art.* Austin, 1994.

Rosenbaum, Ron. "The Great Ivy League Nude Posture Photo Scandal." *New York Times Magazine*, 15 January 1995. 26ff.

Rosenberg, Alfred. *Des Mythos des 20. Jahrhunderts: eine Wertung der seelisch-geistigen Gestaltenkämpfe unserer Zeit.* Munich, 1930.

Rosenberg, Alfred. *Revolution in der bildenden Kunst?* Munich, 1934.

Ruggeri, Giorgio. *Saette e carezze di un ironico libertino: Giovanni Boldini (1842–1931).* Bologna, 1980.

Rykwert, Joseph. *The Dancing Column: On the Orders of Architecture.* Cambridge, Mass., 1996.

Säfflund, Gösta. *Aphrodite Kallipygos.* Stockholm, 1963.

Salerno, Luigi. *I dipinti del Guercino.* Rome, 1988.

Savage, Thomas S., M.D. "Notice of the External Characters and Habits of Troglodytes Gorilla, a New Species of Orang from the Gaboon River." *Boston Journal of Natural History* 5 (December 1847), 417ff.

Scaglia, Gustina. "Instruments Perfected for Measurements of Man and Statues Illustrated in Leon Battista Alberti's *De statua.*" *Nuncia: Annali di storia della scienza* 8 (1993), 555ff.

Schadow, J. G. *Polyclet oder von den Maassen des Menschen, nach dem Geschlechte und Alter mit Angabe der wirklichen Naturgrösse.* Berlin, 1834.

Schmoll gen. Eisenwerth, J. A. *Rodin-Studien.* Munich, 1983.

Schultz, Bernard. *Art and Anatomy in Renaissance Italy.* Ann Arbor, Mich., 1985.

Schultze-Naumburg, Paul. *Kunst als Blut und Boden.* Leipzig, 1934.

Schultze-Naumburg, Paul. *Kunst und Rasse.* Munich, 1928.

Schultze-Naumburg, Paul. *Nordische Schönheit: ihr Wunschbild im Leben und in der Kunst.* Munich and Berlin, 1937.

Sheldon, William H. *An Atlas of Men.* New York, 1954.

Sheldon, William H. *Psychology and the Promethean Will: A Constructive Study of the Acute Common Problem of Education, Medicine and Religion.* New York, 1936.

Sheldon, William H. "The Somatotype, the Morphophenotype, and the Morphogenotype." *Cold Spring Harbor Symposium on Quantitative Biology* 15 (1950), 373ff.

Sheldon, William H. *Varieties of Temperament: A Psychology of Constitutional Differences.* New York, 1942.

Sheldon, William H., with Emil M. Hartl and Eugene McDermott. *Varieties of Delinquent Youth: An Introduction to Constitutional Psychiatry.* New York, 1949.

Sheldon, William H., with S. S. Stevens and B. B. Tucker. *Varieties of Human Physique: An Introduction to Constitutional Psychology.* New York, 1940.

Silber, Evelyn. *The Sculpture of Epstein.* Oxford, 1986.

Siraisi, Nancy G. "Vesalius and Human Diversity in *De humani corporis fabrica.*" *Journal of the Warburg and Courtauld Institutes* 57 (1994), 60ff.

Smuts, R. W. "Fat, Sex, Class, Adaptive Flexibility, and Cultural Change." *Ethology and Sociobiology* 13 (1992), 523ff.

Soloway, Richard A. *Demography and Degeneration: Eugenics and the Declining Birthrate in Twentieth-Century Britain.* Chapel Hill, N.C., 1990.

Sommer, Johannes. *Arno Breker.* Bonn, 1943.

Spear, Richard E. *Domenichino.* New Haven, 1982.

Spengler, Oswald. *The Decline of the West* (1918). New York, 1957.

Stafford, Barbara Maria. *Body Criticism: Imaging the Unseen in Enlightenment Art and Medicine.* Cambridge, Mass., 1991.

Steinberg, Leo. *The Sexuality of Christ in Renaissance Art and in Modern Oblivion.* New York, 1983.

Stemmler, Joan K. "The Physiognomical Portraits of Johann Caspar Lavater." *Art Bulletin* 75 (1993), 151ff.

Stern, Fritz. *The Politics of Cultural Despair: A Study in the Rise of Germanic Ideology* (1961). New York, 1965.

Stewart, Andrew. "The Canon of Polykleitos: A Question of Evidence." *Journal of Hellenic Studies* 98 (1978), 122ff.

Stewart, Andrew. *Greek Sculpture.* 2 vols. New Haven, 1990.

Story, William Wetmore. *Poems.* Boston, 1886.

Story, William Wetmore. *The Proportions of the Human Figure, According to a New Canon, for Practical Use; with a Critical Notice of the Canon of Polycletus, and of the Principal Ancient and Modern Systems.* London, 1864.

Stowe, Harriet Beecher. "Sojourner Truth, the Libyan Sibyl." *Atlantic Monthly* 11 (1863), 480ff.

Strasser, Peter. "Cesare Lombroso: l'homme délinquent ou la bête sauvage au naturel." In *L'Ame au corps: arts et sciences 1793–1993.* Exhibition catalogue, Grand Palais. Paris, 1994. 352ff.

Taylor, Brandon, and Wilfried van der Will, eds. *The Nazification of Art: Art, Music, Architecture, and Film in the Third Reich.* Winchester, England, 1990.

Thompson, Thomas. *James Anthony Froude on Nation and Empire: A Study in Victorian Racialism.* New York, 1987.

Thornhill, Randy, and Steven W. Gangestad, "Human Fluctuating Asymmetry and Sexual Behavior." *Biological Abstracts* 97.8 (1994), 21ff.

Thornhill, Randy, Steven W. Gangestad, and Randall Comer. "Human Female Orgasm and Male Fluctuating Asymmetry." *Animal Behavior* (in press).

Tönnies, F. "Ammons Gesellschaftstheorie." *Archiv für Sozialwissenschaft und Sozialpolitik* 19 [n.s., 1] (1904).

Topinard, P. *Eléments d'anthropologie générale.* Paris, 1885.

Vasari, Giorgio. *Le vite dei più eccellenti pittori, scultori, ed architettori.* Ed. Rosanna Bettarini and Paola Barocchi. Florence, 1966–.

Verdon, Timothy R., ed. *Monasticism and the Arts.* Syracuse, 1984.

Viola, G. *La costituzione individuale.* Bologna, 1933.

Viola, G. "Il mio metodo di valutazione della costituzione individuale." *Riforma medicale* 51 (1935), 1635ff.

Viola, G. "L'Habitus phthisicus et l'habitus apoplecticus comme conséquence d'une loi qui déforme normalement le type moyen de la race en ces deux types antithétiques." *Comptes rendus de l'association des anatomistes.* Turin, 1925.

Virchow, Rudolf. *Collected Essays on Public Health and Epidemiology.* Ed. L. J. Rather. Canton, Mass., 1985.

Virchow, Rudolf. *Disease, Life, and Man.* Stanford, Calif., 1958.

Von Steuben, H. *Der Kanon des Polyklet: Doryphoros und Amazon.* Tübingen, 1973.

Watson, P. J., and R. Thornhill. "Fluctuating Asymmetry and Sexual Selection." *Trends in Ecology and Evolution* 9 (1994), 21ff.

Weindling, Paul. *Health, Race, and German Politics between National Unification and Nazism, 1870–1945.* Cambridge, 1989.

Weingart, Peter, Jürgen Kroll, and Kurt Bayertz. *Rasse, Blut und Gene: Geschichte der Eugenik und Rassenhygiene in Deutschland.* Frankfurt am Main, 1988.

Westermarck, Edward A. *A History of Human Marriage.* London, 1891.

Wickler, Wolfgang. *The Sexual Code.* Garden City, N.Y., 1972.

Wickler, Wolfgang. "Socio-Sexual Signals and Their Intraspecific Imitation among Primates." In *Primate Ethology,* ed. Desmond Morris. Chicago, 1967. 89ff.

Wickler, Wolfgang. "Ursprung und biologische Deutung des Genitalpraesentierens männlicher Primaten." *Zeitschrift für Tierpsychologie* 23 (1966), 422ff.

Winckelmann, Johann Joachim. *Reflections on the Imitation of Greek Works in Painting and Sculpture* (1755). Ed. and trans. Elfriede Heyer and Roger C. Norton. La Salle, Ill., 1987.

Wistrich, Robert. *Weekend in Munich: Art, Propaganda, and Terror in the Third Reich.* London, 1995.

Wollheim, Richard. "Giovanni Morelli and the Origins of Scientific Connoisseurship." In *On Art and the Mind: Essays and Lectures.* London, 1974. 177ff.

Wood, Christopher. *Olympian Dreamers: Victorian Classical Painters, 1860–1914.* London, 1983.

Zavrel, B. John. *Arno Breker, His Art and Life.* Amherst, N.Y., 1985.

Zerner, Henri. "Morelli et la science de l'art." *Revue de l'art* 40–41 (1978), 209ff.

Zöllner, Frank. *Vitruvs Proportionsfigur.* Worms, 1987.

Index